Praise for *The Participatory Museum*

"I predict that in the future this book will be a classic work of museology."
— *Elizabeth Merritt, Founding Director, Center for the Future of Museums*

"As I read this book, there were about twenty times when I thought 'we should try this!'... *The Participatory Museum* has the resonance of a manifesto and the potential to make a transformative impact on museum practice and visitors' experiences in museums in the coming decades."
— *Eric Siegel, Director and Chief Content Officer, New York Hall of Science*

"In readable and engaging prose, Simon provides a multiplicity of practical, real-world examples and strategies for eliciting and enhancing public participation in ways that deliver real value to museum-goers and museums alike. This book will prove essential for any museum seeking to affirm its connection to the public in new ways relevant to the times in which we live." — *Daniel Spock, Director, Minnesota History Center*

"Simon is an excellent teacher; she gently leads her readers through what is likely to be new and intimidating territory. She articulates a useful set of intelligent principles, grounded in research and theory, of the sort that promotes reflective and effective practice." — *Leslie Bedford, Director, Leadership in Museum Education graduate program, Bank Street College*

"The tone and enthusiasm of this book engages and empowers a new generation of museum professionals to reinterpret how we interact with our visitors. Included throughout are thoughtful case studies, interviews, and personal experiences which guide us along a new path of participatory design. This book intrigues, delights, and kept me coming back for more."
— *Bruce Wyman, Director of Technology, Denver Art Museum*

THE PARTICIPATORY MUSEUM

by Nina Simon

17 16 15 14 13 12 11 10   1 2 3 4 5

ISBN-13: 978-0-615-34650-2

Published by MUSEUM 2.0

Santa Cruz, California

To my poppa, who taught me
everyone can do the hand jive

TABLE OF CONTENTS

PREFACE
WHY PARTICIPATE? i

CHAPTER 1
PRINCIPLES OF PARTICIPATION 1
    Making Participation Physical and Scalable 3
    Participation at its Best 6
    What Does Participation Look Like? 8
    Who's Involved in Participation? 13
    Outcomes for Participants and Audiences 16
    How Does Participation Work? 22

CHAPTER 2
PARTICIPATION BEGINS WITH ME 33
    Audience First 34
    Treating People as Individuals 39
    Profiles in the Real World 41
    Designing Profiles for Cultural Institutions 45
    Putting Personalization to Work in Cultural Institutions 54
    Personalized Onsite Experiences 58
    Personalization over Multiple Visits 75
    Making Membership Matter 78

CHAPTER 3
FROM ME TO WE 85
    The Network Effect 88
    Designing Mediating Technology for Social Experiences 97
    Platforms and Values 105
    Creative Approaches to Platform Design 110
    Platforms and Power 120

CHAPTER 4

SOCIAL OBJECTS **127**

What Makes an Object Social? 129
Designing Platforms for Social Objects 133
Social Platforms in the Real World 137
Asking Visitors Questions 139
Tours and Facilitated Social Experiences 152
Provocative Exhibition Design 158
Giving Visitors Instructions for Social Engagement 164
Making Objects Shareable 172

CHAPTER 5

DEFINING PARTICIPATION AT YOUR INSTITUTION . **183**

Models for Participation 184
Participation and Mission 192
The Strategic Value of Participation 197

CHAPTER 6

VISITORS AS CONTRIBUTORS **203**

Three Approaches to Contributory Projects 207
Modeling Desired Participant Behavior 213
Curating Contributions 221
Audience Response to Contributory Projects 225

CHAPTER 7

COLLABORATING WITH VISITORS **231**

Two Kinds of Collaboration 235
Structuring Collaboration 238
Staff Roles in Collaborative Projects 243
Collaborating on Research Projects 253
Collaborating with Casual Visitors 256
Audience Response to Collaborative Projects 261

CHAPTER 8

CO-CREATING WITH VISITORS **263**

Designing Platforms for Co-Creation 268
Co-Creation and Institutional Culture 274

CHAPTER 9
HOSTING PARTICIPANTS 281
    Hosting as a Launch Point for Deeper Engagement 292
    Hosting Exhibitions in Community Galleries 295

CHAPTER 10
EVALUATING PARTICIPATORY PROJECTS 301
    Evaluating Impact 303
    Developing Meaningful Measurement Tools 306
    Incremental and Adaptive Participatory Techniques 314
    Involving Participants in Evaluation 317

CHAPTER 11
MANAGING & SUSTAINING PARTICIPATION 321
    Participation and Institutional Culture 323
    Participation Starts with Staff 327
    Staff Strategies for Managing Participation 332
    Managing Participatory Projects Over Time 338
    Sustaining Participation 343

IMAGINING THE PARTICIPATORY MUSEUM 349

PREFACE

WHY
PARTICIPATE?

AT THE END OF 2009, the National Endowment for the Arts released a so-
bering report on the state of arts attendance in the United States. The authors
didn't mince words; in the preface, they wrote, "The 2008 survey results
are, at a glance, disappointing."[1] Over the last twenty years, audiences for
museums, galleries, and performing arts institutions have decreased, and
the audiences that remain are older and whiter than the overall popula-
tion. Cultural institutions argue that their programs provide unique cultural
and civic value, but increasingly people have turned to other sources for
entertainment, learning, and dialogue. They share their artwork, music, and
stories with each other on the Web. They participate in politics and volunteer in record numbers. They even read more. But they don't attend museum
exhibits and performances like they used to.

How can cultural institutions reconnect with the public and demonstrate their value and relevance in contemporary life? I believe they can do

---

1   Download the 2008 NEA Survey of Public Participation in the Arts report
[PDF] at http://www.participatorymuseum.org/refp-1/

this by inviting people to actively engage as cultural participants, not passive consumers. As more people enjoy and become accustomed to participatory learning and entertainment experiences, they want to do more than just "attend" cultural events and institutions. The social Web has ushered in a dizzying set of tools and design patterns that make participation more accessible than ever. Visitors expect access to a broad spectrum of information sources and cultural perspectives. They expect the ability to respond and be taken seriously. They expect the ability to discuss, share, and remix what they consume. When people can actively participate with cultural institutions, those places become central to cultural and community life.

This book presents techniques for cultural institutions to invite visitor participation while promoting institutional goals. Community engagement is especially relevant in a world of increasing participatory opportunities on the social Web, but it is not new. Arguments for audience participation in cultural institutions trace back at least a hundred years. There are three fundamental theories underpinning this book:

1. The idea of the *audience-centered* institution that is as relevant, useful, and accessible as a shopping mall or train station (with thanks to John Cotton Dana, Elaine Heumann Gurian, and Stephen Weil).

2. The idea that visitors *construct their own meaning* from cultural experiences (with thanks to George Hein, John Falk, and Lynn Dierking).

3. The idea that *users' voices can inform and invigorate* both project design and public-facing programs (with thanks to Kathleen McLean, Wendy Pollock, and the design firm IDEO).

I wrote this book not to update or stake claim to these ideas, but to present specific techniques and case studies to make them actionable in contemporary institutions. This doesn't require flashy theaters or blockbuster exhibits. It requires institutions that have genuine respect for and interest in the experiences, stories, and abilities of visitors.

I define a participatory cultural institution as a place where visitors can create, share, and connect with each other around content. *Create* means that visitors contribute their own ideas, objects, and creative expression to the institution and to each other. *Share* means that people discuss, take home, remix, and redistribute both what they see and what they make during their visit. *Connect* means that visitors socialize with other people—staff and visitors—who share their particular interests. *Around content* means that visitors' conversations and creations focus on the evidence, objects, and ideas most important to the institution in question.

The goal of participatory techniques is both to meet visitors' expectations for active engagement and to do so in a way that furthers the mission and core values of the institution. Rather than delivering the same content to everyone, a participatory institution collects and shares diverse, personalized, and changing content co-produced with visitors. It invites visitors to respond and add to cultural artifacts, scientific evidence, and historical records on display. It showcases the diverse creations and opinions of nonexperts. People use the institution as meeting grounds for dialogue around the content presented. Instead of being "about" something or "for" someone, participatory institutions are created and managed "with" visitors.

Why would a cultural institution want to invite visitors to participate? Like all design techniques, participation is a strategy that addresses specific problems. I see participatory strategies as practical ways to enhance, not replace, traditional cultural institutions.

There are five commonly-expressed forms of public dissatisfaction that participatory techniques address:

1. *Cultural institutions are irrelevant to my life.* By actively soliciting and responding to visitors' ideas, stories, and creative work, cultural institutions can help audiences become personally invested in both the content and the health of the organization.

2. *The institution never changes - I've visited once and I have no reason to return.* By developing platforms in which visitors can share ideas and connect with each other in real-time, cultural institutions can offer changing experiences without incurring heavy ongoing content production costs.

3. *The authoritative voice of the institution doesn't include my view or give me context for understanding what's presented.* By

presenting multiple stories and voices, cultural institutions can help audiences prioritize and understand their own view in the context of diverse perspectives.

4. *The institution is not a creative place where I can express myself and contribute to history, science, and art.* By inviting visitors to participate, institutions can support the interests of those who prefer to make and do rather than just watch.

5. *The institution is not a comfortable social place for me to talk about ideas with friends and strangers.* By designing explicit opportunities for interpersonal dialogue, cultural institutions can distinguish themselves as desirable real-world venues for discussion about important issues related to the content presented.

These five challenges are all reasons to pursue participation, whether on the scale of a single educational program or the entire visitor experience. The challenge—and the focus of this book—is how to do it. By pursuing participatory techniques that align with institutional core values, it is possible to make your institution more relevant and essential to your communities than ever before.

————————

This book is organized into two parts. The first part, *Design for Participation*, introduces core principles of participation in cultural institutions and presents three approaches to making exhibitions, educational programs, and visitor services more participatory. The second part, *Participation in Practice*, presents four models for participatory projects and provides specific recommendations for how to develop, evaluate, manage, and sustain participation in ways that advance institutional missions.

This book is accompanied by a website at **www.participatorymuseum.org**.

The website provides the full text of the book, links to all references, and multi-media content that was not possible to present in printed form. You can also add comments and new case studies to the website, which may impact subsequent editions and will certainly influence those who choose to read the book online.

I wrote this book using a participatory process in which hundreds of people contributed their opinions and professional experiences related to visitor participation. This discussion is not over. I hope you will share your own thoughts and questions at www.participatorymuseum.org so we can continue to build a community of practice around participation in cultural institutions.

CHAPTER 6

PRINCIPLES OF PARTICIPATION

IT's 2004. I'm in Chicago with my family, visiting a museum. We're checking out the final exhibit—a comment station where visitors can make their own videos in response to the exhibition. I'm flipping through videos that visitors have made about freedom, and they are really, really bad. The videos fall into two categories:

1. Person stares at camera and mumbles something incomprehensible.
2. Group of teens, overflowing with enthusiasm, "express themselves" via shout-outs and walk-ons.

This is not the participatory museum experience of my dreams. But I don't blame the participants. I blame the design.

How can cultural institutions use participatory techniques not just to give visitors a voice, but to develop experiences that are more valuable and compelling for everyone? This is not a question of intention or desire; it's a question of design. Whether the goal is to promote dialogue or creative expression, shared learning or co-creative work, the design process starts with a simple question: which tool or technique will produce the desired participatory experience?

Designers have answered versions of this question for many kinds of visitor experiences and goals in cultural institutions. Professionals know how to write labels for different audiences. They know what kinds of physical interactions promote competitive play and which promote contemplative exploration. And while they may not always get it right, they are guided by the expectation that design decisions can help them successfully achieve content and experience goals.

When it comes to developing participatory experiences in which visitors create, share, and connect with each other around content the same design thinking applies. The chief difference between traditional and participatory design techniques is the way that information flows between institutions and users. In traditional exhibits and programs, the institution provides content for visitors to consume. Designers focus on making the content consistent and high quality, so that every visitor, regardless of her background or interests, receives a reliably good experience.

In contrast, in participatory projects, the institution supports multi-directional content experiences. The institution serves as a "platform" that connects different users who act as content creators, distributors, consumers, critics, and collaborators. This means the institution cannot guarantee the consistency of visitor experiences. Instead, the institution provides opportunities for diverse visitor co-produced experiences.

TRADITIONAL INSTITUTION   PARTICIPATORY INSTITUTION

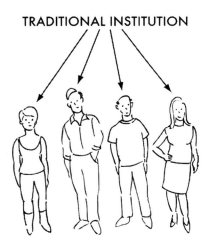
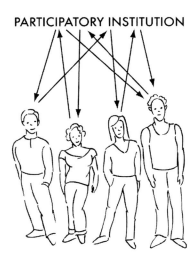

This may sound messy. It may sound tremendously exciting. The key is to harness the mess in support of the excitement. Being successful with a participatory model means finding ways to design participatory platforms so the content that amateurs create and share is communicated and displayed attractively. This is a fundamental shift; in addition to producing consistent content, participatory institutions must also design opportunities for visitors to share their own content in meaningful and appealing ways.

Supporting participation means trusting visitors' abilities as creators, remixers, and redistributors of content. It means being open to the possibility that a project can grow and change post-launch beyond the institution's original intent. Participatory projects make relationships among staff members, visitors, community participants, and stakeholders more fluid and equitable. They open up new ways for diverse people to express themselves and engage with institutional practice.

Making Participation Physical and Scalable

Most institutions prefer to experiment with participation behind closed doors. Cultural institutions have a long history of prototyping new projects with focus groups. Some museums co-develop exhibitions with community members, whether to represent the unique experience of certain ethnic groups or to showcase works of amateur art. These participatory design processes are often institutionally defined, time-limited, and involve a small number of participants.

The growth of social Web technologies in the mid-2000s transformed participation from something limited and infrequent to something possible anytime, for anyone, anywhere. We entered what MIT researcher Henry Jenkins calls a "convergence culture" in which regular people—not just artists or academics—appropriate cultural artifacts for their own derivative works and discussions.[1] Some cultural institutions responded, as did some music and television studios, by locking down their content so it couldn't be used in this way. But as time has gone on, more and more content providers

---

1   Learn more about convergence culture and Jenkins' book with that title at http://www.participatorymuseum.org/ref1-1/

have opened up their material and have invited people to create, share, and connect around it. Particularly for cultural institutions with a mandate to use their collections for public good, digitization and accessibility of content has become a top priority.

But participating with visitors on the Web is just a start. There are also incredible opportunities for cultural institutions to distinguish themselves by encouraging participation in the physical environments of museums, libraries, and arts centers. These institutions have something few Web companies can offer: physical venues, authentic objects, and experienced real-world designers. By combining professional design skills with the lessons of participation pouring out of the social Web, cultural institutions can become leading participatory venues in our cities, towns, and neighborhoods.

For an institution to manage participation, staff members need to be able to design experiences that invite ongoing audience participation sustainably. Traditional participatory bodies like community advisory boards and prototyping focus groups are important, but those forms of participation are limited by design. Participation has the most impact when designers can scale up collaborative opportunities to all interested visitors. This means offering every visitor a legitimate way to contribute to the institution, share things of interest, connect with other people, and feel like an engaged and respected participant.

This leads to an obvious question: does every visitor really want to participate in this manner in cultural institutions? No. Just as there are visitors who will never pull the lever on an interactive and those who prefer to ignore the labels, there are many visitors who will not choose to share their story, talk with a stranger, or consume visitor-generated content. There will always be visitors who enjoy static exhibitions conferring authoritative knowledge. There will always be visitors who enjoy interactive programs that allow them to test that knowledge for themselves. And there will increasingly be visitors—perhaps new ones—who enjoy the opportunity to add their own voices to ongoing discussions about the knowledge presented.

Many museum professionals argue that there are some visitors for whom participatory experiences might be entirely off-putting. This is true, but the converse is also true. There are many people who engage heavily with social media and are incredibly comfortable using participatory platforms to connect with friends, activity partners, and potential dates. There are people who prefer social and creative recreational activities and avoid museums because they perceive them as non-social, non-dynamic, non-participatory places. Just as interactive exhibits were introduced in museums to accommodate the presumed educational needs and active desires of young audiences, participatory elements may draw in audiences for whom creative activities and social connection are preconditions for cultural engagement.

In 1992, Elaine Heumann Gurian wrote an essay entitled "The Importance of 'And'" to address the need for museum practice to accommodate many different and potentially conflicting goals, including scholarship, education, inclusion, and conservation. She commented that we too often think of different institutional goals as oppositional rather than additive, and that "complex organizations must and should espouse the coexistence of more than one primary mission."[2] While the addition of new pursuits to an institutional plan does force some either/or decisions around policies and resources, it need not inhibit the ability to deliver on multiple promises to multiple audiences.

Participatory techniques are another "and" for the cultural professional's toolbox. They are tools that can be used to address particular institutional aspirations to be relevant, multi-vocal, dynamic, responsive, community spaces. Again, I come back to the analogy with interactive exhibits. Interactive design techniques are additive methods that supplement traditional didactic content presentation. Interactive exhibits, when successfully executed, promote learning experiences that are unique and specific to the two-way nature of their design. And while there are some institutions, notably children's and science museums, that have become primarily associated with interactive exhibits, there are other types of museums, notably art and history museums, in which interactives play a supporting role. The introduction of interactive exhibits does not require an entire institutional shift, and in most cultural institutions, interactive exhibits are just one of many interpretative techniques employed.

---

2   See pages 14-18 in Elaine Heumann Gurian's book, *Civilizing the Museum* (2006).

I believe the majority of museums will integrate participatory experiences as one of many types of experiences available to visitors in the next twenty years. There may be a few institutions that become wholly participatory and see their entire institutional culture and community image transformed by this adoption.[3] But in most cases, participation is just one design technique among many, one with a particular ability to enhance the social experience of the institution. Implementing participatory techniques requires some changes to institutional perspectives on authority and audience roles, but these changes may be as small or large as a particular organization's commitment.

Participation at its Best

Whatever role they play in your institution, participatory elements must be well designed to be useful. Poorly designed participatory experiences such as the video comment station mentioned at the beginning of this chapter do little to enhance anyone's experience.

The best participatory projects create new value for the institution, participants, and non-participating audience members. When you are driven by the desire to create new value, you end up with products that are transformative, not frivolous. Consider the story of Bibliotheek Haarlem Oost, a branch library in the Netherlands. The library wanted to find a way to invite readers to assign tags to the books they read.[4] By describing books with phrases like "great for kids," "boring," or "funny," readers could contribute knowledge to the institutional catalogue system while also providing recommendations and opinions for future readers. The participatory act of tagging thus would add benefit to institution and audience alike.

The challenge was how to design the tagging activity. The most obvious way would be to ask readers to type the tags into the library's online catalog, either from home or at the library. But the architect designing the

3   For an example of a radically participatory institution, check out the case study on page 264 on the Wing Luke Asian Museum.
4   Tagging is a term that refers to a collecting activity in which people assign descriptive keywords ("tags") to items.

library, Jan David Hanrath, knew that very few readers would do that. So Hanrath's team did something very clever: they installed more book drops.

The library created a book drop for each of a set of predefined tags. They also built shelves inside the library for the individual tags. When patrons returned books, they placed them on the shelves or in the drops that appropriately described the books. The tags were electronically connected to the books in the catalog, and the new opinions were made immediately available both to in-person and online visitors.

No patron would call the activity of putting their books in book drops "tagging," and that's a good thing. Participation at Haarlem Oost was made easy and its rewards for the next set of visitors searching for a good book were immediate. There were few barriers to adoption or significant infrastructure or support costs. It worked because it was a clever, simple distillation of the core idea of tagging. That's what I call good design.

Doing a sorting activity is a constrained form of participation, but that doesn't diminish its ability to be useful. When I shared the story of the book drops with Daniel Spock, director of the Minnesota Historical Society's History Center (MHC), he was inspired to adapt their model to his institution. Visitors to the MHC wear buttons in the galleries to show that they have paid admission. On their way out, visitors often throw away the buttons, and some end up littering the exit. Spock's team designed a very simple voting mechanism so that instead of littering, visitors could toss their buttons into one of several bins to "vote" for their favorite exhibit they'd seen that day. The simple participatory activity invites people to share their opinions and gives the staff feedback instead of trash. That's what I call value.

Exhibit voting bins outside the Minnesota History Center exit, inspired by the Haarlem Oost book drops.

What Does Participation Look Like?

Dropping buttons into bins may not sound like substantive participation. Many cultural professionals focus on just one kind of participation: the creation of user-generated content. But people who create content represent a narrow slice of the participatory landscape, which also includes people who consume user-generated content, comment on it, organize it, remix it, and redistribute it to other consumers. In 2008, along with the release of the book *Groundswell: Winning in a World Transformed by Social Technologies*, Forrester Research released a "social technographics" profile tool to help businesses understand the way different audiences engage with social media online. The researchers grouped participatory online audiences into six categories by activity:

1. *Creators (24%)* who produce content, upload videos, write blogs
2. *Critics (37%)* who submit reviews, rate content, and comment on social media sites
3. *Collectors (21%)* who organize links and aggregate content for personal or social consumption
4. *Joiners (51%)* who maintain accounts on social networking sites like Facebook and LinkedIn
5. *Spectators (73%)* who read blogs, watch YouTube videos, visit social sites
6. *Inactives (18%)* who don't visit social sites[5]

These percentages add up to more than one hundred percent because the categorizations are fluid and many people fall into several categories at once. I fall into all of the first five categories. I'm a creator when I blog, a critic when I make comments on others' sites, a collector when I assemble "favorites," a joiner on many social networks, and a spectator when I consume social media. The percentages keep changing (and are different for every country, gender, and age group), but one thing stays constant: creators are a small part of the landscape. You are far more likely to join a social network, watch a video on YouTube, make a collection of things you'd like

---

5   The statistics shown here are for adults over 18 in the US as of August 2009. Up-to-date data for different countries, genders, and ages are available at http://www.participatorymuseum.org/ref1-5/

on a shopping site, or review a book than you are to produce a movie, write a blog, or post photos online.

And while 24% of people who engage in the social Web are creators in some capacity, on any given participatory site, the representation of creators is much smaller. Only 0.16% of visitors to YouTube will ever upload a video. Only 0.2% of visitors to Flickr will ever post a photo.[6] In 2006, researcher Jakob Nielsen wrote a landmark paper on participation inequality, introducing the "90-9-1" principle. This principle states: "In most online communities, 90% of users are lurkers who never contribute, 9% of users contribute a little, and 1% of users account for almost all the action."[7]

Participation inequality isn't limited to the Web. Even the most popular participatory opportunities in cultural institutions attract a small number of people who want to draw a picture, make a comment, or contribute to an exhibition. The surprising thing about participation inequality is not that it exists in the real world but that it exists on the Web. Some people believed that the ease of Web-based publishing tools would turn everyone into a journalist, a musician, or a contributor to a wiki. But that's not the case. There are some people who are drawn to create, but many more prefer to participate in other ways, by critiquing, organizing, and spectating social content. This isn't just a question of making creative tools as easy to use as possible. There are some people who will never choose to upload content to the Web, no matter how easy it is. Fortunately, there are other participatory options for them.

Encouraging Diverse Forms of Participation

When museum professionals express objections to participatory practice, one of the most frequent claims is "we don't want to be like YouTube." While I agree that museums should not focus on showcasing videos of cats doing silly things, as a platform, YouTube is an extraordinary service that carefully and deliberately caters to all kinds of social media participants.

---

6   These statistics come from the "Principle in Action" page on the 90-9-1 website at http://www.participatorymuseum.org/ref1-6/

7   Read Jakob Nielsen's October 2006 article, "Participation Inequality: Encouraging More Users to Contribute" at http://www.participatorymuseum.org/ref1-7/

At first glance, YouTube looks like it is made primarily for two audiences: creators, who make and upload videos, and spectators, who watch them. YouTube's tagline—"Broadcast Yourself"—is targeted to the creator audience. Even though only 0.16% of visitors to the site will ever upload a video, YouTube's designers know that the participation of these creators drives the content and the experience of everyone else who visits the site. That's why, despite the fact that the vast majority of their audience are spectators, YouTube's tagline is not "watch funny videos of cats."

A deeper look at the YouTube homepage reveals ways that other types of participation are encouraged as well. Prime real estate is devoted not to creators but to other kinds of participants. You can join YouTube and collect favorite videos across the site. You can critique videos by commenting, rating them, and posting follow-up video responses if desired. These ratings are shown on the homepage, which means that critics and their opinions get top billing alongside the video creators themselves. Finally, YouTube displays the number of times every video has been viewed. Your participation as a viewer affects the status of each video in the system. Just by watching, you are an important participant.

YouTube provides appealing services to all kinds of participants, but the platform's designers spend more time trying to convert spectators into joiners, collectors, and critics than they do trying to encourage more people to become creators. Why focus on these "intermediate" participatory behaviors? First, these behaviors have relatively low barriers to adoption. It's much easier to rate a video than it is to make one—and so conversion is more likely to be successful. But the other key reason is that the platform's value is more dependent on the number of active critics, collectors, and joiners than the number of creators. YouTube doesn't need ten percent or even two percent of its audience to make and upload videos. The overall YouTube experience would likely be worse for spectators if the service was glutted with millions more low-quality videos. The more content there is, the more content there is. In contrast, the more interpretation, prioritization, and discussion there is around the content, the more people can access the videos (and the conversations) that are most valuable to them.

While the top navigation bar invites users to upload videos, the majority of the YouTube homepage is geared toward watching and rating videos. The main area displays "featured videos" to watch, not tools to share your own videos.

Despite the diversity and popularity of participatory options, many museums are fixated on creators. I share Forrester's statistics with colleagues, and they say, "Yes, but we really want people to share their own stories about biodiversity," or, "We think our visitors can make amazing videos about justice." Many cultural professionals see open-ended self-expression as the paragon of participatory experiences. Allowing visitors to select their favorite exhibits in a gallery or comment on the content of the labels isn't considered as valuable as inviting them to produce their own content.

This is a problem for two reasons. First, exhibits that invite self-expression appeal to a tiny percentage of museum audiences. Less than one percent of the users of most social Web platforms create original content. Would you design an interactive exhibit that only one percent of visitors would want to use? Maybe—but only if it was complemented by other exhibits with wider appeal. When I encounter a video talkback kiosk in a museum as a visitor, I never want to make my own video. I don't choose to be a creator in those environments, and thus my only other option is to be a spectator. But I would love to rate the videos on display (as a critic) or group them (as a collector). Unfortunately, those potentially rich participatory experiences—ones which would develop my ability to detect patterns, compare and contrast items, and express my opinion—are not available to me in most museum settings. By making it easy to create content but impossible to sort or prioritize it, many cultural institutions end up with what they fear most: a jumbled mass of low-quality content.

The second problem with focusing on creators is that open-ended self-expression requires self-directed creativity. Much of contemporary learning theory rests on the idea of "instructional scaffolding," by which educators or educational material provides supportive resources, tasks, and guidance upon which learners can build their confidence and abilities.[8] When it comes to participatory activities, many educators feel that they should deliberately remove scaffolding to allow participants to fully control their creative experience. This creates an open-ended environment that can feel daunting to would-be participants. In an open-ended activity, participants have to have

---

8   Consult the work of Lev Vygotsky for foundational material on instructional scaffolding. For a museum-focused discussion, see George Hein's *Learning in the Museum* (1998).

an idea of what they'd like to say or make, and then they have to produce it in a way that satisfies their standards of quality. In other words, it's hard, and it's especially hard on the spot in the context of a casual museum visit. What if I walked up to you on the street and asked you to make a video about your ideas of justice in the next three minutes? Does that sound like a fun and rewarding casual activity to you?

The best participatory experiences are not wide open. They are scaffolded to help people feel comfortable engaging in the activity. There are many ways to scaffold experiences without prescribing the result. For example, a comment board that provides ballots for people to vote for favorite objects and explain the reason behind their preferences offers a better-scaffolded experience than an open-ended board with blank cards and a question like "What do you think?" A supportive starting point can help people participate confidently—whether as creators, critics, collectors, joiners, or spectators.

Who's Involved in Participation?

Participatory projects aren't just about empowering visitors. Every participatory project has three core stakeholders: the institution, participants, and the audience. The audience may mean the institution's visitors, but it can also include other constituencies who might have a particular interest in the outcomes of the project—for example, participants' neighbors or associates. For a project to be successful, the project staff should be able to articulate and satisfy the interests of each group.

From the institutional perspective, participatory projects have value when they satisfy aspects of the mission. Institutions do not engage in participatory projects because they are fun or exciting but because they can serve institutional goals.

This is easier said than done. Many cultural professionals are more familiar with providing visitor experiences than thinking about how visitors can usefully contribute to the institution. When designing participatory components to exhibitions, I always ask myself: how can we use this? What can visitors provide that staff can't? How can they do some meaningful work that supports the institution overall? When staff can answer these questions easily and confidently, participation can yield powerful results for institutions and participants alike.

CASE STUDY
CLIMATE CONFERENCES AT THE WILD CENTER

At The Wild Center in Tupper Lake, New York, participatory engagement is tightly tied to the institutional mission. The Wild Center is a small natural history museum with a mostly seasonal tourist audience, but its mission is quite ambitious: to "ignite an enduring passion for the Adirondacks where people and nature can thrive together and set an example for the world." Executive Director Stephanie Ratcliffe believes that igniting passions and setting examples cannot happen without community participation, and her team identified climate change as a key contemporary issue of interest relating to human coexistence with nature. Staff members felt climate change was not receiving the local attention it deserved from both a business and environmental perspective, and they saw the opportunity to become a place for dialogue around the issue.

In 2008, the institution started inviting builders, politicians, and scientists to come together in dialogue in a series of climate conferences. These conferences served as a hub for locals to understand and act on specific threats that climate change poses to the Adirondacks. The underlying message was that positive action on climate issues could improve town function and business efficiency.

Local citizens responded enthusiastically. After an event focused on "Building a Greener Adirondacks," blogger John Warren wrote:

> Two years ago I was lamenting that no local public leaders were stepping up to the plate on trying to understand what global climate change would mean for the Adirondacks (and its ski-tourism industry) - thankfully, that has changed. The Wild Center in Tupper Lake has taken on the lead role of informing their neighbors about the potential impacts of global warming (such as the impact on amphibians), showing local builders what they can do to mitigate those affects, and organizing sci-

entific meetings to discuss and assess the progress of climate change in the Adirondacks.[9]

Climate conferences are now a core part of The Wild Center's strategic efforts to accomplish its mission.[10] The institution has hosted national and regional conferences for policy-makers and has distributed reports and videos from these events on the Web. In 2009, The Wild Center initiated a yearly Adirondack Youth Climate Summit to bring together educators, high school students, and college students in dialogue about research and action on climate change. The institution has also has become a lead partner in a local coalition to produce an Adirondack Climate and Energy Action Plan.

Over 200 students and school administrators gathered at The Wild Center in November 2009 for an Adirondack Youth Climate Summit. Each school team developed a climate action plan with measurable steps to reduce its carbon footprint.

9   Read John Warren's October 2008 blog post, "Wild Center: Local Leader on Adirondack Climate Change," at http://www.participatorymuseum.org/ref1-9/
10 Explore the full slate of The Wild Center's climate initiatives at http://www.participatorymuseum.org/ref1-10/

The climate events helped established The Wild Center as a national player, and equally importantly, as a local community resource. Participating in this highly strategic way with community members in The Wild Center's geographic area enabled this small, young institution to become a powerful voice of and for its constituents.

Outcomes for Participants and Audiences

Outcomes of participation may be as diverse as the goals of the institution overall. These outcomes include: to attract new audiences, to collect and preserve visitor-contributed content, to provide educational experiences for visitors, to produce appealing marketing campaigns, to display locally-relevant exhibitions, and to become a town square for conversation.

You should be able to define the specific way that a participatory project can benefit your institution and be ready to connect that value to your institution's mission statement. It may be valuable for one museum to receive lots of snail shells collected from visitors, whereas another institution may find value in providing a forum where visitors discuss their opinions on racism. It's also important to clearly state what kinds of participation would *not* be useful. Contributed snail shells that would thrill one institution might be a nuisance for another.

Unfortunately, many cultural professionals settle for an unambitious value of participation that is not compelling to institutional directors nor stakeholders: *visitors will like it*. This is not a robust value. It trivializes the mission-relevance of participatory projects. If you focus solely on participation as a "fun activity," you will do a disservice both to yourself as a professional and to visitors as participants.

Yes, it is fun to help paint a mural or construct a giant model of a molecule. But these activities also promote particular learning skills, create outputs that are usable by others, and promote the institution as a social place. The more you think about which mission-relevant goals you want to support, the more likely you are to design a project that satisfies more than the visitors' desires to be entertained. As Geoff Godbey, professor of leisure studies at Pennsylvania State University, commented in a Wall Street Journal article: "To be most satisfying, leisure should resemble the best aspects of work: challenges, skills and important relationships."[11] Participatory projects can accommodate these interests and are often better suited to providing visitors with meaningful work than traditional museum experiences.

Participatory projects suffer when visitors perceive that the staff is pandering to them or wasting their time with trivialities. Participatory activities should never be a "dumping ground" for interactivity or visitor dialogue. In cases where visitors are actually asked to "do work," that work should be useful to the institution. It's fine to design participatory projects in which visitors produce work that could more quickly or accurately be completed by internal staff members; however, the work should still be of value to the institution ultimately.[12] If the museum doesn't care about the outcomes of visitors' participation, why should visitors participate?

Meeting Participants' Needs

In the book *Here Comes Everybody*, technologist Clay Shirky argued that there are three necessary components for a participatory mechanism to be successful: "a plausible promise, an effective tool, and an acceptable bargain with the [participants]."[13] The institution must *promise* an appealing participant experience. The institution must provide access to *tools* for participation that are easy to understand and use. And the *bargain* between institution and participants—regarding management of intellectual property, outcomes of the project, and feedback to participants—should accommodate participants' needs. Even if your promise, tools, or bargains have to change over the course of a project, you should always be able to articulate what you offer and expect clearly and openly. Doing so demonstrates your respect for participants' time and abilities.

Note that you can substitute the word "volunteer" for "participant" for a snapshot of the ways an institution's most dedicated supporters would like to be engaged. Volunteers and members are people who express

11 Read Jared Sandberg's July 2006 *Wall Street Journal* article on active leisure at http://www.participatorymuseum.org/ref1-11/
12 For a longer discussion on the multiple values of participation, see page 193.
13 See Chapter 11 in Shirky, *Here Comes Everybody: The Power of Organizing without Organizations* (2008).

self-motivated commitment and interest to dedicate time and resources to institutions. Too often, staff members struggle to find fulfilling and substantive activities for volunteers to do. But when institutions can clearly convey how participants' actions will contribute positively to the institution and to future audiences, volunteers of all types respond enthusiastically.

When it comes to the promise, staff members need to offer participants something fundamental: personal fulfillment. Institutions have explicit mission-related goals that dictate which activities are valuable to pursue, but individuals don't have mission statements. Instead, participants have a wide range of personal goals and interests that motivate behavior. John Falk's research into visitors and identity-fulfillment indicates that visitors select and enjoy museum experiences based on their perceived ability to reflect and enhance particular self-concepts.[14] If you think of yourself as creative, you will be fulfilled by the opportunity to contribute a self-portrait to a crowd-sourced exhibition. If you see yourself as someone with valuable stories to share, you will be fulfilled by the chance to record your own recollections related to content on display. If you perceive yourself as helpful, you will be fulfilled by the opportunity to pitch in on tasks that clearly support a larger goal.

Watching a performance or passively walking through an exhibition does not give people this kind of social, active fulfillment. Especially for adult visitors, museums rarely offer challenges that encourage participants to work hard and demonstrate their creative, physical, or cognitive ability. Games researcher Jane McGonigal has stated that people need four things to be happy: "satisfying work to do, the experience of being good at something, time spent with people we like, and the chance to be part of something bigger."[15] Many people visit museums in social groups to spend time with people they like in the context of something bigger. Creating content can give visitors satisfying work and the experience of being good at something. When you put these together and invite people to participate, the institution can meet all four of these needs.

---

14 See John Falk's book, *Identity and the Museum Visitor Experience* (2009).
15 McGonigal shared this list in a cultural context in a December 2008 lecture, "Gaming the Future of Museums." See slide 22 in this presentation for the list: http://www.participatorymuseum.org/ref1-15/

When presenting participatory opportunities to would-be partici-pants, be explicit about how they can fulfill their own needs and contribute to a project with larger impact. Just as casting activities as being "just for fun" devalues the mission-relevance of participation, it also minimizes visitors' understanding of how they can make a meaningful and exciting contribution to the greater community. If you need participants to make a project suc-cessful—whether a research project that requires distributed volunteers, a feedback project that requires diverse opinions, or a creative project that re-quires many hands on deck—say so. The most compelling promises emerge from genuine needs on the part of the institution.

When it comes to the tool, participants need clear roles and informa-tion about how to participate. The tool should also be as flexible as possible. Participants don't need to engage with the same project in a uniform way or at the same level of commitment. You may not want staff members coming in whenever they feel like it, but flexibility is an asset when it comes to participation—you want participants to be able to engage when and how they are most able.

When participants contribute to institutions, they want to see their work integrated in a timely, attractive, respectful way. Too many participa-tory projects have broken feedback loops, where the ability to see the results of participation are stalled by opaque and slow-moving staff activities like content moderation or editing. In some cases, it is completely acceptable to have a lag between participatory action and outcome for intermediate processing. But if a delay is required, it should be communicated clearly to participants. This can even be turned to the institution's advantage. For example, the museum may send an email to a visitor days or weeks after the visit to inform her that her sculpture is now on display or her story integrated into an audio tour.

Regardless of the timeline, rewarding participants involves three steps that should remain consistent. First, the institution should clearly explain how and when visitors will be rewarded for participating. Second, it should thank visitors immediately upon participating, even if their content will now go into a holding pattern. And third, the staff should develop some workable process to display, integrate, or distribute the participatory content—and ideally, inform participants when their work is shared.

At their best, these three steps are immediate, automatic, and obvious to visitors. Imagine a children's museum that includes an area where visitors can build sculptures or toys out of found objects. Visitors can place their creations on a conveyor belt that moves throughout the museum for all to see. In this case, there are no labels necessary. Visitors see what will happen to their sculptures when they put them on the belt, and they understand of how that might fulfill their self-interest in sharing their work with their community of fellow-visitors.

Providing a good bargain for participation means valuing participants' work. This doesn't require giving every visitor a gold star for participating. It means listening to participants, providing feedback on their efforts, and demonstrating how the institution will use their contributions.

Whether the institution asks for a long commitment or a brief encounter, clarity and honesty are the keys to helping participants feel comfortable contributing. This includes addressing issues of privacy and intellectual property. What happens to the videos that participants record in the gallery? Who owns the ideas they share with the institution? Being clear, specific, and honest about participants' roles in participatory projects helps people know what to expect and evaluate whether an opportunity is right for them.

Lack of clarity erodes trust between institutions and participants and can lead to substandard experiences for both. In August of 2008, I worked with the Chabot Space & Science Center on a participatory design institute in which eleven teenagers designed media pieces for an upcoming Harvard-Smithsonian exhibition on black holes. Unfortunately, while the Harvard-Smithsonian representatives were enthusiastic about encouraging teens to "be creative," they were unable to give the teens any specific information about how their work would be integrated into the final exhibit. There was no initial design, no graphics, and no idea of where the teens' work would fit into the overall website. This lack of clarity made teens suspicious that the client was "hiding" the goals from them and preventing them from meeting the criteria for success. In the end, the teens' work was not in line with the client's final website design, and their work was marginalized rather than being featured in the final product. Lack of clarity at the beginning led to a somewhat frustrating experience for participants and an unsatisfactory product for the institution.

When complete clarity is not possible, honesty suffices. The Chabot project was not a failure. While we could not give the teenagers the answers they wanted, we were direct with them about what we did and didn't know and supported them as best we could. Staff members can change their mind, make mistakes, and evolve with participants if they are honest every step of the way. And the more the staff can express to participants—in actions as well as words—how their work helps the institution or other visitors, the more participants will see themselves as partners and co-owners of the project and the institution by extension.

Creating Quality Outcomes for Audiences

Participatory projects are not solely for institutions and participants. There is another populous constituency: the audience of non-participating visitors. How can a participatory project produce outcomes that are valuable and interesting to the larger institutional audience? Some participatory environments are continually open and evolving, so that any audience member can electively become a participant, but most projects limit participation to a small group. It is simpler to say, "You can submit your idea until the end of the year" or "We will work with twenty teenagers from a local high school to develop this project," than it is to construct a system that can let anyone participate at any time. For many institutions, constraining the scope of participation is an appropriate starting point for collaborative engagement.

No matter how large the participating group, the audience for their work matters. Participants' experiences, no matter how superlative, must be weighed against the experience that others will have with the outcome of their work. A mural isn't just for those who painted it; it must bring pleasure to others as an art object as well. Likewise, exhibits, research, marketing materials, programs, and experiences produced in collaboration with visitors must be compelling outputs in their own right. That is not to say they can't be different from standard institutional programs. Ideally, projects developed using participatory models will have unique value that cannot be achieved by traditional processes.

Audience goals, like participant goals, are based on individuals' diverse and idiosyncratic criteria for fulfillment. You can't please everyone, but staff can decide what kind of experiences they want to offer and design participatory platforms to accommodate those. Some visitors are looking for high-quality consumer experiences and do not care about the process by which those experiences are developed. For those visitors, project staff need to make sure the participatory process can deliver a product at the desired levels of rigor, design, and content. Other visitors want to familiarize themselves with participation from the "safe space" of spectating before jumping in. For those would-be participants, staff members should design in mechanisms that celebrate, encourage, model, and value participants' work. The more specifically you can define the intended audience for a project, the more successful you will be at designing a participatory project that will satisfy their needs.

How Does Participation Work?

There are two counter-intuitive design principles at the heart of successful participatory projects. First, participants thrive on constraints, not open-ended opportunities for self-expression. And second, to collaborate confidently with strangers, participants need to engage through personal, not social, entry points. These design principles are both based on the concept of scaffolding. Constraints help scaffold creative experiences. Personal entry points scaffold social experiences. Together, these principles set the stage for visitors to feel confident participating in creative work with strangers.

Participation Thrives on Constraints

If your goal is to invite visitors to share their experiences in a way that celebrates and respects their unique contributions to your institution, you need to design more constraints, not fewer, on visitor self-expression. Consider a mural. If given the chance, very few people would opt to paint a mural on their own. The materials are not the barriers—the ideas and the confidence are. You have to have an idea of what you want to paint and how to do it.

But now imagine being invited to participate in the creation of a mural. You are handed a pre-mixed color and a brush and a set of instructions. You know what you are supposed to do to be successful. You get to contribute to a collaborative project that produces something beautiful. You see the overall value of the project. You can point out your work in the final product with pride. You have been elevated by the opportunity to contribute to the project.

This is a well-scaffolded participatory experience. In successful participatory projects, visitors don't build exhibits from scratch or design their own science experiments. Instead, they participate in larger projects: joining the team, doing their part. Constrained projects often provide opportunities for partial self-expression—a flourishing brush stroke here, a witty sentence there—but the overall expressive element is tightly constrained by the participatory platform at hand. Meaningful constraints motivate and focus participation. As Orson Welles put it, "the enemy of art is the absence of limitations."

The Denver Art Museum (DAM) provided an excellent example of a constrained participatory museum experience in their *Side Trip* gallery on display in the spring of 2009. *Side Trip* was an interactive space that accompanied an exhibition of psychedelic rock music posters called *The Psychedelic Experience*. In one *Side Trip* activity, museum educators invited visitors to make their own rock music posters. Rather than giving people blank sheets of paper and markers (and reaching a narrow audience of self-motivated creators), the DAM educators devised an activity that blended collecting, critiquing, and creating. Visitors were offered clipboards with transparencies attached. There were stacks of graphics—cut-out reproductions from the real rock posters on display next door—which visitors could place under the transparencies to rearrange and remix into poster designs of their own choosing. Visitors then used dry erase markers to trace over the graphics, augment them, and add their own creative flair. When a visitor was satisfied with her recombined poster, she handed it to a staff member, who put it in a color copier to create a completed composite. Each visitor

Visitors carefully constructed their own rock music posters at the Denver Art Museum by placing graphics under transparencies and drawing additions on top. *Side Trip's* immersive environment encouraged visitors both to connect to the pscyhedelic era and to behave differently than they would in other galleries.

Visitors' posters demonstrated an attractive blend of creative appropriation and remix.

was given a copy of her poster and was given the option to display a copy in the gallery.

The results of this physical "remix" activity were beautiful, intricate posters. As a *Side Trip* visitor, I couldn't easily tell where the remixed artifacts ended and the participants' additions began. 37,000 posters were made over the run of the show, compared to total exhibit attendance of 90,000. The average amount of time spent making a poster was twenty-five minutes. This was a popular activity that visitors took seriously.

The poster-making activity was successful because visitors didn't have to start with a blank slate. Their creativity was scaffolded by graphic cut-outs that also tied their creative experience to the artifacts in the show. The constraints gave participants a comfortable entry point to engagement without limiting their creative potential. It invited visitors who did not think they could make art to engage confidently with a positive result. It created an attractive, high quality body of visitor-generated content for spectators to enjoy.

Why aren't more museums designing highly constrained participatory platforms in which visitors contribute to collaborative projects? The misguided perception is that it's more respectful to allow visitors to do their own thing—that the highest-value participatory experiences will emerge from unfettered self-expression. But that idea reflects a misunderstanding of what motivates participation. Visitors don't want a blank slate for participation. They need well-scaffolded experiences that put their contributions to meaningful use.

Going Social

So far, we've looked at a few techniques for designing experiences that invite diverse participation and produce meaningful work. But another key focus of this book is the design of experiences that encourage people to participate socially with each other. To design successful social experiences, you don't start by designing "for the crowd." Instead, think of yourself as a cocktail party host. Your job is to graciously and warmly welcome each individual, and then to connect her with other people whom she might connect with particularly well. When you connect enough individuals to each other, they start feeling like they are part of a communal experience. I call this "me-to-we" design, which builds on individual (me) experiences to support collective (we) engagement.

In other words, you don't start from the top down to design a participatory space. Transforming a cultural institution into a social hub requires engaging individual users and supporting connections among them. While at a party a host might connect people for a variety of reasons—shared professional fields, shared love of Basset Hounds, common personality traits— in a museum, staff members should connect people through the content on display. By introducing individual visitors through the content they both love, hate, or have a personal connection to, staff can motivate dialogue and relationship building around the core focus of the institution.

This evolution of the visitor experience from personal to communal interactions can be expressed via five stages of interface between institution and visitor. The foundation of all five stages is content. What changes is how visitors interact with content and how the content helps them connect socially with other people.

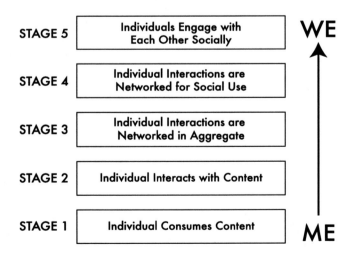

Each stage has something special to offer visitors. *Stage one* provides visitors with access to the content that they seek. *Stage two* provides an opportunity for inquiry and for visitors to take action and ask questions. *Stage three* lets visitors see where their interests and actions fit in the wider community of visitors to the institution. *Stage four* helps visitors connect with particular people—staff members and other visitors—who share their content and activity interests. *Stage five* makes the entire institution feel like a social place, full of potentially interesting, challenging, enriching encounters with other people.

These stages are progressive in that you cannot consistently design physical environments for a stage five experience without providing the groundwork of stages one through four. They are somewhat flexible; there are some highly social people who can easily jump from stage two to stage five, whereas other people may feel most comfortable never moving beyond stage three. Not all institutional projects should be designed for upper-stage experiences. Each stage affords a different kind of visitor experience, and most visitors experience multiple stages in a given cultural experience.

At present, most institutionally designed experiences are on stages one and two. I do not advocate a re-staging of all visitor experiences but rather the inclusion of a greater diversity of experience types, including some that promote the social over the personal. While many traditional museum visitors may be happy with a blend of stage one and two experiences, there are other potential visitors for whom the introduction of stage three, four, and five experiences can make the institution more enticing and meaningful.

Many cultural institutions provide facilitated experiences on all five stages. Tour guides and educators frequently help visitors feel comfortable and confident engaging socially with each other. Facilitated educational programs like camps or reenactments provide stage five opportunities to work in a team or group.[16] The problem is that when the facilitator isn't there or the event isn't happening that social engagement ceases to exist. Designing stage three and four experiences can lay the groundwork to support and encourage unfacilitated social experiences. These frameworks enable visitors to do it for themselves whenever they like.

---

16 See page 153 for an example of a stage five program at the Conner Prairie historic park called *Follow the North Star*.

For example, consider the experience of visiting a historic house on a guided tour. There are many stage one experiences in which visitors can look at things and learn information about the house. There are some stage two opportunities for visitors to touch things, ask questions, and dig into personal interests. Because many visitors tour historic houses in groups with strangers, there is the potential for experiences on stages three to five. Guides can ask individuals to vote for the room they'd most like to live in and see how they compare to others in the group (stage three). Guides can encourage subsets of people who have particular interests, say, in the lives of servants, to spend time in dialogue with each other around artifacts related to that interest (stage four). And the best guides make the group feel like a close-knit team, working together to answer each other's questions and discover new surprises (stage five).

Without a guide, a visit to a historic house is much less social. Visitors look and learn on their own with the companions who accompany them on their visit. The institution makes stage one and two experiences available, but not upper-level social engagement. If visitors engage with strangers, it is based entirely on personal initiative.

How could a historic house encourage visitors to have social experiences with each other outside the guided tour? Stage three and four activities can be designed as unfacilitated experiences. The stage three "vote for your favorite room" mechanism could be a cardboard floor plan on which visitors vote by sticking a pin on their favorite rooms. Visitors could have stage four interactions with other people with similar interests prompted by labels that encourage visitors to share personal memories with strangers through audio-recordings or letter-writing stations.

Designing unfacilitated opportunities for social engagement makes visitors more likely to see each other as potential sources of information and enjoyment in the house. Once this feeling is widespread, the house is ripe for stage five experiences, in which visitors feel comfortable pointing things out to strangers, having brief discussions about their own memories, and so on.

I'm not suggesting that institutions replace educators, front-line staff, or volunteers with exhibitry. Staff interactions provide the most consistent kinds of social experiences, and staff can be an important bridge to support and enhance even the most social exhibit design. Indeed, many of the examples in this book rely on staff or volunteers to work successfully.

But staff cannot be everywhere. Designing physical spaces to support interaction means that it can happen anytime, even when guides or staff members are not available. The goal is not to replace staff but to scale up the opportunity for social engagement. This is what the social Web does so well. It leverages the interests and profiles of individuals to create opportunities for new connections and social experiences.

Let's look at an example of me-to-we design from the corporate world that successfully provides experiences at all stages around a frequently disliked, voluntary activity that takes place all over the world. No, I'm not talking about visiting museums. I'm talking about running, and a platform called Nike Plus.

CASE STUDY
FROM ME-TO-WE WITH NIKE PLUS

Nike Plus (Nike+) is a combined iPod and shoe sensor product for tracking personal running. It provides real-time data about your progress as you run and stores your data for later review online. You can create goals for yourself and challenge other users (both friends and strangers) to run at your pace or complete a target number of miles. You can also create motivational playlists for the iPod to give you a "power-up" audio boost when you most need it. When you start to lag, your favorite song will get you back on track.

Nike+ uses me-to-we design brilliantly to support a product, an activity, a community, and ultimately, a healthy lifestyle. It offers experiences on all five stages of user engagement.

Nike+ is built on two basic products: shoes and music. These provide a stage one experience—you consume music as the pavement consumes your shoes. There's nothing special about Nike+ on stage one.

On stage two, Nike+ distinguishes itself by providing real-time data tracking. It is responsive to your actions and provides you with feedback to influence further action. Nike+ users report that the experience of being tracked actually improves their performance. The real-time statistics help motivate people along their runs, and reviewing the data later helps them spot their weaknesses and set future goals for improvement.

Nike+ gives users points and virtual trophies for completing personal goals. The game-like tracking system makes for an addictive individual stage two experience. But the individual experience with the system can only take you so far. If you take a break from running or stop looking at your statistics on the Web, the memories of trophies and goals slip away. Why run? It's not even a human encouraging you—just a stupid machine.

And that's where stage three comes in. In the online environment for Nike+, users can see the goals and runs set by other people, and use them as inspiration. Seeing the aggregate actions of other runners in the stage three environment helps people see themselves as part of a community, even if they don't connect with other individuals directly. If fifty thousand other people can run ten miles, maybe you can too.

Then Nike+ goes further, offering "collective challenges," in which users team up based on a wide range of similarities or affinities (gender, age, political affiliation, athletic ability) to accomplish shared running goals. This is a stage four experience. When you engage in a collective challenge, you don't just focus on your own running goals or compare yourself to the masses. You have external goals for which you are accountable to virtual teammates. You're motivated to run so you can meet the challenge and contribute to the team. Here's how one enthusiastic blogger, Caleb Sasser, put it:

> And the coolest part about Nike+ running? Like any good online game, you can challenge your friends. First to 100 miles? Fastest 5-mile time? Your call. These challenges wind up being incredibly inspiring — running against good friend and athletic powerhouse J. John Afryl kept me on my toes — and they're also incredibly fun. Logging in after a long run, uploading your data, and seeing where you are in the standings, is a pretty awesome way to wrap up your exercise. And more importantly, sitting around the house, wondering what to do, thinking about jogging, and then realizing that if you don't go jogging tonight you're going to lose points and slip in the standings — now that's true, videogame motivation.[17]

---

17 Read Cabel Sasser's effusive August 2006 blog post, "Multiplayer Game of the Year," at http://www.participatorymuseum.org/ref1-17/

The combination of game mechanics with social challenges makes Nike+ a powerful stage four experience. But what about stage five? One of Nike's goals—and a major component of their online presence—is to encourage people to run together. The company sponsors races and running groups all over the world.

There are many Nike+ online forums and opportunities for meeting up with real people in your real neighborhood to go running. But there are also Nike+ users who have clamored for ways to run with their distant virtual teammates. It's not crazy to imagine a future version of Nike+ that allows you to talk real-time to a running partner halfway around the world as you both navigate the streets.

Think about what a strange feat Nike pulled off with this product. Nike took a non-screen-based, often anti-social, occasionally loathed or feared activity—running—and turned it into a screen-supported social game. It transformed the motivation to run from being about exercise to being about social competition. Nike+ took an uncontrolled venue—the streets and trails used by runners all over the world—and created a compelling experience around it. For its users, Nike+ transforms running into a pervasive, fun, socially driven experience. And if Nike could do it for something as feared and despised as running often is, surely you can do it for your cultural institution.

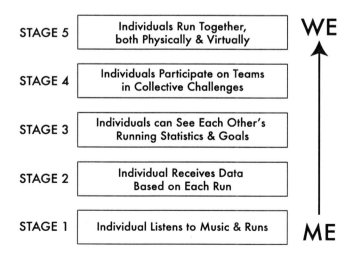

The five stages of me-to-we design for Nike Plus.

Where do you start in designing systems that can help visitors connect to each other through their content interests? Before considering social opportunities for stage three, four, and five experiences, it's important to begin by getting to know visitors as individuals. Remember the cocktail party analogy. If you want to help visitors and staff members connect with the people who will be most interesting and useful to them, you need to welcome them personally and acknowledge their individual interests and abilities. Chapter 2 is all about ways to make cultural institutions more personal so that visitors can feel comfortable, confident, and motivate to participate.

CHAPTER 2

PARTICIPATION BEGINS WITH ME

IN THE SUMMER OF 2009, I took up beach volleyball. My first day of adult beginner volleyball class, the instructor, Phil Kaplan, said, "You're all a little nervous today. You don't know anyone. You don't know how to play. It's ok. By the time you leave you will have lots of friends to play volleyball with." In week one, Kaplan learned all thirty-five of our names. He split us into groups by skill level and gave each group instruction based on their needs. He asked a volunteer to set up an email list and encouraged us to schedule other times to practice together. Some of us used the list to start playing on our own, and by the fall, we had formed a tight group of friends who played together weekly. Almost a year later, I still play volleyball and socialize with many of these folks.

We went from being isolated strangers led by a strong instructor to becoming a self-organized group who are socially and substantively connected to each other through a new activity. We didn't leave the class, thank the teacher, and fall back into our private lives—which is what usually happens when I take a course or a guided tour. How did this happen?

Kaplan did a few key things that differentiated this experience:

1. *His class was audience-centered.* He grouped us by our needs and abilities, provided customized instruction to each group, and shifted us from group to group as our individual needs changed.
2. *He treated us as individuals instead of a crowd of students.* I didn't see the other people in the class as a bunch of people who also wanted to play volleyball. I saw them as Pam the rower, Max the dentist, and Roger the dancer. Kaplan encouraged us to get to know each other personally and make new social connections.
3. *He gave us tools to connect with each other.* During class, Kaplan asked us to pair up with different individuals to play and learn together. He modeled a friendly, social attitude that we emulated. But he also made it easy for us to access each other and the volleyball courts outside of class. He encouraged us to manage our own correspondence and keep playing and learning together.

Cultural institutions are like volleyball courts. Expert visitors and staff already know how to play. They are confident about how to use the space, what's available, and how to connect with content of interest. But there are many casual and infrequent visitors who would like to participate but don't know how to start. These people need friendly hosts like Phil Kaplan who can respond to them personally and help them find the activities, information, and people who will be most relevant to their needs. By welcoming people personally and responding to their specific interests, you can foster an environment in which everyone will feel confident and energized about participating with your institution and with each other.

Audience First

The first step to personalizing cultural institutions is to take an audience-centered approach to the experiences offered. This doesn't mean throwing out the things the staff thinks are important, but it means framing them in the context of what visitors want or need. Instead of starting by describing what an institution or project can provide, audience-centric design processes start by mapping out audiences of interest and brainstorming the experiences, information, and strategies that will resonate most with them.

Traditional points of entry—the admissions desk, the map, the docent tour—are not typically designed to be audience-centric. Ticket transactions occasionally confer information about particular offerings of the day, but not necessarily offerings of interest to the visitors at hand. Maps feature abstractions that reflect institutional organization of content, not visitor interests or needs. Even staff interactions, such as docent tours, can present content in an impersonal (or worse, self-absorbed) manner. While some docents are excellent at adapting their tours responsively to their audiences, eliciting or intuiting visitors' needs can be a challenge. Visitors come in the door knowing who they are, but they may not know what content is of greatest interest to them.

This inattention to visitors' unique needs inordinately affects people who are unfamiliar with cultural institutions—visitors who are still learning to decode what a museum experience is all about. To novice visitors, maps and tours are not obvious starting points full of useful information from which they can dig deeper. These supposed entry techniques introduce further layers of abstraction and ritual to the museum experience that may be confusing or off-putting. These visitors need to see how cultural institutions are relevant and valuable to their own lives, and the easiest way to deliver that is via personalized entry points that speak to people's individual needs and interests. Visitors' varied needs—to accommodate energetic children, to be inspired, to see something novel—are rarely represented on institutional maps and program listings. Labels like "Blue Wing" or "People of the Land" don't help visitors understand what they can see, do, and experience in various places and programs. How can a visitor learn to "make her own meaning" from a museum experience if she cannot make meaning from the map?

Theme parks address this issue well. Like museums, they have aggregated areas with abstract titles (e.g. Tomorrowland) and within those, rides with only slightly more descriptive names (Space Mountain). But on the maps, alongside the names of the rides, there is shorthand information— what kind of ride it is and what ages it's appropriate for. Many theme park maps also feature pop-outs with lists of "must-dos" for visitors of different type—teenagers, people who only have 3 hours, etc. These recommendations are not only based on what visitors might enjoy (roller coasters vs. swings) but also on their particular constraints and situations. And the maps always include information about where to get a snack, find a toilet, or relax between high-impact activities. Theme parks are serious about helping visitors figure out what experiences will be most appropriate for them in all ways.

In 2007, a collection of museums in North East England decided to take an audience-centric approach in a marketing campaign called *I Like Museums*.[1] *I Like Museums* is an online directory of eighty-two museums in North East England that encourages visitors to explore "museum trails"—short lists of institutions—that are based on audience interests, not institutional content. This is the basic premise behind *I Like Museums*: whatever experience you seek, there are museums in North East England that can provide it. Yes, there are content trails, like "I like military history." But there are also trails like "I like keeping the kids happy," for adults facilitating family outings, or "I like a nice cuppa," for people who want to relax with some tea. While staff members and community members developed the initial *I Like Museums* trails, new ones are submitted on a continuous basis by visitors to the site.

In a survey of 2,071 visitors to nine institutions involved in *I Like Museums*, 36% of visitors who were aware of the campaign cited it as influencing their decision to visit. These museum trails were accessible and relevant to people because they started with who they are, not what the institution offers. As a visitor, you don't have to decode whether Lady Waterford Hall or the Centre for Life or any number of enigmatic institutions might accommodate your unique interests. You can find a place to play, a place to be inspired, a place to shop. These are all personalized entry points to museum experiences. And by displaying them all together on one site, *I Like Museums* encourages people to think of museums as multi-use venues, good for different people on different days in different ways. The website subtly gives you more and more reasons to visit a museum beyond viewing its collection.

---

1   Explore the *I Like Museums* trails at http://www.participatorymuseum.org/ref2-1/

Whether potential visitors are seeking inspiration, model trains, or even "places to go with a hangover," the *I Like Museums* website offers museums to satisfy.

The Tate Modern took a similar approach in their physical museum in 2006, when they released a set of quirky pamphlets featuring different tours of the museum based on emotional mood. Visitors could pick up the "I've just split up" tour and wallow in angst, or the "I'm an animal freak" tour and explore their wilder sides.[2] Like the *I Like Museums* trails, these pamphlets allow visitors to quickly select a starting point that in some way reflects personal interests.

Pulling Out Meaning

Both *I Like Museums* and The Tate Modern's pamphlets invite visitors to pull specific content of interest instead of consuming content that is pushed out indiscriminately by the institution. "Pull content" is a term educators use to designate information that learners actively seek or retrieve based on self-interest. Pull techniques emphasize visitors' active roles in seeking out information. Visitors are always somewhat active in their pursuit of interpretation, deciding whether or not to read a label or play with an interactive. But when you invite visitors to retrieve interpretative material rather than laying it out, it gives them a kind of participatory power. They choose what to reveal and explore.

The most familiar pull device in museums is the random access audio tour, in which visitors punch numbers into an audio guide or their phone to selectively listen to interpretative material. "Random access" is a strange term to describe what is really "direct" access—information that can be consumed out of sequence. Random access was the technological

2   Explore the Tate Modern's pamphlets and visitor-created tours of the Tate's collection at http://www.participatorymuseum.org/ref2-2/

innovation that transformed museum audio tours from forced narratives into open-ended explorations. Museums with multiple-channel audio tours geared towards different audiences often use different visual icons for each tour, so you can see that a particular painting has audio commentary on the teen channel and the conservator channel, whereas another sculpture in the same room might just have audio commentary for children. You can pick what you want to hear thanks to random access.

Audio tours, like the Tate Modern's pamphlets, are optional. Pull techniques have the greatest impact when they are integral to the visitor experience. For example, in 2004, a team from the Swedish Interactive Institute created a unique pull device for exploration of a historic blast furnace site in the old steel town of Avesta. The site itself featured no interpretative push material—no labels or media elements. Instead, each visitor was given a special flashlight that could trigger interpretative material when pointed at hotspots painted around the site.[3] The flashlights activated interpretative experiences including light projections, audio tracks, and occasional physical experiences (i.e. smoke and heat). There were two layers of content in the hotspots: educational (how the blast furnace works, explanation of certain elements and history) and poetic (imagistic stories from the perspective of steel workers based on historical sources). Visitors could walk through the blast furnace site and receive none of the interpretative material if they chose, or they could use the flashlights to activate content. The flashlights were both a figurative and literal tool for visitors to illuminate the blast furnace and its stories.

This technique, like all audience-centric initiatives, requires staff members to trust that visitors can and will find the content that is most useful to them. When staff members put their confidence in visitors in this way, it signals that visitors' preconceptions, interests, and choices are good and valid in the world of the museum. And that makes visitors feel like the owners of their experiences.

---

3   Explore a digital model of the Avesta experience at http://www.participatory-museum.org/ref2-3/

Treating People as Individuals

Providing audience-centric ways to enter and access cultural experiences is the first building block in personalizing the institution. The next step is to take a more individualized approach to identifying, acknowledging, and responding to people and their interests.

There are some social venues, like rock concerts, where people enjoy being anonymous members of the crowd. But in most social environments, it's lonely, even terrifying. The fictional bar *Cheers* was "the place where everybody knows your name" for a reason—being treated as an individual is the starting point for enjoyable community experiences.

Cultural institutions are often terrible at this, especially when it comes to visitors. Even at museums where I'm a member, I am rarely welcomed as anything but another body through the gate. This lack of personalization at entry sets an expectation that I am not valued as an individual by the institution. I am just a faceless visitor.

To some extent, ameliorating that facelessness is a simple matter of providing good guest service. Vishnu Ramcharan manages the front-line staff (called "hosts") at the Ontario Science Centre. He trains hosts with a simple principle: hosts should make every visitor feel wanted. As Ramcharan put it: "The hosts shouldn't just be excited generally that visitors are there, but that you specifically showed up today. They should make you feel that *you* are someone they are thrilled to see at the Science Centre." This may sound trite, but when you see Ramcharan's smile, you feel as you do in the hands of any accomplished party host—desired, special, and ready to engage.

Personal Profiles

While kind welcomes are a good start, you can't treat visitors as individuals until you actually know what is unique about each of them. To do that, you need a way for visitors to express their own identities relative to your institution.

Treating people as individuals is at the heart of strong social networks. Whether online or in the physical world, personal self-expression—through appearance, preferences, and actions—allows people to express themselves relative to others. We all use our personal identities to signal who we are, who we want to meet, what we want and don't want. The more clearly and exhaustively you self-identify, the easier it is for an organization, community leader, or online service to connect you to people and experiences that are appropriate for and compelling to you.

In online social networks, the user experience centers on the personal profile. Websites like Facebook and LinkedIn require users to start with an exhaustive profile-making activity in which they detail their interests and affinities. The point of profiles is to give users value by connecting them to relevant people, products, institutions, and ideas. Some sites, such as LinkedIn, very explicitly show the path of "links" between you and others. The expectation is that you are not interested in everyone in the universe of LinkedIn. You are interested in users who are relevant to your self-determined interests and pre-existing contacts.

For example, I use an online social network called LibraryThing to get recommendations for books to read.[4] I'm an avid reader. I use the library frequently, and I'm often frustrated by the lack of personalized recommenda-tions available. Beyond the rack cards with the National Book Award win-ners or best beach mysteries, I have little information to help me in my hunt for great books. There's no section for "literary, plot-driven stories with strong female characters" or "ironic and wacky but not too over-the-top romps." Nor can I turn to the other people in the library for assistance. The librarians are often busy or are not available if I'm searching the online catalog from home. And while there are always lots of people in the library who like books, I have no confidence that a random member of the book-reading community will belong to my particular sub-community of interests—or that they'd respond positively to an advance from a stranger.

And so I rely on LibraryThing. My profile on LibraryThing is my library of books. I type in the titles I've read, and LibraryThing constructs a library-quality catalog of my books. My personal catalog is a node in the social network of LibraryThing, along with every other user's library. LibraryThing automatically recommends books to me based on the pattern of books I've read. It connects me with other users who have books in common with mine

---

4   Explore LibraryThing at http://www.participatorymuseum.org/ref2-4/

based on the theory that we might have similar taste in books. I often end up directly contacting other users to learn more about other books in their libraries. My interest in those individuals is mediated by the network that ties us together.

The resultant experience is incredibly powerful. The more books I add to my library, the better recommendations I receive. I'm unlikely to switch my allegiance to another book-cataloging system because LibraryThing has evolved to be more than just a piece of functional software. It's responsive. It values my personal interests. And it connects me to other people who enrich my reading.

Of course some libraries have wonderful staff members who can help people find books they might like. But relying on staff and even volunteers is not scalable. That's like me calling my volleyball instructor every time I want to organize a game. It's ultimately more valuable for users, and more sustainable for everyone, if the system is set up to be responsive to individuals on demand.

Profiles in the Real World

I don't walk around town wearing the list of books I've read on my sleeve. Online, I can construct complex personal profiles, but in the physical world, I have fewer explicit signifiers I can use to express my unique identity. I can wear a t-shirt for a band I like. I can walk my dog around town. I can display my tattoo. Each of these types of self-identification can lead to social interactions with people who belong to the communities of rockabilly lovers or dog owners or inked folk. The small presentation of self-expression becomes a kind of beacon that links me to others in a loose social network of affinity.

But my "sidewalk profile" is limited to my personal appearance and objects I carry. It is much more difficult for me to display my love of backpacking or Reconstructionist Judaism or off-grid living as I walk down the street. On the Web, I can display all of these. I can use different websites to express myself relative to different types of experiences and content. The people who I trust for book recommendations on LibraryThing are not the same as the people I am professionally connected to on LinkedIn. I can express the aspect of my self-identity appropriate to the situation, and then I can use that personal profile as the basis for a social experience.

Why does this matter when it comes to participation in cultural institutions? If you want to create opportunities for customized content or high-value social interactions, you need to provide visitors with a way to self-identify relative to your institution. This doesn't mean letting them tell their life story. It means designing profiles that are specific to the experiences available at the institution. If the institution offers programs in multiple languages, visitor profiles should include their preferred language of engagement. If the collection is vast and varied, visitor profiles might include favorite iconic objects or themes. The right profile-making activity solicits just enough personal information to deliver high-value outcomes.

Let's take a look at three very different systems for creating visitor profiles in museums.

At the Sony Wonder Technology Lab in New York City, visitors create comprehensive digital profiles they use to access and manipulate exhibits. The Wonder Technology Lab is a hands-on science center focused on creative use of digital technologies. When visitors enter, they start by "logging in" at a kiosk that records their name, voice, photo, favorite color, and preferred music genre. Then, each visitor's profile is saved onto an RFID card that is used to access all the interactive exhibits. Each exhibit greets visitors by name at the beginning of the experience. When a visitor augments an image, he distorts his own face. When he makes an audio mashup, his voice is part of the mix. This may sound gimmicky, but it is emotionally powerful. It draws visitors into every exhibit via their own narcissism. What could be more personally relevant—and compelling—than your own image and voice?

Visitor profiles need not be high-tech to be useful. In the temporary exhibition *Heroes: Mortals and Myths in Ancient Greece* at the Walters Art Museum in Baltimore, visitors created profiles by picking a character from Greek mythology with whom they self-identified. Visitors could take a quick personality quiz at kiosks near the exhibition entrance to determine which of eight Greek heroes, gods, or monsters they were most like. The kiosks prompted visitors to take a personalized tag and ID card from bins nearby for "their" hero. The cards provided more information about the heroes and connected them to specific artifacts in the exhibition. In this case, the profile didn't change the exhibition content, but it served as a personal filter that drove recommendations for how to navigate *Heroes.*

Finally, at the New York Hall of Science, visitors receive different entrance stickers based on their membership level. Non-members receive one color, members another, donors a third, and so on. That way, every passing staff member can visually identify and respond to guests uniquely based on whether they are new or returning visitors. In this case, the visitor profile is a single data point represented by a colored sticker. But it still gives visitors an experience that is somewhat customized to their history with the institution.

Each of these profile systems is different, but they all add value to the visitor experience. A successful personal profile accomplishes three goals:

1. *It frames the entry experience in a way that makes visitors feel valued.* If a staff member greets a visitor by name or attends to her particular interests, she is more likely to feel comfortable in the institution. When an employee shows respect for her background and abilities, he bolsters her confidence as a potential participant and contributor. Self-identity is particularly important when it comes to participatory experiences. If you want visitors to share stories, ideas, or creative work, you need to respect them as individuals who have something of value to contribute.

2. *It gives people opportunities to deepen and satisfy their pre-existing interests.* If someone comes in who is fascinated by trains, the right profile can expose that interest and help the staff provide custom experiences to satisfy it. John Falk's research has demonstrated that museum visitors evaluate their experiences based on institutions' abilities to accommodate unique identity needs.[5] The better you can identify a visitor's need, the more likely you are to fulfill it.

3. *It gives people confidence to branch out to challenging and unfamiliar opportunities.* In the book *Bowling Alone,* political scientist

---

5   Falk, *Identity and the Museum Visitor Experience,* (2009).

Robert Putnam argued that shared experiences around personal interests (like bowling) can help people connect across great diversity in race, wealth, and social class.[6] Bowling leagues, knitting circles, and amateur astronomy clubs all help people enjoy their personal interests while connecting with new experiences and ideas.

Profiles aren't just for visitors. They can also be used to help employees and volunteers express their own personal interests relative to the institution. One of the simplest ways to do this is via "staff picks." Walk into almost any locally owned bookstore, and you are likely to find handwritten cards featuring a few sentences from a staff member expressing his or her ardor for particular books. These picks focus on personal and informal commentary on books rather than formal or hierarchical information.

Staff picks in bookstores highlight specific volumes in a personal, friendly way.

Museums have a long history of inviting curators or guest artists to design custom shows that highlight their idiosyncratic perspectives on the collection. These can be done formally, as in Fred Wilson's *Mining the Museum* exhibition at the Maryland Historical Society (1992) or Damien Hirst's exhibit of favored works at the Rijksmuseum (2008). But this can also be done internally with staff members and volunteers. In 2008, the Exploratorium launched prototype *Staff Picks* signs featuring diverse members of the staff sharing informal thoughts on what they love about particular exhibits.

Museums with wide-ranging content typically group exhibits by topic, with curators writing labels about their areas of expertise. But culture is interdisciplinary, and it can be quite interesting to see how a design curator

---

6   See Putnam's discussion on bridging social capital on pages 22-23 of *Bowling Alone*, (2000).

interprets a historical piece of furniture, or how a scientist sees a piece of landscape art. Because the roles among museum staff are more varied than those in the bookstore, there's an opportunity to promote learning from multiple perspectives using staff picks. Highlighting the unique perspectives of scientists, designers, and educators in cultural institutions can give those individuals unique identities and offers visitors a more nuanced blend of interpretative material.

When staff members are encouraged to express themselves personally, it models respect for diverse individual preferences and opinions. When front-line employees feel confident sharing their personal thoughts on the institution and its content, it gives visitors permission to do the same.

Designing Profiles for Cultural Institutions

There is no single right way to construct a user profile. While many profile-making activities are creative, with users inputting unique content about themselves, others are selective, with users picking from among a few options. The key is to make sure that the institution is able to be responsive to people based on their profiles. There is waste in over-profiling—both for visitors whose time is squandered answering profile questions and for institutions that can't meaningfully use the data gathered.

There are two basic kinds of profiles: *aspirational* and *you are what you do*. Aspirational profiles are those in which people express themselves based on their own self-concept. This is the kind of profile that people create via their clothes, personal statements, or status updates. The Walters Art Museum's *Heroes* exhibition tags were a kind of aspirational profile; each visitor picked the hero who appealed most to her or was most related to her interests.

Aspirational profiles are fundamentally different from the profiles that visitors receive in the United States Holocaust Memorial Museum or the *Titanic* traveling exhibition. Those exhibitions offer visitors the opportunity to randomly identify with a historic person who was affected by the Holocaust or traveled on the *Titanic*. While those kinds of activities do help visitors connect with powerful stories of individuals from the past, the profiles do

not reflect anything personal about the visitors themselves. Aspirational profiles, in contrast, are based on visitors' own personalities, preferences, and
interests.

"You are what you do" profiles are based not on what users say about
themselves but what they actually do. For example, I have a "you are what
you do" profile at my local rock climbing gym. When I walk into the gym,
the staff member at the desk asks me for my member number and then greets
me by name. On the screen in front of him, he can see how often I come,
what classes I've taken, and any issues on record. Beyond my name, no part
of my profile is self-defined. He knows me by my actions relative to the gym,
and he offers me personalized information based on my past behavior.

"You are what you do" profiles have great potential in cultural institutions. If you can find ways to capture even a small amount of the data
generated by visitors' experiences—the exhibitions they visit, the amount of
time they spend looking at different objects, the blend of experiences they
pursue, the amount of money they spend on food or the gift shop—you will
understand them better and be able to respond accordingly.

Many profiles blend these two types, providing value to users based
both on what they say about themselves and what they do. In 2009, I
worked with the Boston Children's Museum to develop a blended onsite
and online experience, *Our Green Trail*, to encourage visitors to be more
environmentally conscious in their everyday lives. We decided that the
online component would serve as a profile reflecting and rewarding green
behaviors performed in real life. The online environment was designed as a
"green village" in which each user has a virtual home.[7] In the initial setup,
users create aspirational profiles. They pick their homes and name them.
The homes start as normal-looking buildings but can transform into "green"
houses with various environmental improvements. People don't improve
their virtual homes by interacting online; instead, their homes advance when
they perform green activities in the real world—taking a reusable lunch bag
to school, turning off the lights, conserving water. Users can express commitment to take on a particular challenge aspirationally, but their virtual
homes only change when they self-report completion of the activity. In this

7   Build your own house in *Our Green Trail* at http://www.participatorymuseum.
org/ref2-7/

way, the virtual homes serve as "you are what you do" profiles for the players' real lives. A quick glance around the green village lets people see who is excelling at living a green lifestyle.

When it comes to staff, most institutions maintain extensive "you are what you do" profiles in personnel files but do not give staff the opportunity to self-identify aspirationally as well. In 2004, I visited the Center Of Science and Industry (COSI) in Columbus, Ohio. In the staff break room, they had a wall of photos, names, and titles of all staff members so that people could easily identify each other across the institution. This is a great (and typical) way for staff members who work in a large organization to recognize each other as individuals. But COSI took it one step further. Each nameplate featured the staff photo, name, title, and "dream title." One educator's dream title was "chief banana eater." A visitor service representative proclaimed herself "queen of bubbles," and so on. This very simple addition allowed staff members to express their aspirational (and creative) selves along with functional information about their work.

Wearable Profiles

When the staff at the Walters Art Museum decided to invite visitors to create profiles for their *Heroes* exhibition, they did not want to deal with the logistical complexity or cost of a long profile-making activity. They wanted profile making to be fun, easy, optional, and high-value. So the staff created a simple wearable identity system. They provided bins with small metal tags featuring eight characters from Greek mythology. Visitors self-identified with one of the eight and wore tags indicating their preferences. Many visitors, strangers and friends alike, used these tags as the basis for conversation and to seek out content in the exhibition about their selected heroes.

Wearable identity is one of the simplest and most flexible forms of self-identification. Many museums already require visitors to wear buttons or stickers to indicate that they have purchased tickets to enter the galleries. Why not use this wearable identification as a way to personalize the experience? Admissions staff can offer visitors different colored stickers or wristbands based on a simple one-selection question. Alternatively, visitors

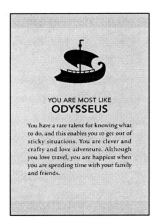

Cards and tags from *Heroes* related to the Greek hero Odysseus. Each double-sided card featured personality information (left) and object information (middle). Visitors wore the tags (right) on their lapels to identify with their heroes of choice.

can personalize their profiles with a word or phrase selected quickly and printed onto a sticker.

Wearable identification acknowledges visitors as individuals by encouraging them to share something unique about themselves. It provides opportunities for deepening because staff can give tailored recommendations and information based on visitors' profiles. It also encourages social bridging among visitors who are strangers by giving them external tools to identify those who share their interests.

These kinds of profiles are only useful if the institution can deliver an enhanced experience based on them. In *Heroes*, the enhancement was the opportunity to find and explore hero-specific content threads throughout the exhibition, and to connect with other people about their different identities.

Imagine you have just one question to ask visitors that can be used to contextualize their experience relative to your museum. What would you ask them?

Profile questions should help frame the specific experience available at particular institutions. If you walk into a space and someone asks you what relaxes you, you shift into a relaxed state of mind. If you walk into a space and someone asks you what challenges you, your adrenaline rises. Questions as simple as "What era in history do you wish you could visit?" in a history museum or "What's your favorite color?" in an art center can help people express themselves uniquely and get in the mindset of the institution.

Wearable profiles can be content-related (i.e. different colors for different content interests), knowledge- or skill-based (different colors for people who self-identify as novices, students, amateurs, or experts), or social (one color for people who are interested in engaging with strangers, another for people who aren't). In a music center, for example, you might offer name-etags that read "Country Western," "Punk Rock," and so on to allow visitors to self-identify relative to their musical preferences.

For more general situations, prompts like, "I'm interested in…" or "I'm inspired by…" can allow visitors and staff to express their affinities and meet people with shared interests. Jay Cousins, a German technologist, has been experimenting with "talk to me about…" stickers to promote social interaction at conferences. People write about their interests and slap the stickers on the backs of their shirts or laptops.

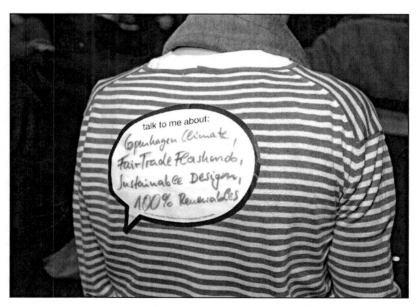

A participant in the Palomar5 Innovation Camp in Berlin, Germany, advertised his social interests with a simple "talk to me" sticker.

Commenting on their popularity even in the most unlikely situations, Cousins noted:

> Deutsche Telecoms Innovation Day – Will men in suits wear stupid look-
> ing bubbles expressing their passions – 8/10 said yes.[8]

These are all aspirational examples, but you can also develop "you are what you do" wearable identity that reflects the exhibits visitors have used, the art they've enjoyed, or the concerts they've attended. "You are what you do" profiles can also indicate the status of members, supporters, collaborators, or other special visitors, as at the New York Hall of Science with their color-coded entrance stickers.

Wearable identification is not just for visitors. It's likely that staff and volunteers in your institution already wear some kind of "you are what you do" item that identifies them as an employee, whether a nametag or a uni-form. When I worked on the front line at a small science center, I wore a blue polyester vest that I fondly remember as a "magic vest." The vest identi-fied me as a safe person with whom to talk and play.

Wearable identification can also reduce staff members to a generic role. At the New York Hall of Science, Preeti Gupta, Senior Vice President of Education & Family Programs, reflected on her anxiety at donning the front line's red apron after years at the institution this way:

> Usually I have my name tag and a set of keys which identify me as staff.
> I comfortably interact with visitors. Why then, with this apron on, was
> I feeling anxious? I realized it was because now I hadn't just put on an
> apron, I actually put on a "role" or an "identity." People would see me in
> the red apron and knew they could ask me anything and it was my job
> to help them, to be accountable to them. It is how I knew they would
> view me, as someone who is supposed to work with them, that made
> me anxious.[9]

When working with wearable identification, it's important that peo-ple feel confident and positive about their profile item rather than feeling wedged into a box or tricked in some way. This is true both for staff members

8   Read Cousins' December 2009 blog post, "Talk to Me Bubbles update," at
http://www.participatorymuseum.org/ref2-8/
9   Read Gupta's complete comment on my February 2009 blog post, "The Magic
Vest Phenomenon and Other Wearable Tools for Talking to Strangers," at http://
www.participatorymuseum.org/ref2-9/

and visitors alike. Wearing your personality on your sleeve should give you a feeling of pride and self-expression. Some people wear colored wristbands that indicate their support for various political and social movements. They wear them to feel the powerful emotional connection with the concept they represent. They wear them to demonstrate their affinity to the world. And they wear them to identify themselves as part of a tribe of like-minded supporters.

What are the tribes of people at your institution? More importantly, what are the tribes who might want to identify with like-minded visitors? The most fertile tribes are not readily obvious from personal appearance. It's not useful to have a blue sticker for men and a red one for women, or to have a green band for people over 65 and a yellow band for children. But it might be useful to have a special sticker for staff members who speak another language, or for people at a military museum who have served their country, or for visitors to a science center who like explosions.

Avoiding Prescriptive Profiles

When designing user profiles, there are two pitfalls to avoid: putting people in overly prescriptive boxes, and not respecting their privacy.

Profiles should be flexible. Many people have experienced the frustration of overly prescriptive profiles on shopping websites. You buy one colander and suddenly the site recommends every kitchen implement under the sun. Buy a book of poetry on a whim and you'll receive reminders every time that poet spits out another verse. When a profile system is too prescriptive, recommendations become laughably inappropriate, and the whole value of personalization turns into an annoyance.

We all exhibit a complex and shifting range of identity-related needs and aspirations when we visit museums.[10] On one visit I may accompany my young nephews on a romp through the space, facilitating their learning experience and bopping from one novel activity to another. Another time I may visit on my own, looking for a more leisurely, intimate opportunity to explore my own content interests. If my profile is locked in from the first visit

---

10 Falk, *Identity and the Museum Visitor Experience* (2009).

as a woman with small children, I won't be necessarily be well-served on subsequent visits, even though the initial profile was constructed accurately.

Finally, profile-making activities should be designed with clear information about what the institution will do with the profile data. There are some institutions, like public libraries, that intentionally avoid collecting data about patrons to protect their privacy. If visitors generate data through their profiles—especially personal data like name, photo, or contact information—the institution should explain in clear language where and how that information will be stored and shared.

Confrontational Profiles

There is one special case in which profile systems that are highly prescriptive or reveal private information can be employed successfully: to provoke confrontational experiences. The Smithsonian National Museum of American History's *Field to Factory* exhibition (1987) typified this approach. To enter *Field to Factory*, visitors had to walk through one of two doors labeled WHITE and COLORED. You had to choose which prescriptive term defined you, and that uncomfortable selection framed the way you experienced the rest of the exhibition.

This "two doors" device has been reinterpreted to great effect at other institutions. The Apartheid Museum in Johannesburg frames the entire visit experience in this way by forcing visitors to enter the museum through two separate paths depending on whether they are white or non-white. Visitors are issued admission tickets that feature their presumed racial identity, and then are shepherded into separate entrances and introductory exhibits, separated by a fence that clearly suggests that the non-whites are on the inferior side. This profile activity intentionally alienates people, makes them frustrated, and can generate discussion out of that frustration. While this profiling technique is certainly powerful, it induces stress that may not be desirable in less provocative exhibitions.

In Switzerland in 2006, the Stapferhaus Lenzberg presented an exhibition called *A Matter of Faith* that used confrontational profiling as an unsettling first step to a more nuanced personalized experience. Visitors were required to enter the exhibition as "believers" or "non-believers." They

A guard checks visitors' racial identity outside the Apartheid
Museum and directs them to the corresponding entrances.

received USB-data sticks to wear that were marked with their choice, creating a wearable identity piece that some wore proudly and others hid in their jackets. Co-director Beat Hächler referred to this as "the principle of exposure," in which visitors were "forced" to become "subjects of exhibition."[11] Again, this is not a desirable feeling for all visitors.

The uncomfortably limiting profiles assigned at entry became more complex as visitors navigated the exhibition. Throughout the exhibition, there were kiosks where visitors could construct more comprehensive personal profiles by responding to a questionnaire about religious faith. Visitors ultimately were segmented into five profiles based on their relationship to faith. They could choose whether to release their personal data to the larger audience of visitors or not, and 95% chose to share their responses to the questions. In a final room, visitors stood around a large round table segmented into five parts, each of which provided more information about a

---

11 These quotes come from Hächler's article, "Capturing the Present in Exhibition Design," in *Exhibitionist* 27, no. 2 (2008): 45-50.

particular profile. As Hächler noted, most visitors went directly to the area of the table related to their own profiles to learn more about themselves and ended up sharing space with strangers who shared their profile. Hächler said, "On several occasions, this special situation was powerful enough to provoke spontaneous conversations among visitors in the same faith segment of the table." What started with unsettling personal exposure ended in dialogue.

Putting Personalization to Work in Cultural Institutions

Personalization is powerful when it responds to visitors based on their unique identities. We've already seen some examples of how profiles allow visitors to feel valued, get access to deeper content, and connect with challenging ideas. Since profile making requires a time investment by visitors and a resource investment by institutions, it shouldn't be limited to single visit experiences. Personalization can become a starting point for deeper personal relationships among visitors and institutions, not just one-off interactions.

Museums already establish deep relationships with very small subsets of visitors: donors, researchers, and community partners. The more money a donor gives, the more personal attention she receives from the development office. The more time a researcher spends examining artifacts, the deeper his relationship with collections staff. And when people are hand-selected for community advisory boards or collaborations, they are likely to work very closely with the institution and staff, expressing interests and needs in response to a sincere desire for their engagement.

These niche groups are necessarily small and it would not be manageable to scale up the personalized attention that a major donor, researcher, or community advisor receives to every member or visitor walking through the door. Institutional patterns for treating individuals personally are based on a scarcity model, since each requires direct human contact with a staff member. Community advisory boards in particular are often seen as requiring a monumental amount of added staff time. It is not practical to apply traditional models for these partnerships broadly.

But what about everyone else—the visitors without deep pockets, relevant PhDs, or programmatic connections? Deeper relationships with regular visitors are possible, but they require less resource-intensive models to support them. Fostering deeper relationships offers obvious benefits to devoted visitors, who become more engaged in ways that connect to their intellectual and creative interests. It also serves the bottom line. If visitors perceive that an institution is personally responsive to their changing needs and interests, they are more likely to visit again, become members, renew their memberships, and donate time and money to the institution.[12]

In the next few sections, we'll look at how institutions can develop scalable systems to provide visitors with the experiences they seek onsite, connect with them outside of visiting hours, motivate repeat visitation, and offer meaningful forms of institutional membership. I like to think of individual visits or transactions as "pearls" of experience. Building strong relationships with visitors means providing a string to tie those pearls together.

Empowering Front-Line Staff as Relationship Brokers

The most effective place to start supporting deeper relationships among visitors and staff is on the front line. Front-line staff and volunteers, whether cashiers or roving educators, security guards or greeters, are the face and voice of cultural institutions to the vast majority of visitors. They have the most immediate understanding of visitors' needs, and they are the most publicly accessible. When front-line staff members are empowered to express their unique personalities and engage with visitors personally, it sets the stage for a personal experience throughout the institution.

When I was a teenager, I worked at a roadside flower shop with a relationship-first approach to doing business. On my first day, Chris, the owner, told me:

> Everyone who comes in here has a story. People don't buy flowers like you'd buy a book or piece of pizza. Every customer has a specific story to

---

12 For more on the business case for developing meaningful personal relationships with visitors, consult John Falk and Beverly Sheppard, *Thriving in the Knowledge Age: New Business Models for Museums and Other Cultural Institutions*, 2006.

tell and a need to fulfill. It's your job to figure out that need and sell them
the flowers that will make them happy.[13]

I did my job, which meant doing things that would be frowned upon
in other retail establishments. I spent time with customers talking about who
their flowers were for and helped them find the right ones for a girlfriend or
a boss or a funeral. If someone was a good customer or spent a lot of money,
I gave her a free vase. Cute kids got a flower to take home. If someone was
a jerk, I upped the price or refused to sell to him. It wasn't a fancy place, but
we built strong relationships with our customers.

I was able to do all these things because they were in line with the
way Chris did business. Unfortunately, most front-line employees are trained
to conduct transactions, not to foster relationships. They are evaluated on
the ability to quickly rip tickets and provide accurate and consistent information. If you are marketing your institution as a transformational place,
you need to include staff in that equation and find ways, as Chris did, to
empower them as such.

The Museum of Life and Science in North Carolina is one institution that is trying to use the admissions desk as a point of engagement and
not just a ticket counter. The sales team has started offering professional
development to front-line staff about the art of engaging with visitors. Front-
line staff members engage first-time visitors in conversation about what they
might enjoy at the museum, and they go out of their way both to greet and
say goodbye to members. The staff goes on field trips to other institutions to
explore ways to make visitors feel welcome and well served. As Director of
Membership Advancement Jeff Stern explained to me, "We want to show
staff that we value the thought process that goes into customer service and
we take it seriously." Internal blogs or all-staff meetings that feature observations and feedback from front-line staff members and volunteers can also
help low-level employees feel like valued members of the team—and help
other staff members who don't spend time on the floor connect with the
visitor experience.

Staff members can also make personal connections with visitors by
sharing their unique voices in exhibitions. For example, when the Monterey

---

13 While every other person in this book is referred to by last name, I know Chris
only as Chris. You can buy flowers from him at Hollyworld Flowers in Los Angeles.

Bay Aquarium mounted a temporary exhibition called *Fishing for Solutions* in 1997, they integrated staff voices as well as visitors' into a comment board. The board invited visitors to share their own solutions for helping fish populations thrive, and it showcased handwritten comments from employees about their own personal solutions and choices. Staff members didn't write about how the work of the institution was helping solve the problem; instead, they wrote about their own transportation, food, and family planning strategies. Staff members signed their comments with their names and positions at the Aquarium, which further personalized the connection between visitors and the real people who worked at the museum. This technique was effective in modeling desired results because it demonstrated that the same staff members who wrote the labels were willing to put their money where their mouths were and talk about their own personal lives and choices.[14]

Putting the Front Line Online

Where possible, front-line staff members are frequently the best people to engage with visitors online. If a visitor forms a relationship with a staff member online, she is most likely to be able continue that relationship in person if that employee works in the galleries. For example, a woman once connected with a staff member with an unusual name (Thor) on the Science Museum of Minnesota's *Science Buzz* blog, and then later had an in-person follow-up discussion with him on the floor at the museum. That relationship was only possible because Thor was able to express his unique voice on the museum's website—and because he had a nametag that identified him onsite.

A group of front-line staff at the Exploratorium, the Exploratorium Explainers, has been running a blog about their work since 2007.[15] Their topics range from favorite exhibits to behind-the-scenes grunt work to funny interactions with visitors on the floor. Their tone is often irreverent, but they do a wonderful job communicating their energy and love of the institution

---

14 Learn more about *Fishing for Solutions* in Jenny Sayre Ramberg's article, "From Comment to Commitment at the Monterey Bay Aquarium," in *Visitor Voices in Museum Exhibitions,* ed. Kathleen McLean and Wendy Pollock (2007): 37-44.
15 Visit the Exploratorium Explainers' blog at: http://www.participatorymuseum. org/ref2-15/

through the posts. The Explainers' blog showcases a group of people who are dedicated to their institution and grateful for the opportunity to be one of its mouthpieces. As one Explainer/blogger, Ryan Jenkins, put it when reflecting on the experience of writing for the blog: "Finally, I want to say how proud it made me feel that the Explainers, on our own, had continued the spirit of innovation that defines the special place we work at."

Encouraging front-line staff members and volunteers to blog in a professional capacity is a win-win for the participants and the institution. It encourages the development and maintenance of institutional memory and helps new employees learn the ropes in the visitor services departments. It values their knowledge and funnels their enthusiasm into a public-facing product. If staff maintain personal blogs, who knows how kindly or unkindly they will reference their workplace. But if they are blogging under the masthead of the institution, they go from being freelancers to staff reporters. They want to further the institution, and to do so without fear of being shut down or fired.

Encouraging staff to engage in participatory activities that highlight their individuality helps connect them to participatory efforts overall. Personalization is the first step to visitors seeing themselves as potentially active, social members of the institutional community. Don't you want staff members to see themselves that way, too?

Personalized Onsite Experiences

How can cultural institutions be responsive to visitors' diverse and shifting needs and interests across a visit? Designers and educators do this in aggregate for all visitors by designing varied spaces, punctuating object experiences with interactives, and offering different kinds of programs. But people derive meaning from different aspects of the museum experience. While one visitor may be fascinated by a blacksmith's tools, another may be more interested in the labor politics of his trade. How can institutions serve the "right" content to each visitor?

This is a question not only of satisfying different types of visitors but of serving visitors over time as their needs and interests evolve. The ability to "grow with visitors" is particularly important for institutions that are perceived as demographic-limited, such as children's museums and science centers. My first museum job was in the Acton Science Discovery Museum, a small hands-on science center in Acton, Massachusetts. The museum was filled with fascinating interactive exhibits, including many whose explanations eluded me despite having a degree in engineering. I found the exhibits to be beautiful and mysterious. But label text was only offered at a child's level, and the resulting experience attracted families with young children exclusively. Families "aged out" when the kids reached age eight or nine. If we could have offered a different track featuring scientists' takes on the interactives, or more complex levels of interactive challenge and explanation, the same interactives might have been able to serve visitors over more life stages.

Serving people custom content requires two things: a rich content base of different types of interpretation for any given exhibit or artifact, and a mechanism by which visitors can retrieve content of interest.

What should go into this "rich content base?" There are many ways to expand the interpretation available around each exhibit, artifact, or program. You can offer designer's insights, insider stories from collectors or performers, contextual information about the time, poetic interpretations of the content, visitors' impressions—the list goes on. People are most likely to use extra interpretation if it is appealing or relevant to them, so it makes sense to take an audience-centric approach to deciding what content to add. For example, an art museum may decide that it is lacking in material specifically for children, or a history museum may decide to use first-person oral histories to enliven a third-person interpretative approach.

Multi-vocal interpretation can also be a way for staff members to express their own particular fetishes. At the Indianapolis Museum of Art, a charismatic groundskeeper named Rhett Reed worked with the museum's new media team to create videos featuring him interviewing staff in the security and collections management departments. Reed's personable, non-expert manner made him the ideal person to introduce visitors to the arcane worlds of the security control room and art packing crew.[16]

16 Watch IMA groundskeeper Rhett Reed in action in *The Need for Reed* video series at http://www.participatorymuseum.org/ref2-16/

Producing additional interpretative content can be a challenge, but it's a known challenge. The trickier part is finding a distribution mechanism that won't introduce too much clutter or complexity to the visit experience. Imagine doing the Herculean effort of collecting a diverse multiplicity of interpretations—expert and novice, artist and scientist, visitor and guard—on institutional content. How would you display them? And how would visitors determine which ones they'd like to access?

A multi-channel audio tour or multi-panel label is manageable on the scale of a few perspectives, but is unsustainable for more than five or six alternatives. Visitors would have to remember the icons or codes and confront a boggling multitude of choices at each exhibit. They might just give up.

This problem of information overload leads to an argument for simplicity, for fewer channels, fewer stops, shorter labels, less interpretative material. But there are other ways to solve the problem, to have your thirty-seven "channels" of content and consume them happily too. What you need now is a recommendation engine.

Recommendation Engines

Recommendation engines are systems that recommend content to you based on your personal profile. This is the heart of what makes services like LibraryThing useful. Anyone can check out the staff picks in a bookstore. But which ones will be right for *you*? That's what recommendation engines try to figure out.

Recommendation engines thrive on robust personal profiles that often incorporate both self-designated and "you are what you do" data. For example, consider Netflix, the dominant US online movie rental company. Netflix provides movie recommendations based on your ratings—both of broad genres and styles and the films you actually watch. Netflix makes a game out of rating movies, encouraging you to do so upon initial account registration and on subsequent logins as part of the profile-building experience so the system can supply you with lists of "Movies You'll Love." The underlying message is that the more complete your profile, the more easily Netflix can help you find a movie you'll enjoy.

This implicit promise of responsiveness motivates people to rate hundreds of movies at will. The more you use it, the better it gets—a symbiotic relationship that serves customer and vendor alike.

For Netflix, improving the recommendation system and motivating people to rate videos is essential to financial success. Netflix is in the business of selling monthly subscriptions. They do not want users to cancel subscriptions because they've seen all the movies they want to see or can't find an appealing flick. They don't want to leave it to chance that friends and family will continually suggest movies users might like, or that people will studiously scan the film reviews for ones they haven't seen. And so Netflix spends a lot of money and energy improving its recommendation system so it can keep suggesting movies that users might like to see. In October 2006, Netflix even offered a million dollar prize to the first team who could improve their recommendation system by ten percent.

Netflix's recommendation engine is tuned to provide customers with more of the things they like most—to provide users with deepening, but not necessarily broadening, experiences. One of the concerns about deploying recommendation engines in museums is that visitors will only be exposed to the narrow window of things they like and will not have "off path" experiences that are surprising, uncomfortable, and potentially valuable. Fortunately, cultural institutions are not in the business of selling movie rental subscriptions. While online retail recommendation engines are typically optimized to present people with things they will like, there are other ways to filter customized information.

For example, LibraryThing has a "books you'll hate" feature called the Unsuggester. The Unsuggester does the opposite of what LibraryThing's traditional recommendation engine does; it recommends books that are *least* likely to be found in your LibraryThing collection or the collections of other users who also have your books. The Unsuggester doesn't so much give you books you'll hate as books that you'd never otherwise encounter.

While the Unsuggester is silly, it's also a valuable set of responsive content to your profile. It's a window into a distant and somewhat unknowable world. And users have responded positively. When programmer Tim Spaulding suggested that few people were likely to actually read books on the Unsuggester list, an anonymous user responded:

> You underestimate Thingamabrarians. Some of us are just looking for new ways to branch out from our old ruts... and something flagged as "opposite" to our normal reading might just be what we're all looking for.[17]

After noting the patterns of opposition between philosophy and chick lit, programming manuals and literature, Spaulding wrote:

> These disconnects sadden me. Of course readers have tastes, and nearly everyone has books they'd never read. But, as serious readers, books make our world. A shared book is a sort of shared space between two people. As far as I'm concerned, the more of these the better. So, in the spirit of unity and understanding, why not enter your favorite book, then read its opposite?

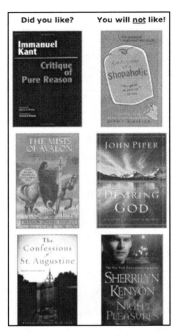

The Unsuggester pairs books with the least in common.

Imagine applying this principle to museum visits. People might be intrigued to learn that "if you always visit the mummies, you may never have explored the fish tanks." Recommendation systems must meaningfully respond to users' profiles, but they don't have to be optimized solely to provide people with more of what they already like.

How could visitors to your institution generate profiles robust enough to be used in recommendation engines like these? While visitors make many active choices across a single cultural experience—what to do, in which order, for how long, with whom—institutions track very few of these choices. Unless your institution is ready to invest in systems to allow visitors to rate exhibits, collect favorites, or register their paths through the institution, recommendation engines may seem out of reach.

---

17 Read Spaulding's November 2006 blog post, "Booksuggester and Unsuggester" and user comments at http://www.participatorymuseum.org/ref2-17/

But don't give up yet. Many recommendation engines (including the Unsuggester) can generate a list of recommendations based on just a single user input. Type in one title, and you'll get a list of "Movies You'll Love" from Netflix, or books you've never heard of from LibraryThing. Responsiveness to user profiles is only one part of what makes recommendation engines successful. They also use institutionally defined connections among objects and content to provide high-quality recommendations.

CASE STUDY
PANDORA—AN EXPERT RECOMMENDATION ENGINE

The online music service Pandora relies on curatorial-style analysis to help users create personalized radio stations and explore new music based on their interests. Here's how it works: you enter a seed artist or song (or several) and Pandora starts playing music that it interprets as related in some way to your selections. User profiles are a mixture of self-expression (seed songs) and "you are what you do" (songs you favorite or skip during playback). You can type in a single song and let it play, or you can keep tweaking a station by adding seed music, skipping over bad songs, and favoriting good ones.[18]

The extraordinary thing about Pandora is the complexity of its filtering. It doesn't just group artists together and play music by similar musicians. Instead, it uses hundreds of signifiers assigned to each song by a team of expert musicians to find correlations among songs. Pandora is a product of the Music Genome Project, in which musicians define the individual "genes" of a song via signifiers and use those to generate song "vectors" that can then be compared to create highly specific and complex musical narratives. Each song takes twenty to thirty minutes for experts to encode. This is a serious data project, not unlike the kinds of categorization and research projects curators perform on museum collections.

For example, I created a radio station based on just one song: *Diamonds on the Soles of Her Shoes* by Paul Simon. That radio station then played:

18 Try Pandora at http://www.participatorymuseum.org/ref2-18/ Note that Pandora is only available in the United States.

- *She's a Yellow Reflector* by Justin Roberts
- *If Only the Moon Were Up* by Field Music
- *She's Going* by The English Beat
- *You're The One* by Paul Simon
- *Withered Hope* by They Might Be Giants
- *Big Dipper* by Elton John
- *Wait Until Tomorrow* by New York Rock and Roll Ensemble
- *The Tide is High* by Blondie

All but one of these songs and half the artists were new to me. I enjoyed seven out of nine. For each song, I could click a "Why?" button to see Pandora's explanation for why it was played. For example, *The Tide is High* was included because it "features acoustic rock instrumentation, reggae influences, a subtle use of vocal harmony, repetitive melodic phrasing and excessive vamping."

There are over four hundred different musical signifiers in the Music Genome Project, ranging from "brisk swing feel" to "lyrics that tell a story" to "sparse tenor sax solo." Pandora and the Music Genome Project are managed by experts who, like curators, are uniquely skilled at describing the indicators of different types of musical expression. Their expertise makes for a better experience for me as a user. As an amateur listener, I could not identify the particular elements of *Diamonds on the Soles of Her Shoes* that appeal to me. Listening and reacting to the Pandora-generated songs allowed me to understand the nuances of what I like and don't like. It turns out I enjoy songs with "excessive vamping." Could I have articulated that at the start? No. Not only did Pandora introduce me to new music, it expanded my vocabulary for discussing music.

Users of Pandora are protective of the Music Genome Project experts. There have been discussions on the Pandora blog about the slow inclusion of user-based filtering, and listeners have shared fears that it will taint the waters of the high-quality expert process. The Music Genome Project involves visitors' ratings in a limited way. The core value is in the professional categorization of the songs.

Imagine a comparable recommendation engine within a cultural institution. Using curatorial records and or staff designations, the institution could generate a list of "genes" present across different objects or content experiences. Imagine a visitor typing the name of a single exhibit or object into her phone and getting a list of related objects, as well as explanations about how the objects are related. The system could provide experiences that are both highly responsive to individual visitors' preferences and which deepen visitors' ability to articulate why they like what they like. In some cases, people might be surprised to learn that they prefer artists whose subject matter comes from childhood memories, or historical stories related to economic crises. While cultural institutions can't be physically rearranged for each visitor or family, the content could be remixed conceptually to present a progressively engrossing, educational experience.

Personalization doesn't just give you what you want. It exposes you to new things, and it gives you a vocabulary for articulating and refining why you like what you like. The world opens a little wider and hopefully, you keep exploring.

Mechanisms for Retrieving Personalized Content

The final piece of the personalization puzzle is the mechanism that visitors use to access recommendations or personalized interpretative content. The ideal mechanism would accommodate both individual and social use. It would respond to visitors' profiles and offer suggestions, but it wouldn't force anyone down a single reductive path.

Some institutions have attempted to solve this problem by creating a physical device—typically associated with a barcode or RFID tag—that visitors carry with them and use to access each exhibit and associate it with their unique identities. This is particularly popular in science centers, and systems of this type have been employed in institutions around the world since the early 2000s.

There are two fundamental difficulties with these systems: they disrupt the social experience of exhibits by forcing groups to use an exhibit one by one (or to watch as a single member of the group uses the exhibit and records her experience), and they force a strict narrative on what is often a highly chaotic exhibit usage pattern. You can't use an exhibit "in the middle" if you must initialize the experience with a swipe of your tag. Particularly for families, the requirement to wait in line until other visitors are done, keep track of the tagged object, associate an exhibit experience with just one member of the family, and swipe it before each exhibit experience can be onerous.

The best mechanisms fit into the ways that people already use cultural institutions rather than forcing new behaviors onto visitors. That's what's so lovely about the flashlight-based interpretative strategy at the blast furnace in Avesta (see page 38)—the flashlight is a familiar tool that fits into the experience of exploring a spooky historic site.

To find a good tool for your institution, think about the ways people currently explore and discover content while visiting. If your visitors frequently use mobile phones onsite, that may be a good solution. For example, in 2009, the Brooklyn Museum launched a pilot version of a text message-based recommendation system. Each artifact was labeled with a text message short code. When a visitor sends a message to that code, it lets the system know that he enjoys that particular artifact and offers him other suggestions for artifacts nearby based on his input. While this system can give more nuanced recommendations as users build their profiles of preferred objects, visitors can use it for single queries and still receive value.

There are also low-tech options for helping visitors connect with deep content throughout cultural institutions. An art museum might offer a "browsing sketchbook" featuring small images of objects (with gallery locations) at the top of each page and notes like, "For more sculpted nudes, go to page 84. For more tortured artists, see page 211." At a transportation museum, visitors might use a ship's logbook or passport to chart where they've been and get suggestions for other places to explore. A science museum might print tiny labels with different perspectives and give visitors magnifying glasses to hunt down preferred interpretation. Even simple labels that read, "if you love this exhibit, you might also enjoy that one down the hall" or "for a contrasting perspective on this story, check out the display on the opposite wall" can help people find custom paths through cultural institutions.

Taking Personalized Content Home with You

The ideal personalized cultural experience doesn't end when visitors leave the institution. Imagine a non-member: a person who visits once, has a great (hopefully personalized) experience, and leaves. What can the institution do to continue engaging with this visitor?

Most cultural institutions treat visitors like one-night stands; they don't call, they don't write, and they don't pine. If visitors sign up for mailing lists or e-newsletters, they will receive announcements of upcoming events, but they won't receive personal communication. While it is unrealistic for staff members to follow up personally with each person who visits once, there are opportunities for personalized connections to follow visitors beyond the exit doors.

Many museums have experimented with exhibits that allow visitors to send home e-cards or bookmarks to content they found compelling or made themselves. Several art, science, and history museums have offered systems since the mid-1990s for visitors to save experiences at the museum for later perusal on the Web. These "do it now, see it on the Web later" activities tend to have a low follow-through rate of less than ten percent.[19]

The numbers are particularly low in institutions in which every visitor receives a personal Web address with her ticket, because these systems "push" personalized take-homes on everybody. A subset of visitors wants to do creative or collecting activities onsite, and a subset of those wants to follow-up later online. There are large numbers of inactive people who are unaware of, uninterested in, or intimidated by these activities. There are also visitors who lose the ticket between the museum and the home computer, or do not realize that they can find the content later online.

In contrast to ticket-based systems, exhibits or systems that invite people to intentionally opt into personalization have higher follow-through rates. When individuals actively choose to participate (or "pull" the experience), they are more likely to follow up than when the experience is pushed out to everyone.

---

19 See the section titled "Do Bookmarking Applications Meet Museums' Expectations?" in Silvia Filippini-Fantoni and Jonathan Bowen's paper, "Bookmarking in Museums: Extending the Museum Experience Beyond the Visit?" available at http://www.participatorymuseum.org/ref2-19/

Beyond inviting visitors to actively elect to participate, there are three factors that positively impact the number of visitors who access content at home that they generated at the institution:

1. The extent to which the content is personalized
2. The amount of investment in the onsite activity
3. The ease with which the content can be accessed at home

The first two of these are often blended. Taking a photo of yourself or writing a personal pledge is an identity-building experience. People are fundamentally self-interested and are more likely to revisit a personal item that commemorates a fun or educational experience than a piece of institutionally-created content. Personalized experiences often promote more emotional connections than traditional content experiences, which also means people are more likely to remember and be interested in re-engaging with their creations.

When it comes to ease of access, sending visitors personal emails instead of directing them to Web addresses makes it easier for visitors to reconnect. For example, visitors who use the Tropenmuseum's "take a photo of yourself with an African hairstyle" interactive exhibit have the option to send the image home to a visitor-supplied email address. Back at home, they are likely to open the email for two reasons. First, the visitors actively opted in to the post-visit experience by supplying an email address onsite rather than passively receiving a ticket with a custom URL on it. And second, accessing the photo at home requires little effort —no codes to type in, just an email waiting in the inbox. Asking for an email address at the exhibit is a kind of test of visitors' investment in the activity. It makes it easier to follow up online, instead of the other way around.

CASE STUDY
USING TAKE-HOMES FOR DEEP ENGAGEMENT AT THE CHICAGO CHILDREN'S MUSEUM

Some "send it home" activities are trivial—take a photo, complete a game—and others are more involved, inviting visitors to collect content throughout the exhibit experience or via a multi-step process. While more time-intensive onsite experiences may not appeal to everyone, visitors who complete complex activities tend to be dedicated to their products. Consider the *Skyscraper Challenge* exhibit at the Chicago Children's Museum. *Skyscraper Challenge* invited visitors to work in groups to construct a mini-skyscraper over several minutes and then create a photo narrative based on their experience. As each team worked, a kiosk snapped timed photographs of them. After the skyscraper was built, the family or group sat down to make a multi-media story about their experiences. The kiosk prompted them to

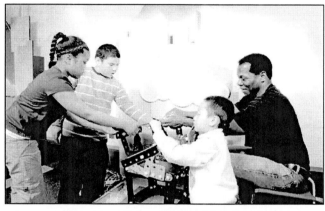

In the *Skyscraper Challenge*, families build a skyscraper (top) and then sit down to construct a digital "book" about their experience (bottom). The book includes photos of the work-in-progress and audio commentary from family members.

select pictures from the bank of photos taken that represented "a time when we worked well together," or "a time when we solved a tough problem."

This clever setup allowed the personalization (the photo-taking) to be automated, and then encouraged visitors to layer on meaning by reflecting on what they were doing and feeling at the different moments caught on camera. This highly personalized photo narrative took a long time to create (median group time on task was fifteen minutes) and about 85% of visitors opted to take their "building permit" home with them to retrieve the digital story via a custom website. Thirty-one percent elected to revisit digital stories on the Web from home—a higher number than is typical, especially considering the very young age of these visitors and the fact that people had to type in a custom URL from the building permit to access them.

Using Take-Homes to Inspire Repeat Visitation

Cultural institutions often have an overly structured concept of the online pre- and post-visit experience that limits the opportunities for repeat engagement. Take-home activities give visitors mementos of fun and educational visits for further reflection, but few explicitly motivate another visit or continued interaction with the museum beyond a few clicks of the mouse. For example, the US Holocaust Museum's *From Memory to Action* exhibition about worldwide genocide allows onsite visitors to swipe a card across a smart table to store videos and multimedia stories for exploration at home via the exhibition website. The idea is for visitors to continue their experience exploring the exhibit's content when at home, where their attention may be more focused on a difficult and highly emotional topic. This is reasonable from a content distribution perspective, but it does little to support relationship building. The planned experience extends engagement with the institution for a short time. The setup is simple: see the exhibit, save the things you like, check them out at home. The end.

These take-home experiences are treated as an epilogue to a visit rather than the hook for a sequel. Rather than focusing on extending single visits with a pre- and post-visit, it can be more valuable to link multiple visits with offsite experiences.

For example, the Chicago Children's Museum occasionally invites visitors to hand-write postcards to themselves about their museum visit. The museum holds the postcards back and mails them a few days later. This activity was originally introduced to encourage visitors to reflect on their experience at the museum and memorialize their learning for later review at home. Cognitive psychologists have shown that reconnecting with educational content at strategic points in time ("spaced repetition") can lead to longer-term retention of the material. In the museum context, that means a postcard can help visitors retain what they learned while onsite—and have stronger recall of their visit experiences.[20]

The postcards don't just serve learning goals; they also create delightful connection points between institutions and visitors. Receiving a postcard in the mail is a special treat, especially for children. A physical, personal, time-delayed artifact like a postcard has much higher potential impact on visitors' relationships with institutions than an email waiting in the inbox when visitors return home from an outing. There's no "delete" button for the postal service: visitors are more likely to read and keep physical items they receive. As Tsivia Cohen, Associate Vice President of Family Learning Initiatives, put it:

> One reason we like to mail the documentation—rather than just handing it to visitors to take home—is to create a delay. We're assuming it will arrive at their house in a few days (let's hope). At the museum, families can also choose to mail the record of their visit to a relative who's not with them, which we hope will result in additional correspondence or a thank you phone call—one more opportunity for conversation.

This activity transforms a take-home item into a surprising, personal gift. From the museum's perspective, the postcard activity prompts the recall of museum experiences that contribute to cementing the learning that started onsite. But it also injects the museum into real life and reminds visitors, via the most personal voice possible, that they liked being there and might like to visit again.

---

20 For more on spaced repetition, read Gary Wolf's fascinating April 2008 article in *Wired*, "Want to Remember Everything You'll Ever Learn? Surrender to This Algorithm," at http://www.participatorymuseum.org/ref2-20/

CASE STUDY

THE 39 CLUES AND CROSS-PLATFORM ENGAGEMENT

When institutions treat visits as "pearls on a string" of an ongoing shared narrative, there is potential to build substantive cross-platform relationships between institutions and individuals. In 2008, Scholastic Books released a new series, *The 39 Clues*, which tied a ten-book mystery to an online gaming environment. *The 39 Clues* experience was devised to foster long-term, progressive relationships with readers. The company paid for ten books written by ten different authors, and the books were released every few months over two years. How could Scholastic keep readers interested enough between releases to bring them back for each subsequent episode?

This problem is analogous to the repeat visit problem for museums and performing arts venues. Museum visits, like book reading, can be intense and wonderful experiences. But they are also punctuated moments in time. Most people don't obsessively reread the same book or visit a particular exhibit or show multiple times. They wait for the next one to come along before they return.

Scholastic didn't want to lose readers from one book to the next. They wanted to build an allegiance to *The 39 Clues* brand that would make more people likely to stick with the series. Rather than trying to increase engagement by releasing longer books or more books, Scholastic shifted to a new medium: online gaming. The online game was the thread that kept readers engaged from one book release to the next.

Here's how *The 39 Clues* cross-platform experience works.[21] There are thirty-nine clues to find across the entire series. Each book unlocks a clue. Each book also comes with 6 game cards to help readers find other clues. These two elements encourage people not only to read but also to purchase books so they can get the cards.

The books follow a team of orphaned siblings who hunt for clues. The online game reveals that you the player are related to them (surprise!) and can hunt alongside the orphans. Online, there are puzzles to solve and exclusive book-related content to absorb and respond to. As readers, users

---

21 As of this printing, *The 39 Clues* is still in progress and can be accessed at http://www.participatorymuseum.org/ref2-21/

The 39 Clues game connects readers to the overarching narrative for
the book series via an interwoven set of virtual and physical clues.

consume the fictitious experiences of the books' characters. But as game
players, readers are able to become active agents in the stories. When combined, both types of experiences enhanced each other.

While Scholastic is focused on selling books, this multi-platform approach need not be limited to commercial enterprise. Scholastic took the
audacious position that people would want to read all ten books, and *The 39
Clues* online experience was unapologetically geared toward that long-term
investment. Imagine a museum game that required visitors to visit six times
in a year to connect with six different exhibits that punctuate a more open-
ended online narrative. Forget "build the exhibit and they will come." This is
"build the narrative and they will return."

Give Visitors a Personal Reason to Return

The simplest way to start thinking like Scholastic is to presume that
your institution has more to offer the first-time visitor striding out the exit
doors. I'm not talking about the next performance or traveling exhibition the
institution will host, but another experience visitors could have in the near
term. There's a restaurant in Santa Cruz with an eccentric owner who says to
every exiting patron, "See you tomorrow!" He knows people aren't actually

likely to come back the next day, but he sets an expectation (and expresses a personal desire) that they might in the near future.

The next step is to act on this expectation by providing visitors opportunities to provide feedback or profile information on the way out. Imagine an e-newsletter sign-up station at which visitors pick one word that best describes their visit ("inspiring," "boring," "fun," "educational," etc.) and another word to describe a new interest motivated by the visit. Visitors could respond digitally, verbally, or by filling out a form. Then, when a visitor goes home, he receives an email from the museum—not a completely impersonal one announcing the next coming attraction, but one that says, "George, we're so glad you were inspired by the museum. Here are a few of the exhibits that other visitors (or staff) have described as 'inspiring' that you might want to check out on your next visit. And since you're interested in learning more about the behind-the-scenes of the museum, here's a blog written by our conservation team, and a couple of dates of upcoming behind-the-scenes tours." These emails could be automated, but writing them could also be a worthwhile activity for volunteers or front-line staff.

Not every visitor will opt in to a feedback experience like this, but for those who do, it's worth making a personal connection. Visitors who willingly give museums their email addresses want a second date. They want to receive follow-up content, and despite all their other e-newsletter experiences to date, they secretly hope that *this* institution can provide something compelling.

Imagine leaving a museum energized. A volunteer at the front door asks you how your experience was and invites you to sign up for the e-newsletter. You do, and then a couple days later, you receive an email from that very person thanking you for coming and making suggestions for your next visit. That's the kind of memorable experience that encourages visitors to return.

Personalization over Multiple Visits

Once an institution can effectively motivate first-time visitors to return, staff members need ways to acknowledge visitors' evolving relationship with the institution. There are some very simple things cultural institutions can do to promote ongoing relationships with visitors who come repeatedly. First, admissions desk computer systems should provide data on the last time a person (or a credit card) has visited the institution. At the least, cashiers should be able to see that the person has visited previously and should be able to smile and say, "Welcome back." You don't need a computer system for this—even a punch card, like those offered at coffee shops—can indicate repeat use and help staff members respond accordingly.

We're all familiar with the basic version of the punch card, ubiquitous in coffee shops, on which you accumulate stamps or hole-punches and receive a free drink after a set number of purchases. There are virtual versions, such as the outdoor store REI's co-op system, in which members of the co-op receive 10% back on all REI purchases available in store credit or cash at the end of the year. There's even a Los Angeles theater that offers a play with forking paths (such that you can't see the whole show on one occasion) and a diminishing ticket price for each subsequent visit.[22]

Punch cards are low-cost relationship-builders that do two important things:

1. They establish an expectation that you might visit multiple times
2. They allow staff to see, with no complex technology, that you have visited previously

Presumably, a membership does these things as well. But many institutions, even those with complex membership database systems, don't prioritize tracking repeat attendance in a way that is usable by front-line staff. Where computers may fall short, punch cards thrive. Seeing that a person's card has been punched several times allows front-line staff to engage in conversation about what visitors liked on previous visits, what's new, and what they might particularly enjoy.

How can coffee shop-style punch cards be redesigned for cultural institutions? People visit museums and performing arts venues infrequently enough that visit-based punch cards may not motivate repeat use. If you buy coffee every day, and your favorite café offers you a free cup for every ten

---

22 Learn more about this unusual play, *Tamara*, at http://www.participatorymuseum.org/ref2-22/

you buy, you can get free coffee every couple of weeks. Cultural institutions don't work that way. Most people (with the exception of enthusiastic young families at children's and science museums) would likely misplace museum punch cards before making it to visit number ten.

There are some clever innovations on the punch card system that may work better in venues that experience infrequent use. Menchies, a frozen yogurt shop in Los Angeles, offers a standard punch card that promises a free yogurt after you've purchased seven. When you enter as a first-time customer and buy a yogurt, instead of receiving an "empty" punch card, you receive one with six punches already completed—functionally, a two-for-one coupon for your next visit. This makes the punch card higher-value for newcomers, and it probably is more effective than a coupon in priming people to return and presumably continue frequenting the shop. Some museums have experimented with sending students home from school trips with a free ticket for a follow-up visit with the family; maybe starting them with a punch card would be a more effective way to connect them to the institution.

Tina, We Salute You, a hip coffee shop in London, turned their punch cards into a social experience. Rather than carrying a card, patrons write their names on the wall and draw a star for every drink consumed. Purchase ten and you receive a free coffee—and a new color to continue advancing your stars. Instead of the loyalty reward being a private transaction, people get to celebrate with staff members and other patrons. This creates a feeling of community and entices new visitors to the shop to add their own name and get involved. There's also a friendly competitive aspect that motivates some people to get more stars or have a more adorned name because their participation is publicly showcased. And it's successful—Tina, We Salute You's initial loyalty wall quickly proved too small for its community of enthusiasts. This could be an easy way, particularly for small institutions, to encourage visitors to think of themselves as part of the cultural community of the place and to desire a "level up" in their nameplate on the wall. It's like a low-budget, dynamic donor wall.

As a final example, The Winking Lizard Tavern is an Ohio-based chain of thirteen restaurants that puts on a yearly "world beer tour," featuring

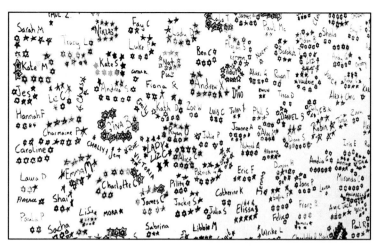

Patrons at Tina, We Salute You keep track of their
purchases by writing on the wall of the coffeeshop.

over 150 international beers. For ten dollars, people can join the tour and
receive a color guidebook of all the beers, a punch card for the beers they've
tried, and access to an online beer-tasting tracking system. When a person
tries fifty beers, she gets a gift, and at one hundred, she receives the "world
tour jacket" featuring the names of the year's beers. This is functionally a
membership, including email newsletters and special events, but it is driven
by the idea that members will keep purchasing new (and different) beers. It's
a brilliant way for each transaction to enhance the value of the punch card
rather than making people wait until the end. You could easily imagine a
similar system to encourage people to visit different institutions, exhibits, or
try new experiences across an institution (educational programs, lectures,
performances, social events).

Making Membership Matter

The ultimate version of the highly engaged visitor is the member.
Members are people who pay upfront for the privilege of being part of the
museum community. Unfortunately, most memberships to cultural institutions have shifted from promoting deep relationships to promoting financial

value. People don't join to express their connection to the institution and its content. They join for free admission.

Why do so many institutions treat membership as an impersonal season pass? As the museum industry has moved towards greater reliance on gate sales, membership has evolved into a commoditized (and successful) product. Membership effectively packages the museum experience—in some cities, a group of local museum experiences—into something repeatable at low cost. The majority of museum members are "value members" who join museums for the cost savings on visits. They do a calculation, realize that a membership is "worth it" if they visit two or three times in a year, and spring for the membership.

What's wrong with value members? From a business perspective, they are a risky long-term investment. Value members are very different from members who join because of strong institutional affinity. Value members are easy to attract but challenging to retain when it comes time for renewal, whereas affinity members exhibit the opposite behavior. If your membership materials are geared towards high-churn value members, you are unlikely to meaningfully serve those members who might be interested in building long-term relationships as donors or highly engaged visitors.

Members are theoretically an institution's best customers—the people who are most motivated to get involved. Treating members as people after a discount effectively denigrates the value of the institution, rather than increasing the value commensurate with those super-visitors' demonstrated interest.

Personalization techniques can improve the effectiveness of both value and affinity memberships. The first step is to separate these. Offer an annual pass to those who want free admission, and offer a different kind of membership to those who want a deeper relationship. This allows institutions to focus specific resources—discounts, personal attention, and opportunities for deeper experiences—towards the people who want them. This reduces institutional waste and is more likely to deliver satisfying experiences to different types of members.

For annual pass holders, personalization techniques should be geared towards motivating repeat visits. These people have purchased based on a calculated expectation that they will return to the institution enough times in the year to "get the value" of their pass. But many annual pass-holders buy the pass on their first visit and may not really understand what the institution can offer them. These people are like those who sign up for a diet because it seems like a good idea. They need feedback and relevant content to stick with it. By explicitly demonstrating that the institution can satisfy these people's individual interests and needs, staff can motivate pass holders to return. When annual pass holders don't renew, it means the institution has not succeeded in demonstrating compelling relevance or value to their lives.

Affinity members are people who express an intention to be more deeply involved with cultural institutions. This desire should be paid in personal attention, not direct mail. Different affinity members have different needs. Some want to contribute to institutions by participating in prototyping or volunteering for special projects. Some want exclusive opportunities, like behind-the-scenes tours, special fast-track lines at events, or early ticket purchasing.

CASE STUDY
NICHE MEMBERSHIPS AT THE BROOKLYN MUSEUM AND THE CENTER OF SCIENCE AND INDUSTRY

In 2009, the Brooklyn Museum launched *1stfans*, a membership targeted at two distinct audiences: people who attend free Target First Saturdays at the museum and those who connect with the institution online. The people who engage in these programs already have pre-existing positive relationships with the institution, but they don't buy memberships because free museum admission is not relevant to their needs. The staff developed a slate of special benefits for this group, including exclusive online content and preferred access to films on free Saturdays. The museum promoted *1stfans* as a "socially networked membership," and staff members host in-person meetups and online discussion groups to encourage *1stfans* to meet each other and connect as a community of members rather than each having a discrete member experience.

At a January 2009 event, street artist Swoon and artists from
her studio made screen-prints for *1stfans* members. The prints
(and the event) were an exclusive *1stfans* benefit.

In the first year of its existence, *1stfans* drew over five hundred members. Though about eighty percent live in New York City, there are 1stfans in twenty-three states and ten countries who support the institution and receive virtual, if not onsite, benefits. While *1stfans* is its first experiment with niche membership, the Brooklyn Museum hopes to offer more customized member packages in the future. When I talked with membership manager Will Cary about *1stfans*, he commented that, "We're hopeful that *1stfans* is just the first step in this direction. We've talked in marketing meetings about creating a package appealing to senior citizens just as we have for the *1stfans*."[23]

The Center of Science and Industry (COSI) in Columbus, Ohio launched a similar experiment to target families with young children, whose needs and interests are slightly different than families with older kids. In the spring of 2009, COSI launched a "premium membership" at $125 (as opposed to $88 for a standard family membership). Premium membership benefits included exclusive early access to COSI's *little kidspace*® gallery on

_____

23 Read the complete February 2009 interview with Cary, Shelley Bernstein, and *1stfans* collaborator An Xiao at http://www.participatorymuseum.org/ref2-23/

weekday mornings, special programs, preferred camp signups, and reciprocity with other children's museums nationwide. In its first eight months, the
premium membership attracted 329 families. This is a small percentage of
the institution's overall member base of 18,000, but it is a first step towards
providing custom services for specific member segments.

These kinds of specialized memberships are personalized to niche audiences, but not to individuals. The top-down structure of member packages
means specialized memberships must appeal to whole groups of people
who want similar benefits. But the ultimate version of this is the personalized
membership—an a la carte suite of benefits that evolves dynamically as the
visitor's needs and relationship to the institution change. For an example of
an institution pursuing this approach to powerful ends, let's turn to a recreational facility with very different values than museums: the casino.

CASE STUDY
PERSONALIZED RELATIONSHIPS WITH HARRAH'S CASINOS

Imagine running a gambling company. How would you encourage
people to feel positive about spending their money in your casino instead of
the one next door?

Harrah's is the world's largest and most geographically diversified
provider of casino entertainment, and they attribute a great deal of their success to "building loyalty and value" for customers through personalization.[24]
Harrah's uses *Total Rewards* loyalty cards to deeply engage gamers as part of
the casino "community," and by doing so, to induce people to play longer
and spend more money.[25]

Total Rewards cards function like bankcards. Users swipe them at
slot machines to play, and the cards register wins and losses. Players accrue
points that can be redeemed for meals and hotel discounts, but the real
power of the *Total Rewards* system is in the comprehensive "you are what
you do" profiles generated for each guest. Harrah's knows what games you
play at which times of the day and for how long. The system keeps track

---

24 See http://www.participatorymuseum.org/ref2-24/
25 For a fascinating radio story on Harrah's *Total Rewards* system, check out
http://www.participatorymuseum.org/ref2-25/

of when you like to take a break and what you like to eat. The cards are integrated across the entire set of Harrah's casinos, hotels, restaurants, and resorts, and the company adjusts its customer service to your preferences. If you tend to book vacations in April, you'll receive an email with hotel discounts in February or March.

Since the loyalty system was launched in the mid-1990s, Harrah's has doubled its share of guests' gaming budgets. It's no coincidence that their system is considered a standout "customer relationship" system as opposed to a rewards card. "The prevailing wisdom in this business is that the attractiveness of a property drives customers," says Gary Loveman, Harrah's CEO. "Our approach is different. We stimulate demand by knowing our customers."[26]

Harrah's knows its customers so well that it can even respond to the emotional roller coaster of gambling. The company maintains real-time data on the actions of every card-holder as they play—dollars in, dollars out, time spent at specific machine—and uses the data to determine individuals' financial "pain points"—i.e. how much money they are willing to spend before leaving the casino. The casino uses those pain points to stage strategic interventions during real-time play. When a player comes close to her quitting point, a staff member on the casino floor receives an alert from a dispatcher, greets the player, and offers her a free meal, a drink, or a few more dollars on the loyalty card. By mitigating the bad experience of losing with a surprise gift, Harrah's extends people beyond their pain points and they stay and play longer. And by combining the action players already do (inserting money) with the desired new action (identifying themselves), the loyalty cards create a deeper relationship without requiring users to substantively change their behavior. In fact, most players prefer to play with loyalty cards because they receive perks for doing so. Players get an easier way to play and receive rewards, and the casino gets unique, trackable data on every player in the room.

While Harrah's goal of promoting gambling and casino loyalty may be unsettling, its loyalty program is an elegant example of a responsive, highly scalable member relationship system. Systems like this need not be focused

---

26 Ibid.

on emptying visitors' wallets or tracking their every move. Personalization isn't just about inspiring multiple visits or purchases; it can also be designed to promote deep engagement with visitors in ways that support their intellectual and creative development.

What might a system like Harrah's look like at a cultural institution?[27] Imagine swiping a member card on entry and gaining access to a tailored set of recommendations based on past onsite and online activities, immediate interests, and institutional offerings. For individual visitors, the system could function like Nike Plus (see page 29), connecting the physical experience to online, tracked progress toward personal experience and learning goals. For educational groups, a personalization system could track students' development and mastery of progressive skills. For families, it could provide a growing body of personal content, an album of shared experiences.

Developing a system as complex as Harrah's may sound like an expensive and daunting task. It is. But you can start small. Identify a single "pain point"—an experience that frequently causes visitors to stop visiting—and try to find ways to build relationships to mitigate that single issue. If your challenge is that families stop coming after their kids turn ten, develop and market programs that explicitly engage ten- and eleven-year-olds. If your challenge is visitors who come for a single event and then never again, try offering explicit information at the event about how that specific program relates to other institutional offerings. Once you do this for one pain point, you'll start noticing others—and eventually, you'll have a system that supports comprehensive relationship building without having to make a major top-down investment. When institutions pursue strategies that support visitors' growth and changing needs, they can grow with visitors instead of visitors outgrowing them.

---

27 For an extended and imaginative answer to this question, consult Chapter 1 of Falk and Sheppard, *Thriving in the Knowledge Age* (2006).

If your participatory goals include social engagement, personalization is only a start. Highly personalized and responsive tools can lead to isolation—me with my customized experience, you with yours. In the beginning of this chapter, I noted that successful social experiences rely on three things: an audience-centric approach, individuals with unique personal profiles, and tools to connect those individuals to each other. This chapter primarily focused on the first two of these. In Chapter 3, we'll look more closely at the tools that connect individuals to each other in a participatory platform and how those tools promote interpersonal dialogue and community engagement.

CHAPTER 3

FROM ME TO WE

THERE ARE MANY TECHNICAL DEFINITIONS FOR WEB 2.0, but in 2006, publisher Tim O'Reilly boiled it down to a single phrase: *an application that gets better the more people use it.* As he explained:

> Google gets smarter every time someone makes a link on the Web. Google gets smarter every time someone makes a search. It gets smarter every time someone clicks on an ad. And it immediately acts on that information to improve the experience for everyone else.[1]

This isn't just true about Google. The more videos you rate on Netflix, the better job it does recommending films—not just to you, but to all its users. The more books in your LibraryThing library, the easier it is for people to find books they might like. These systems provide more than personalized experiences; they also provide community value.

What does a cultural institution look like that gets better the more people use it? Many people—professionals and visitors alike—see museums

---

1   Read O'Reilly's complete 2006 UC Berkeley School of Information commencement address at http://www.participatorymuseum.org/ref3-1/

as getting *worse* the more people use them. More people means crowds between a visitor and her aesthetic experience. More people means more noise, more fingerprints, more mess. While staff members celebrate high visitation as a sign of institutional health, they privately recommend that friends visit during quiet hours for a better experience.

But what if it was possible to design an institution that enabled visitors to enhance each other's experiences? The previous chapter addressed tools that get better the more individuals use them; this chapter explores ways to enhance visitor experiences via interactions with others. This is "me-to-we" design, which enables cultural institutions to move from personal to social engagement.

Designing experiences that get better the more people use them is not simply a question of providing experiences that are well suited to crowds. While many people cite social engagement as a primary reason for visiting museums, they don't necessarily want to spend their entire visit talking or interacting with other visitors in groups. Successful me-to-we experiences coordinate individuals' actions and preferences to create a useful and inter-esting collective result. Technologists often call this "harnessing collective intelligence."

Consider the Ontario Science Centre's *Facing Mars* traveling exhibi-tion. The exhibition opened and closed with a question: "Would you go to Mars?" and visitors entered and exited through turnstiles labeled "yes" and "no." This personalized experience primed visitors emotionally for the exhibit based on their personal identities. But *Facing Mars* went one step further. Above each turnstile an LED display showed the aggregate number of visitors who selected "yes" or "no" to date. Each visitor could watch the number tick up as she walked through her selected turnstile. She had a per-sonal experience answering the question, and her answer made a visible contribution to the exhibition and affected the experience of others.

While the exhibition was on display at the Ontario Science Centre, about two-thirds of entering visitors answered "yes" they would go to Mars. At the exit, the numbers were reversed and only one-third still wanted to visit the red planet. Collective intelligence told visitors something very simple: lots of people think they want to go to Mars, but when they find out what's really involved, they change their minds. This insight is interesting and surprising. And, it was more powerfully conveyed since it was based on data that visitors knew they had contributed to. This message could not be as convincingly offered in label text as it was via the displays, even if it was an underlying focus of the whole exhibit.

The LED displays made visitors aware of themselves as part of a larger social network of visitors—some like them, some unlike them. For visitors whose minds were changed by the exhibition, the displays offered confirmation of a shared social shift. For visitors who did not experience a change of heart, the displays provided information that may have encouraged them to reflect on what made them unique. The LED displays created a social context for what was already a compelling personal experience by networking the individual selections of each visitor.

Visitors entered *Facing Mars* either through the "Yes" or "No" turnstile. The setup was duplicated at the exit so visitors would vote again on their way out.

The Network Effect

The *Facing Mars* turnstiles are an example of the *network effect*, which translates individual actions into community benefits. The network effect is the backbone of social networks. Here's how it works:

1. *Individuals have personalized interactions.* They create content, make choices that generate data, or provide personal information in the form of profiles.

2. *An internal algorithm makes connections among the individuals.* That can mean sorting profiles by interests or types, setting relationship levels among different individuals, or simply aggregating the content.

3. *The networked content is displayed or provided back to the individuals.* In examples like *Facing Mars* or comment boards, everyone gets access to the same content. In systems like LibraryThing or Pandora (see page 40 and page 63 respectively), the content is customized to individuals to provide personalized recommendations or content streams.

The New York Hall of Science's exhibit *Near* is a good physical demonstration of how these networks work.[2] *Near* is a floor-mounted exhibit. When you step on the *Near* mat, you become a node, represented by your location on the mat. Your movement is the individual action. When other people step on the mat, lighted lines indicate abstracted relationships with other nodes/people on the mat. The lights are the content output. The exhibit employs a simple algorithm: it draws a line between each node and the node nearest to it. If there are just two people, there will be two lines, one from me to you, and one from you to me. If there are several people, there will be several lines, and not all nodes will be in reciprocal relationships with just one other close node. As people move around the mat, the lines change as they get closer to some people and further from others. The more people moving on the mat, the more the light display indicates the dynamic ways that nodes can be related in a complex system.

---

2   *Near* is still open at the New York Hall of Science as of this printing.

If you look closely, you can see the lines between the visitors on the *Near* mat.
These lines reposition themselves dynamically based on visitors' movements.

Beyond illustrating how networks work, *Near* demonstrates the power of the network effect in designing multi-person exhibits. The exhibit is flexible and scalable for groups who drift in and out. The activity of walking on the mat is individual, so individuals don't have to worry about how others' contributions might disrupt their personal experience. But the exhibit immediately and transparently communicates the benefits of multiple individuals all acting at once, encouraging group play. *Near* doesn't require visitors to explicitly work together, but it provides additional rewards when people do so.

The Balancing Act Between Networked and Social Experiences

Designing high-quality experiences for multiple users is no easy task, especially if an exhibit has to work as well for thirty people as it does for two or must accommodate both pre-defined and casual groups of users. The most scalable way to do this is to provide many optional individual actions that can add to a social experience but that are not essential to the exhibit's success. Rather than designing exhibits with fixed roles that specific numbers of visitors must fill at the same time, you might design more flexible ways for non-participating visitors to engage peripherally in single-user interactives as spectators, helpers, or partners. For example, some museums have "quiz game" style exhibits at which individuals can answer questions in front of a large projection. While only one visitor can hold a controller, a larger group can crowd around to help him answer questions and play along.

In *Near* and *Facing Mars*, network effects allow any number of visitors' individual actions to combine toward productive shared outputs. To make this work, designers have to respect individuals' actions and personal space so they feel confident jumping into a social environment. If *Near* had required visitors to get uncomfortably close to generate connections, fewer people may have felt comfortable playing with each other on the mat.

This principle is also at work in some of the most successful multi-touch table installations in museums. Well-designed multi-touch tables promote both personal exploration and interpersonal play. People feel comfortable crowding around these tables and engaging with each other because each person can control his own zone of the table with his hand. No one can take over "your spot" but there are often opportunities to work collaboratively to beneficial group results. Everyone comes to the exhibit equally, and it's easy to look up from what you are doing to check out what's going on at another station or talk to another visitor. By entering via their own safe space, visitors are more willing to engage with others.

Recall the stages of social participation introduced on page 25. Most unfacilitated social engagement among visitors starts with a stage three or stage four experience. The *Facing Mars* turnstiles offered a stage three polling experience, in which individual users' actions were networked and presented to each other in aggregate. Most user-generated content experiences in cultural institutions are also on stage three. Visitors can produce content (write their own labels, produce stop-motion videos, etc.) and other visitors can view them. Stage three experiences tend to promote social awareness but not necessarily social engagement among visitors. I can't respond specifically to the person who wrote the provocative message on the comment board—I can only respond to the masses. Others can see my contribution, but they can't talk directly to me.

The difference between stage three and stage four lies in the extent to which the institution serves as a platform that mediates direct social engagement among users. For example, imagine equipping the *Facing Mars* entrance turnstiles with a system that offers each visitor a sticker indicating whether they chose yes or no.[3] Now, visitors who wear the stickers would see not only the aggregate responses of visitors-to-date, they can also approach other visitors in real-time in the exhibition and say, "Hey, I chose yes too!" or "Huh. I chose yes and you chose no. What makes us different?" This is an experience that cannot happen based solely on the LED displays (stage three). It also cannot happen based solely on people making selections privately for themselves (stage two).

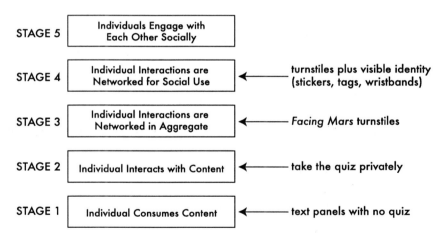

Facing Mars could be designed on any of four stages of me-to-we design.

Stage four experiences are most useful when cultural institutions want to promote direct interpersonal engagement, or when visitors would benefit from knowing more about the unique background or profile of the other visitors using the platform. Visitors may not need a stage four experience to

---

3   This is effectively the same as the scheme for *A Matter of Faith* at Stapferhaus Lenzbergon page 52, but with a less confrontational question and a simpler interface.

read each other's memories about a historic event or find out how they compared to others in a poll. But in situations that feature opinionated content or recommendations, people like to know who's speaking.

CASE STUDY
A NETWORKED SHOW AT THE ANNE FRANK MUSEUM

One of the best illustrations of the hazy boundary between stage three and stage four experiences is the *Free2Choose* experience at the Anne Frank Museum in Amsterdam.[4] *Free2choose* is a very simple interactive show in which visitors vote on their stances on issues related to freedom. It is one room, with a long, semi-circular bench with cushions and room for about 30 people to sit and stand. Every few feet on the bench, there is a small voting box about the size of a light switch with two buttons on it, one red and one green.

The visitors on the bench face a large projection screen that plays a fixed loop. First, a one-minute video clip presents an issue (for example, whether students should be allowed to wear headscarves to school). Then, a statement pops up: "Students should be allowed to wear religious symbols in school." Visitors see a ticking countdown and are told to vote by pressing either the green (yes) or red (no) button on the voting box. At the end of the countdown, the results are shown for both "Visitors Now" and for "All Visitors" (meaning all visitors to date).

The Now vs. All display makes *Free2Choose* a powerful social experience. When you take a poll alone or walk into *Facing Mars*, there's no suspense about the outcome. I voted yes for going to Mars, and then I saw that 65% of other visitors over time agreed with me. In *Free2choose*, I voted yes for headscarves, saw that 65% of all visitors agreed with me, but **also** saw that only 40% of the people currently in the room agreed with me. When the results for "Visitors Now" differed greatly from those of "All Visitors," the surprise was audible. I was in one group where 100% of us voted that Protestants should be able to parade through Catholic areas of Northern Ireland, and we looked around with curiosity and complicity when we saw

---

4   *Free2Choose* is open as of this printing with no scheduled end date.

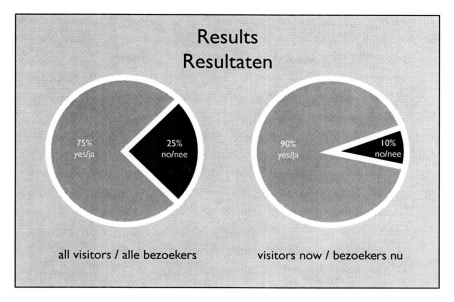

The results screen for the *Free2Choose* show. The greater the difference
between the two graphs, the louder the reaction in the room.

that only 60% of "All Visitors" agreed with us. Every group was different, so
every outcome was different.

Free2choose is powerful because it introduces social tension. When
I voted in the minority, I felt that I was in the minority not just conceptually
but physically, in that crowd, in real-time. Because the room was often full,
I found myself looking for people "like me" in the crowd. But I had no way
to identify them in the faceless group of button-pushers.

And that's where the social dimension of *Free2choose* (and stage three
experiences generally) falls short. There is no component to the *Free2choose*
exhibition that highlights the specific selections made by individuals in the
room, and no vehicle to incite conversation among differing groups. When I
visited *Free2Choose*, there was lots of buzz in the room—but only in whis-
pers among familiars. At one point, I stood next to a group of British visitors
who voted that flag burning should be illegal. I had voted the opposite. We
were standing close enough—a few inches apart—to see each other hit the
button, but I was not comfortable asking them about their decision or having
a discussion about our different choices.

How could *Free2choose* encourage visitors to talk with each other directly about the issues? Here are some design suggestions that could foster stage four or five engagement:

- Voting could be more public. When the results are shown, spotlights in the ceiling could illuminate areas of the room in different colors corresponding to who selected yes or no.
- Instead of voting in place, visitors could be directed to vote by moving to one side of the room or another.
- After the results are shown, the screen could instruct visitors to find someone in the room who voted differently from them, or just to ask their neighbor what they think about the issue or the results.
- Visitors could be instructed to share voting stations and to have a brief discussion to come to a consensus vote. As it was, there were too few stations and people awkwardly looked on as others used them.

Not everyone would want to go to the next level and have a conversation with strangers, but based on their conversations with companions, it was clear that some visitors were deeply engaged and did want to talk about the results. In an international city like Amsterdam, in a museum focused on one girl's extreme story that has touched the whole world, there is an enormous opportunity to go to the next level and facilitate cross-cultural discussion. As it stood, I had an interesting time comparing the results from different groups in my head. But I didn't understand why those groups were different, and I didn't gain more insight into how different people think about complicated human rights issues. I wanted more than just a fun interactive—I wanted to understand the other people in the room. It would have made for an extraordinary and unique experience in line with the overall mission of the Anne Frank House.

Free2choose is a perfect example of the limits of a stage three experience. Even though you are densely packed in a room with other people expressing opinions about important issues, you don't turn to your neighbor and start talking. The stigma is too great, and there is not enough scaffolding to help you cross the social barriers. You vote and see the results (stage three), but the voting mechanism is not a social object that mediates and motivates engagement with others (stage four). And so, even though you are all together in the same room, grappling with tough issues, you will never launch into group discourse (stage five).

Finding Your Own Way In

Not every exhibit benefits from being more socially networked. The Exploratorium's *Spinning Blackboard* exhibit is a good example of an exhibit that had to shift away from a networked setup to provide a high-quality multi-user experience. *Spinning Blackboard* invites visitors to make patterns in a spinning disc of sand. In the exhibit's original version, visitors all worked on the same disc. They were able to easily and unthinkingly mess up each other's patterns, which led both to confusion and frustration. The shared platform hindered rather than improved individual experiences.

The exhibit was redesigned as several adjacent spinning discs, allowing visitors to individually create their own sand patterns while remaining in discussion range with other pattern makers. This reasserted the primacy of the "me" experience while still making social engagement possible. This redesign resulted in a significant increase in number of patterns created, presumably because people were less frustrated by disruption and more able to fulfill their exploratory interests.[5]

In this case, the Exploratorium staff saw their goal as making it easier for visitors to control the sand patterns. But they could have taken a very different approach by prioritizing the social cooperation and competition that occurs when many hands dig in the sand. Consider the multi-player online game *Just Letters*.[6] *Just Letters* is an online version of refrigerator magnets in which you use your cursor to move around letters to make words. There's no goal or score, but the multi-player environment provides diverse opportunities for people to work together or compete. At any time, there may be as many as twenty people logged in, moving around letters. A group will decide to gather together all the blue letters. Then someone else will

5   Sue Allen and Josh Gutwill's excellent article, "Designing Science Museum Exhibits with Multiple Interactive Features: Five Common Pitfalls," appeared in *Curator*, issue 47, no. 2 (2004) and is available for download [PDF] at http://www.participatorymuseum.org/ref3-5/
6   Play *Just Letters* at http://www.participatorymuseum.org/ref3-6/

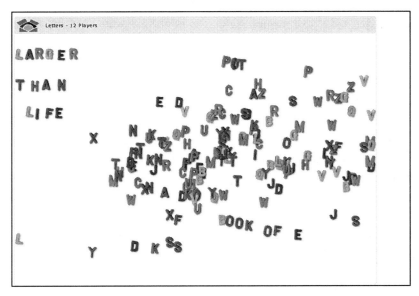

The original version of *Spinning Blackboard* (top) suffered from too many hands in the pot. In contrast, the *Just Letters* game (bottom) deliberately encourages people to disrupt each other's experience.

start stealing letters to spell his name over and over. Since there's no way for people to chat with the other players in the game, those who want to work collaboratively have to find creative ways to intuit each others' goals and help.

The disruptiveness that plagued the original version of *Spinning Blackboard* is the game mechanic that makes *Just Letters* unpredictable, lively, and fun. I'm not suggesting that one of these experiences is better than the other, but that it is possible for social friction to generate positive user experiences. It all depends on the values and behaviors you want to promote.

Designing Mediating Technology for Social Experiences

Just Letters has something that *Spinning Blackboard* does not: the mediating barrier of the Internet. Because people play the game through their own personal computers, they may be more comfortable both disrupting each other's play and collaborating with strangers than they would be in person. In this way, technology that looks like a social barrier leads instead to social engagement.

We're all familiar with the way technological barriers can make us more comfortable socializing with strangers—for good and ill. The same comfort that allows people to bare their souls (and lie) on the Web encourages kids to make funny faces through car windows. When you interact with strangers across barriers, you are more willing to engage in ways that might be considered rude or disruptive if you were together in person. This means that if you design the right barrier, you can invite visitors to engage with each other in some unusual and valuable ways.

Two layers of technology mediate *Just Letters*: the letters and players' computers. Without these barriers, people are probably too polite to make this kind of interaction possible. If you encountered a similar experience in a museum—a giant magnetic poetry wall, perhaps—people would likely interact with the wall singly or in their pre-determined groups, creating their own poems. I doubt that visitors would often interact in real time with other users of the wall—even to ask nicely if they could borrow a word. The social barriers to interaction among strangers are too high.

But imagine constructing a real-world version of *Just Letters* with barrier intact. Picture two magnetic poetry walls, back to back, with rods on the inside connecting words on each side. The walls look disconnected, but as soon as you move a word on one side, a word on the other side moves too. Suddenly, you start peeking around the wall, wondering what the heck that other person is doing. You might start coordinating or competing. The physical barrier between you would create a social environment for play, a bridge for stranger-to-stranger interaction.

CASE STUDY

HOW INTERNET ARM WRESTLING MEDIATES SOCIAL ENGAGEMENT

The *Internet Arm Wrestling* exhibit is a fascinating example of how technology-mediated interaction can lead to direct interpersonal engagement in museums. *Internet Arm Wrestling* was installed in six American science centers in 2004. This exhibit allows people to virtually arm wrestle with people around the country. When you sit down to use it, you grasp a metal arm (meant to simulate your competitor's arm) and are connected to another visitor at an identical kiosk. This visitor may be a few feet from you in the same science center or hundreds of miles away at another science center. You receive a "go" signal, and then you start pushing. The metal arm exerts a force on your arm equal to the force exerted by your remote partner on his own metal arm. Eventually, one competitor overpowers the other, and the game is over.

What makes *Internet Arm Wrestling* incredible—and a bit bizarre—is the extent to which strangers feel comfortable socializing around this game. Each player can communicate through a webcam feed to her partner as they play. Early on, some science centers removed the audio functionality of the webcams because some kids yelled obscenities at each other through the cameras.[7]

---

7   From the institutional perspective, the mediating technology let people cross too many social barriers.

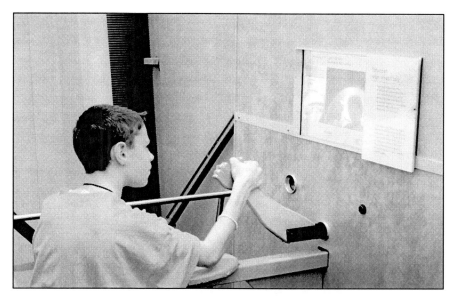

A visitor at the New York Hall of Science focuses intently on his remote arm wrestling competitor, watching him via webcam as he pushes on the metal arm.

I watched piles of kids use this exhibit at the New York Hall of Science in 2007, socializing both at each kiosk and across the kiosks. In some cases, multiple kids would gang up on one kiosk and try to sit on the arm to exert force on it. Kids would push on the arm as hard as they could, then turn their heads to look and laugh at their opponents at the other kiosk, then turn back and shove on. Other times, strangers—adults and kids—would stick out their tongues at each other in the cameras or make funny faces to try to distract their opponents from the task at hand.

Think about how unusual this is. Strangers—adults and children—engaging in silly and competitive social behavior through a set of metal arms. Would you ever challenge an unknown child (or adult, for that matter) to an arm wrestling match in a museum? Would you ever challenge a stranger to an arm wrestling match unprompted, ever? The *Internet Arm Wrestling* exhibit allows people to enjoy an interpersonal experience that otherwise wouldn't happen.

The Experimentarium in Denmark took this one step further with *EgoTrap*, a game visitors can play onsite with their mobile phones. After completing three solo challenges, each player is linked via mobile phone numbers to another who is playing at the same time. The players are in-structed to call each other, and then they meet up in person and play the rest of the game together throughout the science center.

This is not quite as risky as it may sound. Mostly intact groups (stu-dents and families visitors) play *EgoTrap*, so players are likely to be paired with classmates or family members. But this game raises an interesting ques-tion: if you wanted to invite absolute strangers to engage with each other, could you? That's what the next case study is all about.

CASE STUDY
LEARNING WITH STRANGERS IN THE HUMAN LIBRARY

The *Human Library* is an event that gets strangers talking openly and directly with each other about prejudice.[8] The organizers describe *Human Library* as "a tool to foster peaceful cohabitation and bring people closer to-gether in mutual and careful respect for the human dignity of the individual." Visitors sign up with a staff member, look through a catalog of stereotypes, pick one of interest, and enter into a 45-minute conversation with a real person who embodies that stereotype. As its organizers put it:

> The Human Library works exactly like a normal library – readers come and borrow a 'book' for a limited period of time. There is only one difference: the Books in the Human Library are human beings, and the Books and readers enter into a personal dialogue. The Books in the Human Library are people representing groups frequently confronted with prejudices and stereotypes, and who are often victims of discrimination or social exclusion. The 'reader' of the library can be anybody who is ready to talk with his or her own prejudice and stereotype and wants to spend an hour of time on this experience. In the Human Library, Books cannot only speak, but they are able to reply to the readers' questions, and the Books can even ask questions and learn themselves.[9]

A *Human Library* requires three kinds of people:

---

8   Until 2010, this project was called *Living Library*. It was renamed *Human Library* due to a legal conflict. I have changed all references to *Human Library* for clarity, but some of the referenced downloads may include the old term.
9   Download the comprehensive Human Library Organizer's Guide, which is available in eight languages at http://www.participatorymuseum.org/ref3-9/

1. Books who openly and authentically represent certain stereotyped groups (i.e. quadriplegic, Black Muslim, cop, Goth, lesbian)
2. Readers who check out the Books for 45-minute to 2-hour discussions
3. Librarians who facilitate the whole process

The *Human Library* was conceived in Denmark in 2000 as a way to engage youth in dialogue about ending violence by encouraging people to meet their prejudices and fears in a safe, fun, facilitated environment. Since then, *Human Libraries* have been produced all over the world at festivals, in libraries, and in workplaces. While they started as one-off events, *Human Libraries* have increasingly been included in the regular slate of programming at major libraries and educational facilities. Some institutions have expanded their scope beyond the initial focus on prejudice to provide a peer network for learning. For example, the University of Arkansas' Fall 2009 *Human Library* catalog included Books like "Meditation 101" and "Learning about Table Tennis" alongside more traditional volumes like "Christian Female Soldier," and "I am an Atheist."[10]

Where evaluated, Human Libraries have been incredibly successful. In an evaluation of a *Human Library* in Istanbul featuring 21 Books, 481 out of 484 Readers said they would recommend that others try the reading experience.[11] Several readers praised the authentic nature of the encounters as "exciting" and "educational." One reader said: "I could find common grounds with the advocate of an opinion that I do not agree with :)." Another Turkish reader commented:

> I've never had a gay friend. It was unbelievably exciting to find myself facing him with his body, opinions and identity. It seems he was not very different from me and especially he was not an alien. From now on, I will not disrupt my communication with the gays, I will enhance it.

A subway ticket inspector Book at a Danish *Human Library* shared this reflection:

10 See the University of Arkansas' complete catalog at http://www.participatory-museum.org/ref3-10/

11 Download the complete evaluation report from the Turkish *Human Library* [DOC] at http://www.participatorymuseum.org/ref3-11/

It was very interesting to meet and learn about how these young people experienced us (ticket inspectors) on duty in the trains.

Some of the most frequently asked questions were "Do you have to be a bastard to get a job like yours?," "Don't you ever feel sorry for those people who somehow find themselves in a situation without a ticket but needing transportation?," or "Isn't it terribly difficult for you to have to do this to other people?." In several cases they had questions that related to a specific situation they themselves had been involved in. I heard many of the readers' personal experiences with my colleagues, good and bad. But the advantage of the situation was that I was right there, sitting with them and ready to try to answer their questions. I often had to cut the conversation short when the time ran out.

I especially remember one situation with a young couple, sworn members of the Punk scene with their colourful hair and black leather outfits; we had a very interesting discussion and some more people joined us and started to ask questions. It ended up being 20 people joining in and listening to me babble about my work as "the bad guy who writes out the tickets.[12]

Unlike other networks explored in this chapter, the *Human Library* does not function on a proximate model. It doesn't give Readers Books that are most "like them" or related to their lived experience. Instead, it challenges Readers to connect with something foreign and unfamiliar. The value system that underlies the *Human Library* network is one focused on confronting long-held beliefs and moving outside your comfort zone.

The Librarians play a very special role in making this possible. By serving as connectors instead of delivering content, Librarians can spend their time recruiting new and interesting Books, creating a safe space for Books and Readers, evaluating the experience, and refining the setup, rather than learning how to deliver Book content (less authentically) themselves.

Librarians also perpetuate the metaphor of the library, which serves as the platform for the social interactions. The *Human Library* methodology very deliberately mimics traditional library experiences. *Human Library* spaces are often decorated to simulate libraries, or increasingly, are staged in real libraries. Visitors fill out a special library card, talk with the Librarian,

---

12 This excerpt came from the Human Library Organizer's Guide referenced above. For more reflections from Books, check out http://www.participatorymuseum.org/ref3-12/

Llbrarians help eager Readers find Books of interest at a 2009
Human Library in King's Garden in Copenhagen, Demark.

browse the catalog, and spend a significant amount of time with any Book
selected. Librarians maintain these conventions, even in contexts like festivals in which they seem a bit absurd. The creators of the *Human Library*
project recognized that libraries are safe places for learning new things. They
capitalized on that value to make a risky proposition to users. By framing the
whole experience in the context of a library, which has widely understood
implicit rules and expectations, they turned something that could have simply been about provocation and bravado into a true learning opportunity.

I worked with a team of graduate students in 2009 who used a similar
device in *Advice,* a temporary exhibition at the University of Washington
student center.[13] The students designed an advice booth as part of the exhibition and invited volunteers—some of whom signed up entirely spontaneously—to staff it. As in the *Human Library*, the advice booth provided a
familiar infrastructure (a platform) that made people comfortable giving and
getting advice from strangers, including eight year olds, tattoo artists, and
money managers.

These platforms—the library cards, the advice booth—may seem
artificial, but they are deeply important. Imagine the alternative. Imagine
putting out some comfortable couches and a sign that says, "talk to strangers

13   There is a longer case study about *Advice* on page 257.

about your prejudices" or "give advice to each other here." Even in the context of a larger exhibition or comfortable environment, I suspect that very few people would use these spaces. The booth and the library both scaffold the experience, transforming something threatening into an experience that appears appealing and safe.

In contrast, consider British artist Jeremy Deller's open-ended dialogue program, *It Is What It Is: Conversations About Iraq*, which traveled to several museums in the US in 2009. The piece featured two guests, an Iraqi translator and a US Army reservist, who sat on couches in a conversational space, flanked by a powerful artifact—a car that was destroyed in a suicide bomb attack in Baghdad. The goal

This simple plywood advice booth helped *Advice* visitors feel comfortable talking with each other.

was to support "messy, open-ended discussion," and the draw was the idea that visitors could go to the museum and talk about Iraq with someone who had actually been there during the war.

I saw *It Is What It Is* twice at the Hammer Museum in Los Angeles. Both times, the central square it was situated in was crowded with people enjoying art, hanging out with friends, and working. I never saw anyone engage in dialogue with the guest experts. Even with a couple of comfortable couches, a provocative object, and a sign that said, "Talk to X from 3-5," the barriers to participation were high. From my perspective, *It Is What It Is* was not designed with sufficient scaffolding to robustly and consistently support dialogue. It didn't bridge the social barriers that keep people from naturally talking to strangers. It didn't set expectations for what would happen (which was intentional) and that made people more wary about getting involved. Whereas both the *Human Library* and the advice booth were audience-centric, focusing on what visitors wanted to discuss or ask, I felt like *It Is What It Is* was trying to push something at me. It felt like if I sat on that couch, someone might talk at me or try to sell me their view.

By formally linking individual entry points to a social experience, the *Human Library* and the *Advice* booth successfully engaged a stream of diverse users. While the experiences were structured by the platforms, they often evolved into the kind of "messy, open-ended" dialogue that Jeremy Deller sought with *It Is What It Is*. But without designed infrastructure for engagement, the results appeared more haphazard. *It Is What It Is* was an unscaffolded social platform, one in which the connection between individual actions and the shared outcome was not well defined. In open-ended platforms, interesting and surprising social interactions may occur. But they are more likely to occur consistently in well-structured ones.

Platforms and Values

Social platforms need to be well designed to be successful, but that doesn't mean you need to entirely redevelop your institution to make every visitor experience fit into a structured framework. Designing an entire institution that functions like a *Human Library* or an advice booth probably isn't your goal. Your goal is more likely to promote social learning, creative participation, or meaningful conversations about institutional content. There are ways to achieve these goals with low-tech, socially networked platforms, many of which are just as effective as and more natural than their high-tech counterparts.

Designing the best social platform for your institution or project boils down to understanding your participatory goals. How do you want visitors to learn from or interact with each other? Do you want to promote dialogue, as the *Human Library* does? Do you want to promote group collaboration? Do you want visitors to respond to each other, to help each other, to create things together? If you think about network effects in terms of a useful outcome for visitors and institutions rather than in terms of data collection, you can design platforms that reflect your participatory values.

Let's look at three examples of institutions that created simple platforms for three very different participatory goals.

To encourage visitors to develop a stronger emotional connection to Worcester City Gallery and Museum's collection, that institution created an exhibition called *Top 40* in which visitors voted for their favorite paintings by paper ballot. *Top 40* featured forty paintings from the permanent collection, each of which was labeled with a large number indicating its place in the *Top 40* standings. The exhibition ran through the summer of 2009, and the labels were changed weekly to reflect the count from visitors' ballots. Collections Manager Philippa Tinsley wrote:

> Spontaneous discussions broke out in the gallery on the relative merits of different pictures; visitors of all ages came back again and again to see where their favourite was in the chart that week and to cast another vote—at times they were queuing outside before we opened. As well as our existing audience, new visitors came just because they wanted to be part of it.[14]

By developing a platform that was highly responsive to visitor input, the Worcester City Gallery and Museum achieved their goals to connect visitors to the paintings on display and the institution as a whole.

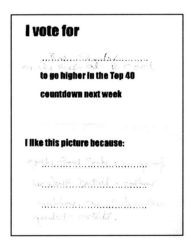

Top 40 visitors voted for favorite paintings with paper ballots (left) which were counted weekly to generate the new rankings for the following week (right).

---

14 Read Tinsley's complete account in a Nov 2009 blog post, "Guest Post: Top 40 Countdown at the Worcester City Museum" at http://www.participatorymuseum.org/ref3-14/

To promote collaboration among teenagers and young adults, the Ontario Science Centre uses front-line staff and labels in an atypical way in their *Weston Family Innovation Centre (WFIC)*. Many exhibits in *WFIC* feature no instructional text or graphics, and visitors struggle to figure out how to use them. *WFIC* staff known as "hosts" mill around engaging visitors casually and socially. When a visitor approaches a host with a question about how something works or what it's for, the host will often pull in another visitor, saying, "Hey, can you help us out? We have a question." The hosts thus link visitors—often strangers—to each other, and provide a supportive environment for those visitors to play and learn together. There are some visitors for whom this strategy would be very off-putting, but it fits in with the overall vibe of *WFIC* and supports its goals for visitor collaboration.

To help visitors connect personally to a formal institution, in 2009 the Dutch ceramics museum Princessehof hosted a seven-month visitor co-created exhibition of wedding china called *Shards & Happiness (Scherven & Geluk)*. The museum invited people from throughout the Netherlands to showcase their wedding china, wedding photos, and celebratory stories at the museum. These diverse personal stories prompted heightened levels of dialogue among visitors about their own family celebrations, and Princessehof engaged in extensive onsite and online programming to promote community conversations and sharing of wedding- and wedding china-related experiences. Staff even hosted a "wedding for a day" event in which visitors could pair off, walk down the aisle, and toss the bouquet just for fun.[15]

Each of these is an example of how an institution designed a platform to translate individual actions into collective benefit. Each of these projects "got better the more people used it." And most importantly, each platform reflected the specific values and goals of the project at hand.

Designing Social Platforms for Specific Values

To design a platform that will reflect the specific values of an institution or project, consider these three questions:

　　1. What individual actions will be available to visitors?

15　Learn more about *Shards & Happiness* and see photos of the 24-hour newly-weds at http://www.participatorymuseum.org/ref3-15/

2. What will staff do with the individual actions, i.e. how will the institution respond to them, incorporate them, and use them?
3. How will the institution display the collective outcome of the individual actions?

Let's look at each of these questions through the lens of a common museum platform: the comment board. While they seem simple, comment boards can be designed in very different ways to achieve different social results.

The individual action:

Comment boards offer visitors specific materials to use to share their thoughts. Different comment board designs bias people toward different results.[16] Sticky notes and pencils signal an easy, quick activity that anyone can do. A typewriter, or fancy markers and drawing paper, signal a more involved activity. In the *Advice* exhibition at the University of Washington, the staff provided visitors both with sticky notes to answer each other's questions and a "bathroom wall" where they could scrawl whatever they wanted. While no one specifically told visitors, "you can write bad words on the bathroom wall but don't do it with the sticky notes," they certainly interpreted the interfaces that way.

The response:

Once visitors write their comments, what happens next? Can they immediately stick them on the wall, or do they drop them in a slot for some kind of staff processing? On some comment boards, staff curate submitted comments and pick a selected few to display for all to see. On others, visitors can place their comments wherever they like, even layering over each other's.

Sometimes the staff is under responsive; visitors place their comments in the box and they languish there for weeks. Other times, staff members

16 For a detailed account of how different comment board prompts and materials affect visitor behavior, consult pages 16-22 of the formative evaluation of the *nano* exhibition at LACMA Lab, available for download [PDF] at http://www.participatorymuseum.org/ref3-16/

respond directly to commenters. When the National Library of Scotland put out a Victorian writing desk for visitors during an exhibition of famous authors' letters to publisher John Murray, librarians committed to responding to letters that visitors wrote. They were shocked to find themselves quickly overloaded with multi-page, personal letters written in longhand to long-dead authors. Fortunately, the staff honored the promise—but they also learned to think more carefully about how they would respond to visitors' contributions in the future.

The display:

Museums tend to use one of two types of platforms for display of visitor-generated content: those that value recency or those that value quality (or a mixture of both). Platforms that value recency put the newest visitor comments front and center, and previous comments are either archived or accessible on secondary layers. Platforms that value quality use some curation system (almost always staff led) to select featured content for presentation to visitors. Recency models may encourage more visitors to contribute because they will receive the immediate satisfaction of seeing their comments on display. In contrast, quality models may motivate less contribution, but those who choose to comment may be more invested in what they share.

Moving Beyond Recency and Quality-based Systems

There is a conflict between recency and quality-based models for showcasing visitor-created content. Recency models let everything through instantly, drowning out the gems. In contrast, quality models require staff time to read, curate, and post the best submissions. This can lead to exhibits piled with contributions languishing for weeks until the staff member in change can sort through them and select the best for display. How could these two models be usefully blended to improve the display on comment boards?

There's no reason that staff members need to do the work of curating visitor-created content alone. As noted in the first chapter, there are many more people who enjoy spectating and critiquing content than there are those who enjoy creating it. Inviting visitors to sort and rate visitor-generated content takes the load off of staff members who rarely have the time to do it. It also provides "critical" visitors with an activity that generates useful collective outcomes from their frustration at poor contributions and delight at quality ones. Curating visitor-generated content is not only about expressing likes and dislikes; it's a useful cognitive activity that promotes learning how to make judgments and connections among content sources. There are many historians, curators, and scientists who spend more time evaluating and analyzing content than generating it. Why not promote a participatory activity that reflects these important learning skills?

By incorporating the networked preferences of visitors over time, a visitor-generated exhibit could dynamically provide higher-quality offerings to spectators. But with this potential comes a worry that visitors will just select the funniest items, or the ones made by their friends, or will generally use criteria that is not in line with museum values.

The best way to address these concerns is by being explicit. If you want to encourage people to curate using particular criteria, give them the criteria. Say, "pick the photos you think best represent the theme," or "pick the comments that are most provocative." Or, you can say, "use your judgment and select the ones you think have the most value." Clear criteria can help reinforce your goals, but they aren't always necessary. Sometimes trusting visitors as participants means accepting that their values are just as valid as those of the staff.

Creative Approaches to Platform Design

With some creative thinking, it is possible to design platforms to meet even the most ambitious goals. In the simple example of sharing visitor-generated content, there are many other values beyond recency and quality that can be emphasized. Let's take a look at how the same system could evoke two different values: diversity and reflective discourse.

Imagine a video kiosk in a history museum intended to invite visitors to "share your story" related to a historic event on display. A platform that values diverse sharing might employ kiosks that use different questions and themes to solicit different perspectives on the same experience. Visitors acting as critics might be asked to sort the videos into different perspective categories rather than rate them or pick their favorites. At another station, critics might be able to then select favorites within each category. In this scenario, spectators would not just see "the best" videos overall, but the best videos reflecting a diversity of perspectives.

Now imagine the same exhibit with a different platform that values reflective discourse. This exhibit might use heavier consistent theming across the video creation kiosks. Visitors might be prompted to select another visitor's video as a starting point and make a video in response to it rather than reacting to an institutionally-provided query. For critics, the system would focus on commenting rather than rating or sorting. Videos might be featured based on the chain of response they generate rather than on the diversity of perspectives represented. In this scenario, spectators would see long multi-vocal dialogues played out across videos and text comments.

Two platforms, two designs, two different goals and desired visitor experiences. Let's leave the world of the theoretical video kiosk and take a look at two real platforms—*Signtific* and *Click!*—that were successfully designed to reflect distinct values.

CASE STUDY
STRUCTURED DIALOGUE IN THE SIGNTIFIC GAME

Signtific was an online game platform that promoted dialogic discourse about wild ideas. The Institute for the Future released *Signtific* in 2009 to help regular people engage in futurecasting, or predicting the future. *Signtific* was not a museum project, but it could easily be adapted to cultural institutions as a low-tech internal or public brainstorming tool. It was, quite simply, a comment board that encouraged people to engage in dialogue with each other.

Here's how it worked. The staff produced a short video introducing a provocative yet possible future scenario in the year 2019. In the first version of the game, the question was: "What will you do when space is as cheap and accessible as the Web is today?" The video explained: "In 2019, cube-sats—space satellites smaller than a shoebox—have become very cheap and very popular. For $100, anyone can put a customized personal satellite into low-earth orbit." It then posed the simple question: "How will the world be different?"

People were not allowed to answer the question generically. They had to pose their answer either in terms of "positive imagination," (i.e. the best thing that could happen) or "dark imagination," (the worst that could happen). Answers had to be brief—140 characters or less—and were displayed to look like index cards. Game designer Jane McGonigal called *Signtific* a platform for "micro-forecasting," explaining "the idea was to make it easier for people to share small, quick ideas about the future."

Spectators could very quickly scan the cards to see both the positive and dark answers and could click on any card of interest to follow up with a response. Players could not respond freely to each other but were required to use one of four types of response: momentum, antagonism, adaptation, or investigation. Players used momentum cards to add additional ideas, antagonism cards to raise disagreements, adaptation cards to suggest other potential manifestations of the same idea, and investigation cards to ask questions. The response cards were also limited to 140 characters.

Multiple response cards could be played on any other card, generating expanding trees of debate and discourse. The result was a network diagram

A "positive imagination" card that spawned responses in all four response categories.
Note at top that this card received a "super interesting" award from staff.

of cards, a threaded dialogue that took place across many nodes. The game masters curated some of the most interesting cards daily and offered frequent rewards for "outlier" ideas that were improbable but fascinating.

Signtific provided a very deliberate framework to prioritize collaborative brainstorming about the future. These four design decisions reinforced their goals:

1. Responses were kept short. This allowed people to scan many cards quickly and focus on responding to the most interesting ideas rather than wading through or generating long personal manifestos. It also made it easy to contribute quickly. Instead of focusing on crafting perfectly-written responses, players focused on the arguments they wanted to make and the cards that represented their interests.

2. The scoring emphasized interpersonal play, not just solo participation. Players were rewarded with points for playing their own cards as well as for motivating others to contribute response cards. Players earned more points for starting a great discussion among many people than for personal pontification.

3. The profile setup encouraged people to experiment with different forms of argumentation. Each player's personal profile tracked the number of each type of cards played and a small message read, "Are you stronger in some areas than others? Play another card to balance your strengths." This simple message set an expectation for players to explore the different types of argumentation rather than sticking with the ones that were easiest for them to use.

4. The "outlier" awards put wild ideas front and center. The scoring system rewarded people with special badges for suggesting ideas that were "super interesting." One of the important techniques of futurecasting is to deliberately seek out aberrant possibilities. Since these more unusual cards were not necessarily going to receive special attention in the flow of the game, staff made sure to feature them wherever possible to encourage people to take risks and think broadly.

Signtific was not an open mushy conversation about the future. It was a structured platform of specific interactions guided by clear values of

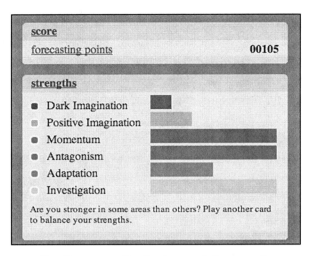

A *Signtific* user profile. The bar graph illustrates how
many cards of different kinds the player has employed.

collaborative discourse and imagining multiple outcomes for a potential
scenario. It was a well-designed platform imbued with the Institute for the
Future's value on "helping people make better, more informed decisions
about the future."

Many civic and cultural institutions share this goal, and the *Signtific*
platform could be adapted to both professional strategic brainstorming and
crowdsourced dialogue about community issues. While *Signtific's* online
platform made it easy to scale the number of cards played, this could easily
be designed as a physical game played with colored sticky notes. Imagine
offering a set of bins with different colored stickies—red for momentum,
green for antagonism, blue for adaptation, and so on. Rather than inviting
visitors to just share their response to an institutionally provided prompt,
a *Signtific*-like platform could encourage visitors to collaboratively address
tough scenarios like the future of transportation, multi-lingual education
systems, or genetic modification of humans.[17]

17 At the 2009 *Museums in Conversation* conference in Tarrytown, NY, Elizabeth
Merritt tested this out during a lunch session about the future of museums.
Colleagues from museums around New York state were quickly able to imagine
some positive and dark futures for museums—and to adapt and investigate them in
some funny and surprising ways.

CASE STUDY

TESTING THE WISDOM OF CROWDS AT THE BROOKLYN MUSEUM

When it comes to cultural institutions taking an ambitious, creative approach to designing a platform with specific values, *Click!* takes the cake. *Click! A Crowd-Curated Exhibition* was developed in 2008 by the Brooklyn Museum to investigate the question of whether crowds could "wisely" judge something as subjective as art.[18] *Click!* happened in three stages: an open call for submissions, online judging of entries, and presentation of the final exhibition. In the open call, people submitted photographs on the theme of "the changing face of Brooklyn." Then, the museum opened an online tool where visitors could judge the photographs on their artistic quality and relevance to the exhibition theme. Finally, staff mounted an exhibition of the photographs with prints scaled in size to match their rank in the judging scheme. The photographs were also displayed online, where visitors could access more information about each photo and how it was judged.

The submission process for *Click!* was fairly standard, but the judging and display were highly unorthodox. Despite the Brooklyn Museum's extensive forays into social media, the team designed the judging platform to intentionally limit the social nature of the experience. Citizen curators made their judgments privately. They could not see cumulative scores for each photo nor the comments others had made. They couldn't skip photos or pick the ones they wanted to judge. They couldn't send links to friends to encourage them to vote for their favorites.

Why did the Brooklyn Museum team deliberately restrict social behaviors? In simple terms, they wanted to build a fair platform to test the wisdom of the crowd. According to social scientist James Surowiecki, crowds are only "wise" if individuals cannot have undue influence on each other. If everyone guesses the number of jellybeans in a jar privately, the average will come very close to the true number. But if everyone shares their guesses,

---

18 *Click!* was inspired by *The Wisdom of Crowds*, a 2004 book by social scientist James Surowiecki, which argued that large groups of non-experts can be collectively "wise" when individuals in the group are able to make decisions without overly influencing each other's choices.

or encourages their friends to guess like them, the average will not be as accurate.

Restricting social behaviors also helped demonstrate respect for the artworks. It helped judges focus on the photographs, not discussion surrounding them. For the same reason, judges moved a bar on a sliding scale to judge each photograph rather than picking "best out of five" or assigning a number to each image. The team felt that a subjective rather than numerical assessment reduced the emphasis on the "score" for each image.

The *Click!* judging interface. Citizen-curators used a sliding scale (top right) to judge each photograph for its artistic quality and relevance to the theme. They could also leave comments, but these would not be revealed until judging was complete. Instead of social content, the judging platform provided personal statistics (bottom right) to encourage judges to continue their work.

The platform also required judges to create profiles with just two data points: geographic location and self-reported art knowledge. The team used these data points later to run comparisons so they could see if self-described experts rated photos differently than their novice counterparts, or whether Brooklyn denizens had different perspectives on the "changing face of Brooklyn" than judges in other areas.

In the end, the photos were displayed, both virtually and physically, sized relative to their rank in the judging scheme. The physical display was not thematic; it was entirely random. In the physical exhibition, the sizes of the prints were fixed, but on the Web, audience members were able to resize the photos contextually by changing data criteria, looking at the photos resized based on geographic location or self-reported art knowledge of judges. Interestingly, the top ten photos selected by judges of all levels of self-reported art knowledge included eight of the same images, suggesting that "crowds" of people with little art knowledge are likely to make comparable choices to those made by experts.

Click! spurred conversation among participants and cultural professionals not just about the photographs' value, but also about the ways cultural institutions might appropriately engage the public as participants. Once mounted, the exhibition was a highly social space. The community of people who had been involved in making it—photographers and judges alike—came to share the experience with each other and with their own networks.

Online, the conversation continued.[19] Users continued to make new comments post-opening, energized by the seeded content from the judging phase. Visitors could surf the images that were "most discussed," which promoted ongoing dialogue around the photographs. The online platform also allowed visitors to compare the relative ratings of different photographs—a flexible opportunity for visitors to practice juxtaposition on their own. Visitors could even view photographs that enjoyed the greatest "divergence of opinion" among the different self-defined geographic and art expertise groups. This prompted yet another discussion about the relative abilities and

---

19 Explore *Click!* online at http://www.participatorymuseum.org/ref3-19/

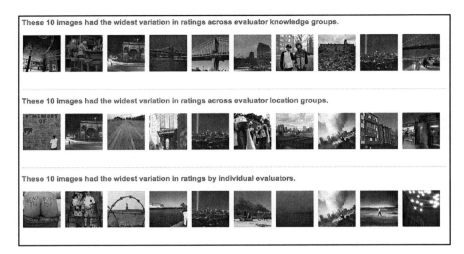

Online, visitors can explore the *Click!* data via a range
of visualizations and photo comparisons.

prejudices of different groups of people in determining the aesthetic value
and relevance of images to a broad public.

    Click! was a controversial experiment because its value system was
so different from that of traditional art institutions (including the Brooklyn
Museum itself). Its goal was not to find and display the best photos submitted
by photographers. Instead, the goal was to perform a public research project
about crowd-based decision-making. As Shelley Bernstein, organizer of the
show, put it, "it's a conceptual idea put on the wall."

    Conceptual ideas don't necessarily make pretty exhibits in a tradition-
al sense. The Museum's contemporary art curator Eugenie Tsai commented
that, "[Click!]'s about data, and making the data visual. It's not really a photography show in the way I would curate a photography show."[20] Bernstein
and Tsai were both explicit about the fact that they made decisions in favor
of research and against the most beautiful exposition of the art. All the photos were printed with the same process, and their sizes were determined
by the judging process rather than aesthetic preferences. Critics from the
New York Times and the *Washington Post* commented that the resulting show
was not that visually impressive, but they were comparing *Click!* to photo

---

20 Listen to a one-hour panel discussion about *Click!* with Tsai, Bernstein, and
technologist Jeff Howe at http://www.participatorymuseum.org/ref3-20/

exhibitions, which Bernstein would deem inappropriate. It would be more correct to compare it to data visualizations like tag clouds or spark charts—whether the audience wanted that or not.

Click! was a deliberate attempt by a museum to test something and present the results, saying, "don't judge this as art." Not everybody believes or wants to hear that. Some of the photographers who submitted their work to *Click!* were not thrilled to learn that they would not be able to control the way their photos would be printed, and some were skeptical about the validity of the public curation platform. As one photographer put it, "Why it is better for the crowd to use this peculiar (annoying and frustrating) method, is beyond me."[21] To some, the collaboration was a force fit to institutional goals. Fortunately, according to Bernstein, her team's open and clear communication with the artists about the project helped keep most participants feeling positive.

Some participants didn't care if their work was being exhibited as data; they were just thrilled to see their photographs up in the museum. This feeling of connection extended to those who had served as online curators as well. As participant Amy Dreher put it: "I felt ownership over what was on those walls because I had been involved in it from the first walk we took to the last photo I ranked."[22]

Click! may have generated dynamic tension between what the museum wanted to present and what some participants and reporters wanted to experience, but the institutional team stood by their initial goals as a valuable experiment and visitors responded positively to the exhibition. Ultimately, experimenting with the questions of how visitors might be engaged in curatorial process and whether crowds of visitors could be "wise" evaluators of art were the most important parts of the *Click!* experience from the institutional perspective. The exhibition was just an output of that research.

---

21 See comment #27 on Shelley Bernstein's June 2008 blog post, "Preparing to Click": http://www.participatorymuseum.org/ref3-21/
22 Dreher described her multi-faceted involvement in *Click!*, which started with exploratory walks with fellow photographers, in "The *Click!* Experience: A Participant's View," in *Exhibitionist*, 28, no. 2 (2009): 55–58.

Platforms and Power

Click! was controversial because it threatened the traditional power relationships in a cultural institution between visitors and staff, experts and amateurs. Socially networked platforms have political implications. If experts, exhibits, and program staff no longer deliver content exclusively but also serve as facilitators connecting one visitor's experience to another's, institutions' roles as content authorities change. This is threatening to the power that staff members have enjoyed for many years in cultural institutions, and it can generate a great deal of fear and resistance.

These power struggles are not new, especially in the educational sector. In the 1960s and 1970s, educational revolutionaries like Paulo Friere and Ivan Illich spoke out against traditional schooling systems, claiming schools were oppressive systems promoting non-reciprocal relationships between teachers and students. Friere and Illich both sought alternatives that would engage equitable communities of learners, and one of the ideas Illich promoted was networked education via what he called "learning webs." In his 1971 manifesto, *Deschooling Society*, Illich suggested an educational model based on a person-to-person network in which each individual would list his skills in a kind of phonebook.[23] The phonebook would serve as the "available curriculum," and people could call or write to each other and solicit instruction from each other on everything from auto mechanics to poetry. Illich argued that this kind of citizen-powered education would be much more powerful and valuable to communities than formal schools.

What Illich didn't discuss was exactly how he would design his hypothetical phone book. As we've seen in the above case studies, there are significant value judgments inherent in the design of participatory platforms. How would you design Illich's educational phone book? Would you organize it by skill offered, location of the instructor, or the name of the person offering it? Would you include information about each person's relevant experience and credentials? Would you encourage learners to rate their learning experiences and use those ratings to reorder the list? Would you introduce a feedback loop to help people find the most popular teachers, or

---

23 See Chapter 6, Illich, *Deschooling Society* (1971), especially the section on "peer-matching networks."

would you design the platform to distribute learning experiences as equitably as possible across participants?[24]

Each of these decisions would send the resulting community experience down a different path. Platform designers have incredible power over the user experience, but it's a kind of power that may be unfamiliar to those accustomed to designing and presenting content experiences. It's not the power to be the only voice in the room but the power to determine who speaks and in what order.

To be successful leaders in a socially networked world, cultural institutions must feel comfortable managing platforms as well as providing content. One of the primary fears museum professionals (and all professionals) have about entering new relationships with audiences is the fear of losing control. However, in most cultural institutions, the professional expertise of the staff—to preserve objects, to design exhibits, to deliver programs—is not based on content control. It's based on expert creation and delivery of experiences. Expertise is valuable, even in a platform-based institution. The problem arises when expertise creates a feeling of entitlement to control the entire visitor experience. Power is attractive. Being in control is pleasant. It lets you be the only expert with a voice. But if your expertise is real, then you don't need to rule content messages with an iron fist. You can manage the phone book instead of directing the classroom.

Developing platforms to harness, prioritize, and present a diversity of voices around content does not mean giving all the power to visitors. Platform designers grant users a few specific, designed opportunities—to create their own content, to prioritize the messages that resonate best for them personally—in the context of a larger overall ecosystem. The platform is what's important. It's a framework that cultural institutions can (and should) control, and there's power in platform management.

Platform managers have four main powers—the power to:
1. Define the types of interaction available to users
2. Set the rules of behavior
3. Preserve and exploit user-generated content

---

24 For one interesting approach to networked learning, check out The Public School at http://www.participatorymuseum.org/ref3-24/

4. Promote and feature preferred content

These powers constitute a set of controls that constitutes a real and valuable authority. Let's take a look at each one and how it applies in cultural institutions.

The power to define available interactions:

This power is so basic that it is often overlooked. On YouTube, users share videos. In *Free2Choose*, visitors vote on questions of personal freedoms. In the *Human Library*, people have one-on-one conversations. On *Signtific*, players debate the future of science. Every platform has a limited feature set and focuses on one or two basic actions that users can take. Cultural institutions don't need to offer every kind of interaction under the sun—they just have to pick the few interactions that most support the kind of behavior and content creation that they value. There's power in the specific decisions about whether users will be allowed to contact each other directly, make comments or ratings, or produce various kinds of digital and physical artifacts. When staff members focus the platform on a very small set of active features, they are able to steer the direction of the overall user experience and the body of growing visitor-driven content.

The power to set the rules of behavior:

Online participatory platforms influence user and community behavior both implicitly through the tools that are and aren't offered and explicitly through community management. Every online social network has rules about acceptable content and ways that users can engage with each other, and those rules have serious implications about the overall tone of interaction on the site.

Most cultural institutions tend to rely on implicit rules of behavior, but it's a good idea to draft community guidelines or information about what is expected from visitors in a participatory environment. For example, the *Make History* story-sharing site for the National September 11th Memorial and Museum informs users that they should only share their personal experience of September 11th and should do so as accurately and honestly as possible.

The community guidelines also note: "Given the intensity of the event, some strong language may be appropriate in certain stories. But consider that this site will be used by people of all ages." The staff set guidelines that honored the emotional nature of September 11th memories while encouraging users not to go overboard.[25]

Differences in community guidelines and rules also often influence the makeup of users who feel welcome and choose to participate. When it comes to cultural institutions, it's important to make sure that staff members' own personal biases toward certain kinds of behavior don't overly dictate who feels comfortable participating. If you have some particular audiences in mind for a project, involve them in deciding what constitutes inappropriate behavior. A platform for parents might have very different community guidelines than one for artists or another for young historians.

The power to use and exploit user-generated content:

Platforms have the power to set rules related to preservation and ownership of the content they display—often with quite strict intellectual property statutes that favor the platform over users. Every time someone posts a video on YouTube, she gives the site the right to use that video in perpetuity however it sees fit. She owns the content, but she grants YouTube:

> A worldwide, non-exclusive, royalty-free, sublicenseable and transferable license to use, reproduce, distribute, prepare derivative works of, display, and perform the User Submissions in connection with the YouTube Website and YouTube's (and its successors' and affiliates') business, including without limitation for promoting and redistributing part or all of the YouTube Website (and derivative works thereof) in any media formats and through any media channels.26

This is a standard clause in the Terms of Service of many online social platforms.

Cultural institutions have different standards for managing intellectual property, protecting visitors' privacy, and monetizing visitors' creations. While museums tend to be more protective of their own and their lenders'

---

25 Read the complete community guidelines for *Make History* at http://www.participatorymuseum.org/ref3-25/

26 Read the complete Terms of Service for YouTube at http://www.participatorymuseum.org/ref3-26/

intellectual property than online social platforms, they are also typically more protective of visitors' rights to control what they make and do. For example, when the Denver Art Museum invited visitors to make their own rock music posters in the *Side Trip* exhibition, staff didn't automatically display copies of each poster on the wall. They asked visitors whether or not they wanted to share their posters publicly.[27]

There are many models for how to share and use visitor-generated content that respect both institutional and visitors' interests. Here are a few examples:

- The Smithsonian American Art Museum's *Ghosts of a Chance* game accessioned player-generated objects into a temporary part of their collection database, with clear rules about what happened to the objects at the end of the game (they became the responsibility of the game designers, a sub-contractor to the museum).
- The Metropolitan Museum used visitor-generated photos from Flickr in the popular "It's Time We Met" advertising campaign, following user-specific licensing requirements to credit visitors properly.[28]
- The Chicago Children's Museum used visitor-generated multimedia stories in their *Skyscraper Challenge* exhibit (see page 68) as the basis for research on cognitive development.
- The Powerhouse Museum and the Brooklyn Museum have both created print-on-demand books of content generated by visitors involved in community exhibits and online projects.
- At the Victoria & Albert Museum in London, Gail Durbin has discussed using content created in museums as the basis for customized on-demand retail items, like personalized calendars showing images of your favorite exhibits, or one-off books of images captured at a fabric-making workshop.

27 Denver Art Museum educators did, however, archive a copy of every poster made for internal evaluation and collection purposes.
28 See the "It's Time We Met" Flickr-based ads at http://www.participatorymuseum.org/ref3-28/

In the same way that Web 2.0 sites display a range of respect for user-retained intellectual property, cultural institutions can navigate and create their own rules—with related powers—for content developed by visitors.

The power to promote and feature preferred content:
One of the greatest powers retained by participatory platform managers is the power to feature content that reflects the values of the platform. Just as the question of which stories to feature and bury in a newspaper is a question of power, so too is the question of how to feature content in social networks. Recall the alternative strategies for how to feature content on comment boards; these strategies are fundamentally about the question of how content will be selected for promotion. Institutions may promote the most popular content, the newest content, staff-selected content, or content that is unique in some way. While some platform designers strive for transparency in promotion systems, most tailor their systems to feature the kind of content and behavior that they want to see modeled for other users.

There was a fascinating example of the power of platform design in the successive redesigns of Facebook from mid-2008 to mid-2009. Over that year, Facebook evolved from focusing on personal profiles shared with small groups of known individuals to focusing on publishing lifestream-style feeds of status updates and short-format content for mass audiences. Whereas previously Facebook was a place to maintain a profile and connect to a web of friends and acquaintances, by the fall of 2009 it had become a personally relevant content stream, a dynamic newspaper created for each user (and shared with the rest of the world by default). Some users complained and left the service, but most remained—and changed their own behavior to match Facebook's new design.

The power to promote and organize users' content may be the most important platform power for cultural institutions because it is the one that most dramatically enables the platform to present its values and model preferred behavior. It is also the most technical power, because it requires understanding how design decisions affect broad patterns of user behavior.

Cultural institutions are still learning to wield this power effectively. When museums do assume this power, it is often in a zero-transparency way that doesn't model behavior for users. Visitors are invited to contribute creative work or data, and then must wait until the end of a contest or submission period to see what the staff selected to feature. In opaque systems, visitors can't adapt their contributions based on staff feedback along the way. Compare this to the Worcester City Gallery and Museum's *Top 40* exhibition in which visitors could access new information about the relative rankings of paintings on display every week. In *Top 40*, the regular refreshment of featured content motivated people to keep visiting and participating throughout the run of the exhibition.

There are real opportunities in a participatory world for cultural institutions to retain authority related to visitor values, experiences, and community behavior. The power of the platform may not let the staff dictate every message that floats through the doors of the institution. But with good, thoughtful design, it can ensure that those messages enhance the overall visitor experience. When you are able to network individual visitors' experiences in ways that are both useful and beautiful, you will motivate new experiences and relationships that are exciting and valuable for the institution and users alike.

This chapter focused on designing platforms for connections among people in cultural institutions. This leads to an obvious and uneasy question for museum professionals: what about the objects? If institutions evolve to support visitors creating, sharing, and learning from each other, where does the collection fit in? Chapter 4 addresses the unique role of objects in participatory institutions. Artifacts can be the heart of platform-based experiences, the "object" of visitors' conversations and creative expression.

CHAPTER 4

SOCIAL OBJECTS

IMAGINE LOOKING AT AN OBJECT not for its artistic or historical significance but for its ability to spark conversation. Every museum has artifacts that lend themselves naturally to social experiences. It might be an old stove that triggers visitors to share memories of their grandmother's kitchen, or an interactive building station that encourages people to play cooperatively. It could be an art piece with a subtle surprise that visitors point out to each other in delight, or an unsettling historical image people feel compelled to discuss. It could be a train whistle calling visitors to join the ride, or an educational program that asks them to team up and compete.

These artifacts and experiences are all social objects. Social objects are the engines of socially networked experiences, the content around which conversation happens.[1] Social objects allow people to focus their attention

---

1 For the purposes of this discussion, I define an object as a physical item that is accessible to visitors, either on display, shared through educational programming, or available for visitors to use. Some of the objects described in this chapter are designed experiences, but mostly, I'm talking about artifacts that cultural institutions collect, preserve, and present.

on a third thing rather than on each other, making interpersonal engagement more comfortable. People can connect with strangers when they have a shared interest in specific objects. Some social networks are about celebrity gossip. Others center around custom car building. Others focus on religion. We connect with people through our interests and shared experiences of the objects around us.

In 2005, engineer and sociologist Jyri Engeström used the term "social objects" and the related phrase "object-centered sociality" to address the distinct role of objects in online social networks.[2] Engeström argued that discrete objects, not general content or interpersonal relationships, form the basis for the most successful social networks. For example, on Flickr you don't socialize generally about photography or pictures, as you might on a photography-focused listserv. Instead, you socialize around specific shared images, discussing discrete photographic objects. Each photo is a node in the social network that triangulates the users who create, critique, and consume it. Just as LibraryThing connects people via books instead of reading, Flickr connects people via photos instead of art-making.

The objects don't have to be physical, but they do have to be distinct entities. Engeström explained object-centered design this way:

> Think about the object as the reason why people affiliate with each specific other and not just anyone. For instance, if the object is a job, it will connect me to one set of people whereas a date will link me to a radically different group. This is common sense but unfortunately it's not included in the image of the network diagram that most people imagine when they hear the term 'social network.' The fallacy is to think that social networks are just made up of people. They're not; *social networks consist of people who are connected by a shared object.*

This is great news for museums, both in the physical and virtual world. While Web developers scramble for object catalogs upon which to base new online ventures, cultural institutions can tap into pre-existing stories and connections between visitors and collections. And that needn't happen solely on the Web. Objects can become the center of dialogue in physical galleries as well. This chapter focuses on how to make this possible in two

---

2   Read Engeström's April 2005 blog post, "Why some social network services work and others don't—Or: the case for object-centered sociality" at http://www. participatorymuseum.org/ref4-2/

ways: by identifying and enhancing pre-existing social objects in the collection, and by offering visitors tools to help them discuss, share, and socialize around the objects.

What Makes an Object Social?

Not all objects are naturally social. A social object is one that connects the people who create, own, use, critique, or consume it. Social objects are transactional, facilitating exchanges among those who encounter them. For example, one of my most reliable social objects is my dog. When I walk around town with my dog, lots of people talk to me, or, more precisely, talk through the dog to me. The dog allows for transference of
attention from person-to-person to person-to-object-to-person. It's much less threatening to engage someone by approaching and interacting with her dog, which will inevitably lead to interaction with its owner. Unsurprisingly, enterprising dog owners looking for dates often use their dogs as social instigators, steering their pups towards attractive people they'd like to meet.

Take a brief mental tour of your cultural institution. Is there an object or experience that consistently draws a talkative crowd? Is there a place where people snap photos of each other, or crowd around pointing and talking? Whether it's a steam engine in action or an enormous whale jaw, a liquid nitrogen demonstration or a sculpture made of chocolate, these are your social objects.

Whether in the real world or the virtual, social objects have a few common qualities. Most social objects are:
1. Personal
2. Active
3. Provocative
4. Relational

Personal Objects

When visitors see an object in a case that they have a personal connection to, they have an immediate story to tell. Whether it's a soup bowl that looks just like grandma's or the first chemistry kit a visitor ever owned, personal objects often trigger natural, enthusiastic sharing. The same is true for objects that people own, produce, or contribute themselves. Recall *Click!* participant Amy Dreher's words about her pleasure in visiting the exhibition repeatedly: "I felt ownership over what was on those walls because I had been involved in it."[3]

Not every artifact automatically stirs a personal response. It's easy for staff members to forget that visitors may not have personal relationships with many artifacts. Staff and volunteers who care for, study, or maintain objects often have very personal connections with them. One of the challenges for cultural professionals is remembering that visitors don't come in the door with the same emotional investment and history with artifacts that professionals have and may not see them as obvious conversation pieces.

Active Objects

Objects that directly and physically insert themselves into the spaces between strangers can serve as shared reference points for discussion. If an ambulance passes by or a fountain splashes you in the breeze, your attention is drawn to it, and you feel complicit with the other people who are similarly imposed upon by the object. Similarly, in bars, darts or ping pong balls that leave their playing fields often generate new social connections between the person looking for the flying object and the people whose space was interrupted by it.

In cultural institutions, active objects often pop into motion intermittently. In some cases, like the changing of the guard at Buckingham Palace, the action is on a fixed schedule, and passersby naturally strike up conversations about when it will happen and what's going on. Other times, the action is more spontaneous. For example, living objects, like animals in zoos, frequently motivate conversation when they move or make surprising sounds.

---

3   See page 115 for the full case study on *Click!*.

Inanimate objects can also exhibit active behavior—think of the discussions among visitors that naturally arise as model trains chug along their tracks or automata perform their dances.

Provocative Objects

An object need not physically insert itself into a social environment to become a topic of discussion if it is a spectacle in its own right. When the Science Museum of Minnesota opened the exhibition *Race: Are We So Different?* in 2007, staff frequently noticed crowds of people gathering, pointing, and talking about some of the objects on display. One of the most discussed exhibits was a vitrine featuring stacks of money representing the average earnings of Americans of different races. Money is somewhat exciting on its own, but the real power in the exhibit was in the shocking disparity among the piles. People were compelled to point out of surprise. The powerful physical metaphor of the stacks made the information presented feel more spectacular without dumbing it down or over-dressing it.

Visitors in *Race: Are We So Different?* discussing the stacks of money demonstrating wealth disparities among different races in the US.

Provocation is tricky to predict. If visitors expect to be shocked or provoked by content on display—as in some contemporary art institutions—they may choose to internalize provocation instead of discussing it. To work well, a provocative object must be genuinely surprising to visitors who encounter it.

Relational Objects

Relational objects explicitly invite interpersonal use. They require several people to use them to work, and their design often implies an invitation for strangers to get involved. Telephones are relational. Pool tables, seesaws, and game boards fall into this category, as do many interactive museum exhibits and participatory sculptures that invite people to work together to solve a problem or generate an effect. For example, many science centers feature exhibits that explicitly state on their labels, "this exhibit requires two people to use." One is the player, the other the tracker, or one on the left and the other on the right. These objects are reliably social because they demand interpersonal engagement to function.

Making Objects More Social

Most social object experiences are fleeting and inconsistent. For social object experiences to work repeatedly for a wide diversity of users or visitors, day after day, design tweaks can make an object more personal, active, provocative, or relational. For example, the Museum of Transport and Technology in Auckland has an old traffic light mounted outside one of many small buildings full of artifacts. When staff members put the lights on a timer (red, yellow, green) and painted a street-style crosswalk to evoke a street scene, they were surprised to discover children using the traffic light for spontaneous games of "Red Light Green Light" (or "Go Stop" as it is called in New Zealand). Turning on the lights transformed the traffic light into an active, relational object that was quickly adopted as part of a game.

The Minnesota Historical Society took a different approach in its *Open House: If Walls Could Talk* exhibition, which opened in 2006.[4] The

---

4   *Open House* is still open as of this printing with no scheduled end date.

exhibition tells the personal stories of fifty families who lived in a single house on the East Side of St. Paul over 118 years. Designers used photos and audio recordings to embed personal narratives of residents directly into artifacts in surprising ways. As visitors touch and explore the objects in the house, they unlock personal stories from the people who lived in the house over time. Everything from the dishes to the furniture tells stories. In summative evaluation, researchers found that visitors engaged in high levels of conversation about their connections to the exhibition, with the average visitor relating personal histories to at least three objects on display.[5] By making common household objects personal and active, *Open House* successfully encouraged people to share their own experiences while visiting.

Physically altering objects is not always the most efficient or practical way to promote social experiences in your institution. It's often more productive to design interpretative tools and platforms that enhance the sociability of pre-existing objects across the collection. That can mean rewriting labels or placing objects in different environments, but it can also mean more explicitly social approaches to presentation. Jyri Engeström argued that there should be active verbs that define the things users can "do" relative to social objects—consume them, comment on them, add to them, etc.—and that all social objects need to be situated in systems that allow users to share them. To make objects social, you need to design platforms that promote them explicitly as the center of conversation.

Designing Platforms for Social Objects

What makes an interpretative strategy explicitly social? Social platforms focus primarily on providing tools for visitors to engage with each other around objects. While attractive and functional presentation of objects is still important, it is secondary to promoting opportunities for visitors to discuss and share them. Let's compare the social behaviors supported by a traditional exhibition to those provided by an online social network, Flickr, in the context of the presentation of photographs.

---

5   Download the December 2006 summative evaluation report on *Open House* here [PDF]: http://www.participatorymuseum.org/ref4-5/

In a traditional museum photo exhibition, visitors can look at photographs hanging on the walls. They can read information about each photo and its creator in label text, and they can probably access information about how the photograph is catalogued in the museum's collection database. Sometimes visitors may take their own pictures of the photographs; other times, they are prohibited from capturing any likeness of the artifacts or even their labels. In some installations, visitors may be able to share personal thoughts about the photographs in a comment book at the entrance or exit to the gallery. The institution also typically offers visitors the chance to buy reproductions of some of the photographs in a catalogue or postcard set in the museum's retail shop.

In a typical photography exhibition, visitors can look and learn, but they can't leave comments or share the images with others as they browse. Social use of the photos is visitor-directed and may or may not be institutionally supported.

Contrast these to the visitor actions supported by Flickr. On Flickr, users can look at photos. They can read information about each photo and its creator. They can leave comments on each photo. They can mark particular images as favorites in their personal collections of favorites. They can make notes directly on sub-areas of photos to mark details of interest. They can add tags and geocodes that serve as descriptive keywords for each photo. They can view the comments, notes, and tags created by other users who have looked at each photo. They can send personal messages to each photo's creator, or to other commenters, with questions or comments. They can invite photographers to submit their photos to special groups or virtual galleries. They can send individual photos to friends by email, or embed them in blog posts or entries on other social networks. They can talk about each photo on Flickr and elsewhere.

Flickr supports a long list of social behaviors that are not available in museums and galleries. This doesn't mean that Flickr provides a better overall photography exhibition experience. From an aesthetic perspective, it is much more appealing to see photographs beautifully mounted and lit than arranged digitally amidst a jumble of text. When activated, the "notes" function on Flickr deliberately obscures the view of a photo by covering the image in rectangles indicating the locations of noted details. Providing social platforms for objects has design implications that can diminish the aesthetic power of the artifact.

But providing social functions around objects promotes other kinds of user experiences that are also incredibly valuable. Consider the photograph on page 136, taken by John Vachon in 1943 and titled "Workers leaving Pennsylvania shipyards, Beaumont, Texas." In January 2008, the Library of Congress offered this image on the Flickr Commons, a special area of Flickr reserved for images in the public domain.[6] This image is not exhibited at the Library of Congress. If you know what you are looking for, you can hunt it down in the Library of Congress online database via long lists of text.[7] In other words, there was no pre-existing way for visitors to experience this image in a designed context that promoted its aesthetic power or historical significance. Then it was uploaded to Flickr.

---

6   See John Vachon's photograph on Flickr: http://www.participatorymuseum.org/ref4-6/

7   View the same photo by searching for it in the Library of Congress database at http://www.participatorymuseum.org/ref4-7/

Vachon's image on Flickr and several comments. The floating text box on the image is one of the user-generated "notes" attached to the photograph.

On Flickr, this photo has an active social life. As of January 2010, it had fifty-three user-supplied tags, eight user-created notes, and seventeen community comments. It was featured by a Peruvian Flickr group called "People—costumes and customs no limits" and another called "Nautical Art." The image was also shared in an unknown number of blog posts and personal emails sent from the site.

The comments and notes on the Flickr page include several compelling and educational discussions. People answered each other's questions about why the "Pennsylvania" shipyards were located in Texas. Two people shared personal recollections of growing up near these shipyards, and one added links to historical information about a race riot that happened in the town of Beaumont the same month the photo was taken.

These Flickr users weren't just saying, "nice pic." They answered each other's questions about the content, shared personal stories, and made sociopolitical commentaries. They did things that are not supported for people who visit the Library of Congress or view the photo in the online database. Flickr arguably supported a more engaging, more educational experience with the content.

Is all of this social value worth the aesthetic tradeoffs that Flickr's design implies? That depends on institutional goals and priorities. If the goal of the Library of Congress is to encourage visitors to engage with each other about the stories and information at hand, then Flickr is the ideal choice. And similarly, if you want to encourage visitors to engage socially around your content, you should consider ways to build social functionality into exhibits, even if it means diminishing other aspects of the design.

Social Platforms in the Real World

How can you translate the social experience on Flickr to one that is possible for visitors to your institution? You don't need to replicate every tool provided by sites like Flickr to create successful physical social platforms. You may not be able to write a note directly on an artifact, but museums and physical environments provide other social design opportunities that are impossible to simulate virtually. People use different social tools and transactions in different environments, and not all activities that work virtually translate well to physical environments.

For example, in the real world, oversized objects often function as social objects because they are surprising and can be experienced by many people at once. There's no way to design a comparable virtual object that suddenly and completely overwhelms several strangers' sensory experience. Highly designed immersive environments, which provide context that may make some artifacts feel more active or provocative, are another example of a physical design platform that can accentuate the sociality of objects.

The rest of this chapter explores five design techniques that can activate artifacts as social objects in physical design:

1. Asking visitors *questions* and prompting them to share their reactions to the objects on display (see page 139)
2. Providing *live interpretation* or performance to help visitors make a personal connection to artifacts (see page 152)
3. Designing exhibitions with *provocative presentation* techniques that display objects in juxtaposition, conflict, or conversation with each other (see page 158)
4. Giving visitors clear *instructions* on how to engage with each other around the object, whether in a game or a guided experience (see page 164)
5. Offering visitors ways to *share* objects either physically or virtually by sending them to friends and family (see page 172)

Which of these interpretative techniques will work best in your institution? That depends partly on the comfort levels of staff members, but even more so on the comfort level of visitors. Museums can be particularly challenging social object platforms, especially those in which visitors often already feel a little uncertain of how to behave. If visitors don't feel comfortable and in control of their environment, they are unlikely to talk with a stranger under any circumstances.

Walk around your institution and listen to the hum. Are people naturally and comfortably talking to each other about the objects on display? Do they point things out, pull friends over to share an experience, or engage with strangers? If you work in a very social place, visitors are likely to respond well to open-ended techniques like provocative presentation, questions, and sharing. If your institution doesn't promote much social activity, then more explicit, directed techniques like instructions and live interpretation might be better starting points.

Asking Visitors Questions

Asking visitors questions is the most common technique used to encourage discussion around objects. Whether via conversations with staff or queries posted on labels, questions are a flexible, simple way to motivate visitors to respond to and engage with objects on display.

There are three basic reasons to ask visitors questions in exhibitions:

1. To encourage visitors to engage deeply and personally with a specific object
2. To motivate interpersonal dialogue among visitors around a particular object or idea
3. To provide feedback or useful information to staff about the object or exhibition

These goals are all valuable, but unfortunately, questions are not always designed to achieve them. Many institutionally-supplied questions are too earnest, too leading, or too obvious to spark interest, let alone engagement. Some questions are nagging parents, asking, "how will your actions affect global warming?" Others are teachers who want parroted answers, inquiring, "what is nanotechnology?" Some pander facetiously. And worse of all, in most cases, there is no intent on the part of the question-asker to listen to the answer. I used to be terrible about this. I'd ask a friend a question, and then I'd get distracted by something else and walk out of the room. I understood the social convention of asking the question, but I didn't actually care about the answer.

Any time you ask a question—in an exhibition or otherwise—you should have a genuine interest in hearing the answer. I think this is a reasonable rule to live by in all venues that promote dialogue. Questions can create new connections between people and objects and people and each other, but only when all parties are invested in the conversation. Staff members don't have to be there physically to receive and respond to every visitor's answer. There don't even have to be physical mechanisms like comment boards for visitors to share their answers with each other. But the design of each question must value visitors' time and intelligence, so that answering the question, or entering dialogue sparked by a question, has clear and appealing rewards.

What Makes a Great Question?

Successful questions that prompt social engagement with objects share two characteristics:

- The question is open to a diversity of responses. If there's a "right answer," it's the wrong question.
- Visitors feel confident and capable of answering the question. The question draws on their knowledge, not their comprehension of institutional knowledge.

How do you design a question with these characteristics? There's a very simple way to test if a question is prescriptive or not, and whether it yields interesting responses: ask it. Take your question out for a spin. Ask it to ten people, and see what kind of responses you get. Pose the question to your colleagues. Ask your family. Ask yourself. Listen to or read the answers you collect. If the answers are different and exciting, you have a good question. If you find yourself dreading asking the tenth person that same question, you have the wrong question.

When designing questions for visitors to answer, I often encourage project teams to get together and write individual questions on pieces of paper and share them around. The staff members then answer each other's questions personally by writing responses on the sheets. After a few rounds of writing answers on the sheets, the team lines them up and looks at the resulting body of content. This simple exercise can help staff members quickly identify the characteristics of questions that elicit a diversity of interesting responses. It also helps staff members understand what kinds of questions are easier or harder to answer.

There are two basic types of questions that are most successful at eliciting authentic, confident, diverse responses: personal questions and speculative questions. *Personal* questions help visitors connect their own experience to the objects on display. *Speculative* questions ask visitors to imagine scenarios involving objects or ideas that are foreign to their experience.

Asking Personal Questions

Personal questions allow visitors to enter the social realm through their own unique experience. Everyone is an expert about himself, and when people speak from personal experience, they tend to be more specific and authentic in their comments. Questions like, "Why is the woman in the painting smiling?" or "What can you figure out about the person who made this object by examining it?" are visitor-agnostic; they are entirely focused on the object. While such questions may encourage people to investigate the object, they are social dead-ends. If your goal is to move towards a social experience, you have to start with a personal question instead.

CASE STUDY
GETTING PERSONAL WITH POSTSECRET

What's a secret you've never told anyone?

That's the question behind artist Frank Warren's *PostSecret* project. Since 2004, Warren has invited people to anonymously share their secrets by sending him postcards in the mail. He encourages people to make their postcards brief, legible, and creative. *PostSecret* quickly became a worldwide phenomenon. Within five years, Warren had received hundreds of thousands of postcards. Warren shares a small selection of the ones he receives through his high-traffic blog (named Weblog of the year in 2006),[8] as well as in best-selling books and exhibitions of the postcards.

The success of *PostSecret* is based on the power of the question, "What is a secret you've never told anyone?" It is, by design, one of the most personal questions there is. It's a question that people are only willing to answer anonymously, and when they do, they generate evocative, haunting

8   Visit the *PostSecret* blog: http://www.participatorymuseum.org/ref4-8/

responses. As Frank put it, "their cour-age makes the art meaningful." The contributors care deeply about their answers, and they labor to create something of value, a worthy vehicle for their secrets. While the postcards may not be aesthetically outstanding, the power of authentic, courageous voices shines through.

PostSecret has two audiences: Frank Warren and a wide world of spectators and participants. One of the reasons people answer the question is that Warren presents himself as a compassionate, interested lis-tener. He publishes his home address for people to mail in their postcards, which helps establish a relationship

While some PostSecret contributors create original art, most remix cultural images to share personal secrets.

of trust and mutual respect between a secret-giver and its recipient. When I heard him speak in 2006, Warren expressed incredible love and apprecia-tion for people who are willing to entrust their secrets to him.[9] But he's not the only listener out there. *PostSecret* keeps growing because the question induces a compelling spectator experience. There's urgency to the secrets—even ones that have been hidden for decades—because each postcard rep-resents the moment at which it was finally let out. And by curating the cards that he releases for mass consumption on the blog and in books, Warren demonstrates which cards that he perceives as most valuable—those that are authentic, diverse, and creative.

Warren commented that he thinks people love the cards not because they're voyeurs, but because the postcards reveal "the essence of human-ity." I'm not sure that's true, but there are certainly hundreds of postcards that resonate with me personally—and I imagine with everyone who views

---

9   I saw Frank Warren in a packed house at the American Visionary Art Museum in Baltimore, one of the first museums to support *PostSecret*.

them. The *PostSecret* postcards are social objects that represent an incredible outpouring in response to a simple question framed well by someone who was whole-heartedly ready to listen.

Personal Questions in Exhibitions

The *PostSecret* question is incredibly personal, but it is not content- or object-specific (unless you run a Museum of Secrets). If you want to use personal questions to engage people with exhibitions or objects, you need to find a connection between visitors' lives and the artifacts on display. For example, the Denver Art Museum's *Side Trip* exhibition of rock music posters asked visitors to share stories of "my first concert," "my first trip," or "the first time I saw... (fill in the musician here)." Another visitor feedback station asked people to reflect on statements like, "I was a roadie," "I was a hippie," or "I was not into it." These were highly personal questions that related to the overall themes of the exhibition and drew compelling, diverse responses. The questions set the stage for interpersonal discussion about individuals' experience with the music, the lifestyles, and the mythology of hippie culture.

Simple rolodexes allowed *Side Trip* visitors to share personal stories across a variety of themes.

Personal questions can also encourage people to be more thoughtful in their engagement with particular objects. In 2007, Exploratorium researcher Joyce Ma published a brief formative study on *Daisy*, an artificially intelligent computer program that engages visitors in text-based conversation. *Daisy* is a "chatbot" with some pre-programmed questions in her repertoire, and Ma was studying the ways different questions affected the richness of visitor responses.[10]

---

10 Download the formative study on *Daisy* [PDF] at http://www.participatorymuseum.org/ref4-10/

In this small study, Ma found that visitors responded at greater length to *Daisy* when the computer program asked personal questions about the visitors than when it asked about itself. For example, the question, "How do I know I'm talking to a human and not just another machine?" prompted more self-reflection than "Are you sure that I'm not a real person talking to you by e-mail? What would it take to convince you?" The first question focused on the visitor, whereas the second question focused on the object.

Ma also discovered that visitors were more likely to provide elaborated responses when questions were posed in two parts. For example, visitors gave more complex responses to the two-part question: "Are you usually a logical person?" <visitor response> "Give me an example." <visitor response> than they did to the single question "Are you usually a logical person, or do you let your feelings affect your decisions? Give an example of a recent logical or emotional decision you made." Simple tasks or questions help build participants' confidence in their ability to engage in more complicated activities.[11]

This use of personal, progressive questions also elicited highly complex responses in two exhibitions at the New York Historical Society: *Slavery in New York* (2005) and its successor, *New York Divided* (2006).[12] These popular temporary exhibitions used artifacts, documents, and media pieces to trace the role of the slave trade in New York City's history and New Yorkers' responses to the Civil War. At the end of each exhibition, there was a story-capture station at which visitors could record video responses to four questions:

1. How did you hear of the exhibit?
2. What was your overall impression?
3. How did the exhibit add to or alter your previous knowledge of the subject?
4. What part of the exhibition was particularly noteworthy?

---

11 For another example of this multi-stage approach to visitor engagement, read about the *MP3 Experiments* on page 169.

12 Except where noted, all quotes in this case study come from articles by Richard Rabinowitz ("Learning from the Visitors to *Slavery in New York*") and Chris Lawrence ("Talk-Back Culture") in *Visitor Voices in Museum Exhibitions,* ed. McLean and Pollock (2007): 62–68.

Visitors had four minutes to respond to each question, and the story capture experience averaged ten minutes. Richard Rabinowitz, curator of *Slavery in New York*, noted that the progressive nature of the questions yielded increasingly complex responses, and that "it was typically in response to the third or fourth question that visitors, now warmed up, typically began relating the exhibition to their previous knowledge and experience." Rabinowitz commented: "as a 40-year veteran of history museum interpretation, I can say that I never learned so much from and about visitors." It was the lengthy progressive response process that turned what is often a series of brief and banal comments into a rich archive of visitor experience.

The visitor responses to *Slavery in New York* also demonstrate the power of exhibits and questions that deal with personal impact rather than external visitor opinions. About three percent of visitors to the exhibition chose to record their reactions to *Slavery in New York*, of whom eighty percent were African-American. This representation was disproportionate relative to the overall demographics of visitors to the exhibition (estimated by Rabinowitz at sixty percent African-American over the course of the exhibition), suggesting that more African-American visitors were moved to share their responses than members of other races. Many visitors explicitly linked the exhibition to their own personal histories and lived experience. A young woman stated she would feel very differently about "returning to work on Wall Street next week, knowing that it was first built by people who looked like me." One man who visited both exhibitions noted that they changed his perception of "how I fit into the American experience, and the New York experience."[13]

Another group of young men internalized *Slavery in New York* in a relational way, saying "After seeing this exhibit I know now why I want to jump you when I see you in the street. I have a better idea about the anger I feel and why I sometimes feel violent towards you." Chris Lawrence, then a student working on the project, commented:

> This visitor addressed the camera as "you," placing the institution as "white" and to a lesser degree as "oppressor." This sentiment was not exclusive to teenagers, as many African Americans referenced the

13 Watch a clip from this video at http://www.participatorymuseum.org/ref4-13/

New-York Historical Society as a white or European-American institution
and took the opportunity to speak directly to that perspective.

These visitors perceived themselves to be in dialogue between "me" the visitor and "you" the museum. The institution responded by posting visitors' videos on YouTube and integrating clips into the introductory videos that framed both *Slavery in New York* and *New York Divided*. By letting visitors "speak first" in a provocative exhibition, the institution demonstrated that it valued their personal experiences as an important part of the dialogue.

Asking Speculative Questions

Personal questions only work when it is reasonable for visitors to speak from their own experiences. If you want to encourage visitors to move away from the world of things they know or experience and into unknown territory, speculative questions are a better approach. You can ask an urban visitor, "what would your life be like if you lived in a log cabin with no electricity?" and she can answer thoughtfully, using her imagination to connect personally with a foreign experience. You can ask an adult, "What would the world be like if you could choose the genetic makeup of your child?" and he can answer without a comprehensive grasp of biochemistry. In cultural institutions, the best "what if" questions encourage visitors to look to objects for inspiration, but not prescriptive answers.

For example, the Powerhouse Museum's *Odditoreum* gallery (see page 161) encouraged visitors to look carefully at strange objects and imagine what they could possibly be. The *Signtific* game (see page 111) asked players to work together to brainstorm potential future scenarios based on scientific prompts. In both cases, people used objects and evidence as the basis for imaginative responses to a speculative question.

CASE STUDY
WHAT IF WE LIVED IN A WORLD WITHOUT OIL?

Speculative questions don't have to be off the wall to induce imaginative play states. In 2007, game designer Ken Eklund launched *World Without Oil*, a collaborative serious game in which people responded to a fictional but plausible oil shock that restricted availability of fuel around the world. The game was very simple: each day, a central website published the fictional price and availability of gasoline, diesel, and jet fuel. The price rose as availability contracted. To play, participants submitted their own personal visions of how they would survive in this speculative reality. People wrote blog posts, sent in videos, and called in voice messages. Many of them created real-world artifacts and documented how the fictitious oil shock was affecting their local gas stations, farmer's markets, and transportation systems.

Player submissions—over 1,500 in all—were distributed across the Web and networked by the *World Without Oil* website. Players built on each other's ideas, intersecting, overlapping, and collaboratively developing a community response to the speculative situation. As one player who called herself KSG commented:

> Rather than just getting people to "think about" the problem, it [World Without Oil] actually gets a large and actively interested community of people to throw ideas off of each other through their in-game blog posts, and the out-of-game Alternate Reality Game community. There's some potential for innovation there, for someone to think up a brilliant lifestyle change for the better that people can start jumping on board with.[14]

The game play motivated people to sample different lifestyles, think differently about resource consumption, and in some cases, change behavior long-term. As another player put it, "We hope that the people who play the game will ultimately live some of what they 'pretend' if they don't already."[15]

Speculative questions can often seem too silly to couple with serious museum content. But there are many questions like the one posed in *World Without Oil* that are just close enough to reality to offer an intriguing window into a likely future. What will a library be like when books are a tiny part of their services? Which historical artifacts will resonate from our time? These questions are ripe for cultural institutions to tackle with visitors.

---

14 Read KSG's complete comment on Brady Forrest's April 2007 blog post, "World Without Oil Launches," at http://www.participatorymuseum.org/ref4-14/. org/ref4-13/

15 You can access *World Without Oil* player's reflections, educational materials, and the game archive at http://www.participatorymuseum.org/ref4-15/

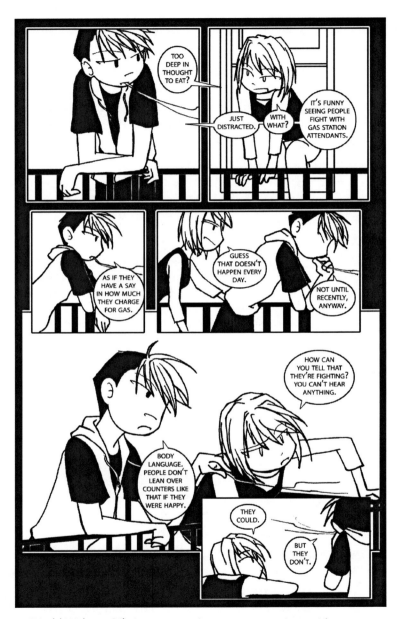

World Without Oil players created game content using a wide range of media. Jennifer Delk created a comic for each of the 32 "weeks" of the game, chronicling how an urban family dealt with the oil shock.

Where Should You Put Your Question?

Once you have a great question in hand, you need to decide how and where to ask it for maximum impact. The most common placement for questions is at the end of content labels, but this location is rarely most effective. Positioning questions at the end of labels accentuates the perception that they are rhetorical, or worse, afterthoughts. To find the best place for a question, you need to be able to articulate the prioritized goals for the question.

Recall the three basic goals for questions in exhibitions:

1. To encourage visitors to engage deeply and personally with a specific object
2. To motivate interpersonal dialogue among visitors around a particular object or idea
3. To provide feedback or useful information to staff about the object or exhibition

If the goal is to encourage visitors to engage deeply with objects, questions and response stations should be as close to the objects of interest as possible. Visitors can speak more comfortably and richly about objects that they are currently looking at than objects they saw 30 minutes earlier in the exhibition.

When these experiences are focused on private, personal responses to objects, enclosed story capture booths such as those used in *Slavery in New York* are effective. When you want visitors to spend a long time reflecting and sharing their thoughts, it's important to design spaces for response that are comfortable and minimize distractions.[16] Some projects, like Wendy Clarke's *Love Tapes*, even go so far as to let people personalize the space in which they respond to the question. Clarke asked participants to pick a visual background and song to accompany highly personal videos in which they talked about love.[17] This personalization allowed participants to take some control over an emotional and potentially revealing experience.

---

16 The booths for the popular StoryCorps project are also designed in this fashion.
17 For more information on this incredible project, read Clarke's article, "Making the 'Love Tapes'" in *Visitor Voices in Museum Exhibitions,* ed. McLean and Pollock (2007): 101–105.

When the goal is to encourage a large percentage of visitors to respond to questions, visitor responses should be of comparable aesthetics to the "official" institutional content on display. If a label is printed beautifully on plexiglass and visitors are expected to write responses in crayon on post-its, they may feel that their contributions are not valued or respected, and will respond accordingly. One of the things that made the visitor stories contributed in the Denver Art Museum's *Side Trip* exhibition so compelling and on-topic was a design approach that elevated visitors' responses to comparable footing with the pre-designed content. The vast majority of the signage in *Side Trip* was handwritten in pen on ripped cardboard, which meant that visitors' contributions (pen on paper) looked consistent in the context of the overall gallery design. By simplifying and personalizing the design technique used for the institutional voice, visitors felt invited into a more natural, equitable conversation.

If the goal is to motivate interpersonal dialogue around an object or subject, the question and answer structure should clearly support visitors building on each other's ideas. The *Signtific* game (page 111) did this virtually by encouraging players to respond to each other by "following up" on other players' entries. You could easily do something similar in a physical space, either by using different color paper or pens for different types of questions and responses, or by explicitly encouraging visitors to comment on each other's responses or to group their thoughts with like-minded (or opposing) visitor contributions.

If the goal is for visitors to consume each other's responses, make sure that questions are posed in a location that makes them most useful to others. If you ask visitors to recommend artifacts or exhibits to each other, their recommendations should be on display near the entrance to the galleries, not the exit. The more visitors can see how their voices add to a larger, growing conversation, the more likely they are to take questions—and their answers—seriously.

Finally, if the goal is for visitors to provide useful feedback to staff, the question station must make its utility clear to visitors. In 2009, the Smithsonian American Art Museum launched *Fill the Gap,* a project in which visitors were invited to suggest which pieces of art might be used to fill vacancies left in the public display when pieces went out on loan or into conservation labs. Visitors could answer in-person by writing on a comment board at the museum, or they could answer online via a Flickr-based version of the project.

The question, "What object would fit best in this spot?" is not a particularly sexy question, but it began a meaningful conversation between staff members and visitors. The institution clearly indicated that staff would listen to and act on visitors' responses. The activity required visitors to carefully examine objects and to advocate for their inclusion by making arguments in a distributed conversation among visitors and staff members. Importantly, the results of the conversation were visible—visitors could return and see which object had been selected and inserted into the gap. Visitors engaged with the objects to answer the question because they understood how it would provide value to the institution.

The *Fill the Gap* activity station clearly communicated a simple, meaningful question.

Tours and Facilitated Social Experiences

While questions may be the most common technique, the most reliable way to encourage visitors to have social experiences with objects is through interactions with staff through performances, tours, and demonstrations. Staff members are uniquely capable of making objects personal, active, provocative, or relational by asking visitors to engage with them in different ways. This section does not focus on the many fabulous ways that live interpretation helps people understand and experience the power of museum objects, but instead looks specifically at ways interpretation can make the visitors' experiences more social.

Making Tours and Presentations More Social

What does it take to make a tour or object demonstration more social? When interpreters personalize the experience and invite visitors to engage actively as participants, they enhance both the social and educational value of cultural experiences. Demonstrations that involve "guests from the audience" or encourage small groups of visitors to handle objects allow visitors to confidently connect with objects in a personal way. Staff members who ask meaningful questions, give visitors time to respond, and facilitate group conversations can make unique and powerful social experiences possible.

In a 2004–6 study at Hebrew University's Nature Park, researchers found that even a few minutes of personalization at the beginning of a tour can enhance visitors' overall enjoyment and learning.[18] A *Discovery Tree Walk* guide was trained to start her tour with a three-minute discussion about visitors' personal experiences and memories of trees. She then lightly wove their "entrance narratives" into the tour itself. Compared to a control group (with whom she chatted casually before the tour, but not about trees), the group who received personalized content was more engaged in the tour and rated the experience more positively after it was over.

In some programmatic experiences, visitors are explicitly encouraged to act like researchers and to develop their own theories and meaning around

---

18 See Dina Tsybulskaya and Jeff Camhi's article, "Accessing and Incorporating Visitors' Entrance Narratives in Guided Museum Tours," in *Curator* 52, no. 1 (2009): 81–100.

objects. In the world of art museums, the *Visual Thinking Strategies (VTS)* interpretative method, developed by museum educator Philip Yenawine and cognitive psychologist Abigail Housen in the late 1980s, is a constructivist teaching technique used to encourage visitors to learn about art by engaging in dialogue with the art itself. *VTS* is simple on the surface. Facilitators use three basic questions: "What's going on in this picture?," "What do you see that makes you say that?," and "What more can we find?" to lead discussion. Staff members listen carefully, rephrase visitors' comments to validate their interpretations, and use the three questions to keep the conversation going.

Unlike traditional museum art tours, *VTS* facilitators do not provide historical context for the works discussed; in most cases, facilitators don't even identify the artist or the piece. The point is not for the guide to confer knowledge, but to encourage visitors to think openly, vocally, and socially about what art means and how it works. Several research studies have demonstrated that students in *VTS* programs increased their visual literacy, critical thinking skills, and respect for others' diverse views.[19] By encouraging visitors to talk through their observations, *VTS* models a kind of dialogue that visitors can continue to employ outside of the facilitated experience.

Provocative Programming

Just as a provocative object can spark dialogue, a provocative staffed experience can give visitors unique social experiences.[20] Perhaps the most famous provocative visitor tour is that in *Dialogue in the Dark (DITD)*, an international traveling exhibition that has been experienced by over 6 million visitors in 30 countries since it opened in 1988. *DITD* is a guided experience in which visitors navigate multi-sensory simulated environments in total darkness. Their guides are blind people. The experience is intensely social; visitors rely on the guides for support as they move into confusing and potentially stressful scenarios like a busy street scene or a supermarket.

The social experience of *DITD* frequently results in sustained visitor impact. In exit interviews, visitors consistently talk about the emotional

---

19 Visit http://www.participatorymuseum.org/ref4-19/ for evaluation reports and research techniques related to *VTS*.

20 In this section, the "object" is the experience itself.

impact of the experience, their newfound appreciation for the world of the blind, and their gratitude and respect for their blind guides. In a 2005 study of 50 random visitors who had attended *DITD* in Hamburg, Germany in the year 2000, one hundred percent remembered the experience, and 98% had talked about it with others. Sixty percent changed their attitude towards blind people, and 28% self-reported changing their behavior towards people with disabilities.[21] A 2007 study of forty-four blind guides at six European *DITD* venues showed that their work with *DITD* led to increased self-confidence, communication skills, and enhanced relationships with friends and family.[22]

While the setting for *Dialogue in the Dark* is intense and unusual, the social experience is safe and supportive. By contrast, the *Follow the North Star* experience at Conner Prairie, a living history site in Indiana, combines a bucolic natural setting with a stressful social experience. *Follow the North Star* is a role-playing experience that takes place in 1836. Visitors portray a group of Kentucky slaves who try to escape while being moved by their owners through the free state of Indiana. In contrast to the common interpretative technique in which staff members portray characters and visitors are observers, *Follow the North Star* puts the visitors in the middle of the action as actors themselves. As historian Carl Weinberg described it, "As visitors, we are not only performing 'old-timey' tasks. We are central actors in a drama, taking on a whole new identity, as well as the risks that identity entails."[23]

This approach leads to powerful interpersonal experiences among visitors in a group. Visitors may be pitted against each other or forced to make decisions about which of them should be sacrificed as bargaining chips with costumed staff members along the way. Hearing a fellow visitor yell at you to move faster can be much more intense than hearing it from a staff member who you know is paid to act that way.

---

21 Download the 2005 report on DITD visitors [PDF] at http://www.participatory-museum.org/ref4-21/

22 Download the 2007 report on DITD blind guides [PDF] at http://www.partici-patorymuseum.org/ref4-22/

23 From Carl Weinberg, "The Discomfort Zone: Reenacting Slavery at Connor Prairie" *OAH Magazine of History* 23, no. 2 (2009). Available at http://www.participatorymuseum.org/ref4-23/

All groups are debriefed after the reenactment is over, which often prompts interpersonal dialogue among visitors. Guest Experience Manager Michelle Evans recounted one particularly heated debriefing:

> A mixed race group began their debriefing on a tense note. After a white participant spoke about his experience, a black woman commented, shaking her head, "You just don't get it." But this fortunately opened up such an engaging conversation that the whole group headed to Steak and Shake afterward to continue to the discussion.[24]

Designing experiences like *Follow the North Star* is incredibly complex. You have to balance the intensity of the planned experience with the social dynamics of strangers working in groups. I was the experience developer for *Operation Spy* at the International Spy Museum, a guided group experience in which visitors portrayed intelligence officers on assignment in a foreign country on a time-sensitive mission. In the design stage, we constantly weighed the desire to have visitors work together against their hesitancy to do so in a high-stakes environment in which each wanted to perform as well as he or she could individually. As in *Follow the North Star*, we had to balance visitors' desires to discuss the experience with the need to keep the story (and the energy) moving. The *Operation Spy* guides are part actor, part facilitator, and it isn't easy to maintain dramatic intensity while managing visitors' interpersonal and individual needs.

CASE STUDY
OBJECT-RICH THEATER AT THE INDIANAPOLIS CHILDREN'S MUSEUM

Follow the North Star and *Operation Spy* are expensive, complicated productions to design and facilitate. But it is also possible to integrate live theater experiences into exhibition spaces, more naturally connecting visitors to important objects and stories.

One of the best examples of this is in *The Power of Children* permanent exhibition at the Indianapolis Children's Museum. *The Power of Children* features the stories of three famous courageous children throughout history: Anne Frank, Ruby Bridges, and Ryan White. Three spaces in the

---

24 Ibid.

exhibit can transition from open exhibit space to closed theater space via a couple of strategically placed doors. There are several ten-to-fifteen-minute live theater shows in the exhibition per day, each of which features a single adult actor. I watched one of the Ruby Bridges shows in an exhibit space designed to simulate the classroom in which Bridges took her first grade classes alone. She spent a year going to school by herself because all the white parents chose to remove their children from school rather than have them contaminated by an African-American classmate.

The Ruby Bridges show treated visitors like participants, not just passive audience members. In the show I experienced, a male actor portrayed a US marshal reflecting on his time protecting Bridges as she walked to school. The actor used objects (photos from the time, props in the room) and questions to connect us with the story and the real person. The choice to use an adult actor who was both a fictitious "insider" to the story and a "real life" outsider like the rest of the audience enabled him to facilitate personal connections among us as a community of observers to the story.

The actor portraying the US marshal delivered his show inside this classroom. The print on the desk and photos in the background are both historic props used to connect visitors to the real story of Ruby Bridges.

We could relate to the personal conflict he was expressing, and he treated us as complicit partners, or confessors, to his experience. Visitors weren't asked to BE Ruby Bridges—instead, we were treated like citizens of her time, scared, confused, uncertain.

The show also explicitly connected us to the objects in the room. We were sitting on the set—in classroom desk chairs facing him at the blackboard. The whole show allowed us to live in the imaginative space of Bridges' classroom. *What if I was the only student in my class? What if people yelled horrible things at me on my walk to get here every day?*

This show didn't separate visitors from the action. It let us onto the stage to share it with the actor, the objects, and the story at hand. And when the show was over, we got to stay onstage. Because the room was both an exhibit space and a theatrical space, visitors could continue to explore it after the show was over. Visitors could connect with the artifacts and props in the space without being rushed out, and there were opportunities to discuss the experience further with the actor and other audience members.

In contrast, there are many painful museum theater experiences that seemed to willfully ignore visitors' desires to participate or engage with each other socially. On a 2009 trip to the National Constitution Center, I joined a small group of visitors for a live theater show about contemporary issues related to constitutional law. Four actors presented a series of vignettes and then concluded by asking us to vote by raising our hands to indicate how we would have decided in each of the cases. There were only ten of us in the audience, and as we dutifully raised and lowered our hands, it was painfully obvious that we could have had interesting dialogue about our different opinions on the issues. Instead, we were thanked, given surveys, and shuttled out. As a small group of adults, it felt condescending and almost bizarre to sit silently through a long show by four actors when they could have easily prompted discussion.

Facilitating Dialogue Instead of Putting on a Show

When staff members are trained to facilitate discussion rather than deliver content, new opportunities for social engagement emerge. When the Levine Museum of the New South mounted a temporary exhibition called *Courage* about the early battles for school desegregation in the United States, they accompanied the exhibition with an unusual programming technique called "talking circles." This Native American-derived dialogue program invited visiting groups to engage in facilitated discussion about race and segregation in an egalitarian, non-confrontational way. The *Courage* talking circles were designed for intact groups—students, corporate groups, civic groups—and have become a core part of how the Levine Museum supports community dialogue and action based on exhibition experiences. When the Science Museum of Minnesota mounted their *Race* exhibition, they also used the talking circle technique with local community and corporate groups to discuss issues of race in their work and lives after viewing the exhibition.

Learning to facilitate dialogue is an art.[25] While there are entire books written on the topic, the general principles are the same as those for designing civic participatory environments. Respect participants' diverse contributions. Listen thoughtfully. Respond to participants' questions and thoughts instead of pushing your own agenda. And provide a safe, structured environment for doing so.

Provocative Exhibition Design

Live interpretation is not always possible, practical, or desired by visitors. Even without live interpreters, there are ways to design provocative, active settings for objects that can generate dialogue. Just as dramatic lighting can give objects emotional power, placing objects in "conversation" with each other can enhance their social use. When visitors encounter surprising design choices or objects that don't seem to go together, it raises questions in their minds, and they frequently seek out opportunities to respond and discuss their experiences.

Provocation through Juxtaposition

One of the most powerful and simple ways to provoke social response is through juxtaposition. Rarely employed in online platforms, juxtaposition of artifacts has been the basis for several groundbreaking exhibitions,

---

25 For more information on facilitating dialogue in cultural institutions, check out *Museums and Social Issues* 2, no. 2: 2007, which focused on civic discourse.

including Fred Wilson's *Mining the Museum*, presented in 1992 at the Maryland Historical Society. Wilson selected artifacts from the Historical Society's collection—objects that were overlooked or might have been perceived to have little evocative power—and used them as the basis for highly provocative, active, relational exhibits. He placed a fancy silver tea set alongside a pair of slave shackles, paired busts of white male statesmen with empty nameplates for African-American heroes, and contrasted a Ku Klux Klan robe with a baby carriage.

While the objects in *Mining the Museum* were (for the most part) unremarkable, the platform on which they were presented added a provocative, relational layer to their presentation. This translated to a more social reception by visitors. Juxtaposition implies obvious questions: "Why are these here and those missing?" "What's going on here?" Curators and museum educators often ask questions like this, but these questions can fall flat when presented as teachable moments. In *Mining the Museum*, these questions were not explicit but bubbled naturally to the top of visitors' minds, and so people sought out opportunities for dialogue.

Mining the Museum generated a great deal of professional and academic conversation that continues to this day. But it also energized visitors to the Maryland Historical Society, who engaged in dialogue with each other and with staff members, both verbally and via written reactions, which were assembled in a community response exhibit. *Mining the Museum* was the most well-attended Maryland Historical Society exhibition to date, and it fundamentally reoriented the institution with respect to its collection and relationship with community.

Several art museum exhibitions have paired objects in a less politicized way to activate visitor engagement. In 1990, the Hirshhorn Museum and Sculpture Garden mounted an exhibition called *Comparisons: An Exercise in Looking* in which pairs of artworks were hung together with a single question in-between. By asking visitors to connect two artifacts via explicitly relational queries, the artworks were activated as social objects in conversation with each other. The questions were subjective, but they all encouraged deep looking. Some were open-ended: "Do you respond more to one work than the other?" whereas others were more educational: "Is it apparent that Liger has changed the composition and painted over areas in either painting?"

From interviews with ninety-three visitors, researchers determined that visitors primarily considered *Comparisons* to be an "educational gallery" and that they wanted to see more such exhibitions. One visitor comment noted that the exhibition was very interesting, but "definitely an exhibit to see <u>with</u> someone." Another visitor observed: "(married) couples had wonderfully disparate views as they saw this exhibit." The questions provided tools for discussion in a venue in which visitors often feel uncertain about how to respond to objects on display.[26]

In 2004, the Cantor Art Center at Stanford University took this idea further and presented *Question*, "an experiment that provokes questions about art and its presentation in museums." Rather than just displaying art in a neutral way along with questions on labels, *Question* featured radical display techniques that were intended to explore but not answer basic questions that visitors have about art, like "What makes it art?," "How much does it cost?," and "What does it mean?" The team mounted artworks by famous artists and children together on a refrigerator. They crowded European paintings against a cramped chain-link fence and mounted other pieces in natural settings with sound environments and comfortable seating. All of these unusual and surprising

Is it art if my kid could draw that? *Question* employed unusual display techniques to encourage discussion and debate.

26 The *Comparisons* 1992 research study, *Appreciating Art: a study of Comparisons, an exercise in looking,* is available in the Smithsonian library at http://www.participatorymuseum.org/ref4-26/

design techniques were meant to provoke dialogue. As exhibit designer Darcie Fohrman commented, "In the museum field, we know that learning happens when there is discussion and conversation. We want people to ask strange questions and say, 'I don't get this.'"

In summative evaluation, researchers found that 64% of visitors discussed exhibit content while in the gallery, which was high relative to typical visitor behavior. Visitors spent twice as much time at exhibits whose labels led with a question than those that did not, and that the interactive or provocative exhibits were more likely to generate conversation than their more traditional counterparts. In addition to verbal conversation, visitors frequently responded to each other through text-based participatory exhibits. For example, the entry to *Question* featured two graffiti walls with peepholes through which people could look at artworks and write up their own questions and responses about art. The walls proved so popular they had to be repainted multiple times over the run of the exhibition.

Provocation through Fiction

Fred Wilson didn't just place objects in dialogue with each other; he also wrote labels and interpretative material that deliberately twisted the meaning of the artifacts on display. Artist David Wilson uses a similar technique at the Museum of Jurassic Technology in Los Angeles, which showcases very odd objects alongside labels that couple an authoritative tone with fantastical content. These artists play games with the ways cultural institutions describe and attribute meaning to artifacts in museums. By doing so, they invite visitors to question what's going on in an exhibition or institution.

CASE STUDY
IMAGINATIVE OBJECT DESCRIPTIONS AT THE POWERHOUSE MUSEUM

Playing games with objects isn't just a high art technique; it can also help visitors construct their own meaning about objects and have some fun while doing so. In the summer of 2009, the Powerhouse Museum opened a temporary gallery called the *Odditoreum*, which presented eighteen very odd objects alongside fanciful (and fictitious) labels written by children's book author Shaun Tan and schoolchildren. While the *Odditoreum* was designed for families on holiday, the Powerhouse described it as being about meaning making, not silliness. The introductory label talked about "strangeness, mystery, and oddity" and noted that, "when things are strange, the brain sends out feelers for meaning." This is a powerful statement that encouraged visitors to think about the "why" of these objects.

The *Odditoreum* featured a participatory area in which visitors could share their reactions by writing their own labels to go with the bizarre objects on display. This component was very popular and well used, and the visitor-submitted labels in the *Odditoreum* were inventive and on-topic.

While many museums have experimented with "write your own label" campaigns, the *Odditoreum* was unique in its request that visitors write imaginative, not descriptive, labels. While many visitors may feel intimidated by the challenge to properly describe an object, everyone can imagine what it *might* be. The speculative nature of the exhibition let visitors at all knowledge levels into the game of making meaning out of the objects. And yet the imaginative activity still required visitors to focus on the artifacts. Every visitor who wrote a label had to engage with the objects deeply to look for details that might support various ideas and develop a story that reasonably fit the object at hand.

The Odditoreum was carefully designed to encourage imaginative play without asking visitors to also absorb the "correct" story of each object. The Powerhouse team dealt delicately with the presentation of the "real" information about each object. As Public Programs Producer Helen Whitty put it: "I didn't want the fantasy label immediately next to the real information, thus spoiling the approach ('really you thought we were going to have fun but really it's business as usual')." Instead, the museum mounted the real information ("What they actually are!") together on one large panel nearby—available, but not the point of the experience.

In all of these examples, design techniques were strategically optimized to promote artifacts as objects of conversation. The objects were not presented in a way that allowed visitors to receive the most accurate

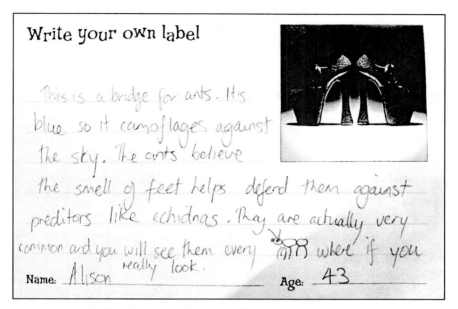

Write your own label

This is a bridge for ants. It's
blue so it camoflages against
the sky. The ants believe
the smell of feet helps defend them against
preditors like echidnas. They are actually very
common and you will see them every [where] where if you
really look.

Name: Alison   Age: 43

Energized by the strange objects and fictitious labels on display, many
Odditoreum visitors shared their own unique object interpretations.

information or the most pleasing aesthetic experience. It's hard to take pleasure in a silver tea set that is forcibly paired with a set of slave shackles, and
a refrigerator is probably not the ideal aesthetic setting for a sketch by Miró.
By designing the exhibitions as successful social platforms, these exhibitions
drew in new and enthusiastic crowds, but they also turned off some visitors for whom the approach was unfamiliar and unappealing. Just as Flickr's
choice to allow users to write notes on photos may be distracting to some
photography buffs who prefer unadulterated images, socializing exhibition
techniques introduce design tradeoffs that may be in conflict with other institutional values or visitors' expectations.

It's no coincidence that these kinds of projects typically involve
outside artists or designers. Even if doing so might invite visitors to spend
time discussing and exploring the objects intently, staff members rarely
give themselves permission to display objects in ways that might be seen as
denigrating their worth or presenting false information about their meaning.
If you want to present objects in a provocative setting, you must feel confi-

dent—as did each of these design teams—that social response is a valuable and valid goal for visitor engagement.

Giving Visitors Instructions for Social Engagement

The easiest way to invite strangers to comfortably engage with each other is to command them to do it. Provocative presentation techniques, even when overt, can be misinterpreted. If you are looking for a more direct way to activate artifacts as social objects, consider writing some rules of engagement with or around the objects.

This may sound prescriptive, but it is something museum professionals are already comfortable with when it comes to individual experiences with interactive elements. Instructional labels explain step-by-step how to stamp a rivet or spin the magnet. Audio tours tell visitors where to look. Educators show people how to play. Many games and experiences use instruction sets as a scaffold that invites visitors into social experiences that become much more open-ended and self-directed.

Exhibits that require more than one person's participation typically employ labels that say, "sit down across from a partner and..." or "stand in a circle around this object." For visitors who arrive with family or social groups (the majority of museum visitors), these instructions are easy to fulfill. But for solo visitors, these labels pose a challenge. Where can I find a partner? How can I get others to stand in a circle with me?

For solo visitors, it's easiest to engage if labels explicitly instruct people to "find a partner," or, even better, to "find someone of your gender," or "find someone who is about your height." Specific instructions give visitors comfortable entry into social encounters that would otherwise feel awkward. A visitor can point back to the instruction label and say to a stranger, "it says I need to find another woman to use this exhibit." The stranger can confirm via the label that this is indeed an institutionally sanctioned interaction. And if the stranger declines to participate, she isn't rejecting the asker—she's rejecting the instruction. It's not that she finds something unsuitable about the other visitor; she just doesn't want to play the game. Clear instructions give both askers and respondents safe opportunities to opt in and out of social experiences.

CASE STUDY
TAKING INSTRUCTIONS AT THE SAN FRANCISCO MUSEUM OF MODERN ART

In some traditional institutions, especially art museums, it can be hard to convince visitors that it is okay to engage directly with the objects, let alone with each other. When the San Francisco Museum of Modern Art (SFMOMA) mounted *The Art of Participation* in 2008, the exhibition included several components in which visitors were explicitly instructed to interact with objects and with each other. Recognizing how unusual these activities were in the face of standard art museum behavior, SFMOMA used orange label text for all of the interactive components. At the entrance to the exhibition was a simple orange label that read:

> Some of the objects in this exhibition are documents of past events, but others rely on your contribution. Watch for the instructions printed in orange on certain object labels—these signal that it is your turn to do, take, or touch something.

In other words, SFMOMA created a special label type for interactive elements. This label set up a casual game for visitors inclined towards participation: look for orange text, do the activity. Had the participatory instructions been integrated into the standard black text labels, visitors might not have be as aware of the commonalities across the interactive art pieces. The repetition of the orange may also have encouraged some reluctant visitors to engage later in their visit, as it suggested multiple opportunities for participation.

I had a powerful social experience in *The Art of Participation* with the interactive *One Minute Sculptures* by artist Erwin Wurm. The artwork was a low, wide stage in the middle of the gallery with some unusual objects on it (broomsticks, fake fruit, a small fridge) and Wurm's handwritten instructions encouraging visitors to balance the objects on their bodies in funny, specific ways. About three people could fit on the stage comfortably, and the evocative, weird instructions naturally led people to try their own combinations of objects and positions.

The orange label for this artwork read:

> Follow the artist's instructions. Take a picture of your One Minute Sculpture and post it to the SFMOMA blog (www.blog.sfmoma.org) Use the tag "SFMOMAparticipation" to help others find it.

Emboldened by this label, I gave my phone to a stranger and asked him to take my picture. He took a picture of me balanced on the fridge and then suggested that I try a slightly different pose. Soon, we were cheerfully art-directing each other into increasingly strange poses. We enticed onlookers to join us and gave them explicit instructions about how to pose with the objects.

The gallery turned into a group social experience in the creation of art. I knew something unusual and powerful was happening when, several minutes into this experience, my new friend George paused mid-pose and said, "I think I'm going to take off my shirt."

One of Erwin Wurm's instructions for the *One Minute Sculptures*.

I don't often meet people in art museums who spontaneously undress. This was an incredible social experience mediated by the objects on display. It was unique; I don't expect to experience this kind of playfulness, intellectual curiosity, and physical intimacy with every visitor with whom I engage socially in museums.

But it need not be an isolated incident. The me-to-we pattern was at work—George and I each engaged first with the exhibit individually. We read specific instructions and then adapted them to create personal expressions of self-identity. The exhibit platform was well positioned and designed to naturally draw in spectators and would-be participants. There was a direct prompt to take pictures of each other (a simple social action). There was also the space and opportunity for the exhibit to encourage open-ended and truly wild social art experiences. What started with clear instructions turned into a strange and memorable event.

The first photograph of me, taken by George.

Three spectators we enticed into participating.

A gallery staff member who joined in the fun.

A year later, I still keep in touch with
George, my partner in crime.

Giving Instructions via Audio

As a further exploration of the use of instructions in motivating social experiences, consider the audio guide. Traditional audio guides use
instructions to help visitors orient themselves, but some artists have used
this medium to great effect to encourage visitors to have surprising, social
experiences. This section compares two such audio experiences: Janet
Cardiff's *Words Drawn on Water* (2005) and Improv Everywhere's *MP3
Experiments* (2004–ongoing). These experiences were both offered for free.
They were both about 35 minutes in length. They took place in major cities—Washington, D.C. and New York City, respectively. But they had very
different social outcomes.

In 2005, the Hirshhorn Museum and Sculpture Garden commissioned sound artist Janet Cardiff to create a 33-minute audio walk, *Words
Drawn on Water*, around the National Mall in Washington, DC.[27] Visitors
put on earphones and listened as Cardiff told them exactly where to go,
step by step. *Words Drawn on Water* used a combination of exacting directions and fictional narrative to draw participants into a series of intimate
object experiences. It was a highly isolating, personal experience. Cardiff
layered strange sounds—bees zooming in, soldiers marching—over a jour-
ney through museums and sculpture gardens, and she interpreted objects
like James Smithson's tomb and the Peacock Room in the Freer Gallery in
an evocative, dreamlike way. Though I experienced it with friends (and we
talked afterwards), throughout the audio walk each of us was lost in the
minutiae of her own augmented experience.

By contrast, Improv Everywhere's *MP3 Experiments* are designed to
encourage social experiences, not personal ones.[28] Like Cardiff, Improv
Everywhere distributes audio files for people to listen to on their own personal
audio devices while navigating urban environments. The *MP3 Experiments*
are event-based. Participants gather in a physical venue at a prescribed time
with their own digital audio players, and everyone hits "play" at the same
time. For about half an hour, hundreds of people play together silently, as

27 Listen to excerpts from *Words Drawn in Water* at http://www.participatorymu-
seum.org/ref4-27/

28 Learn more about the *MP3 Experiments* at http://www.participatorymuseum.
org/ref4-28/

directed by disembodied voices inside their headphones. The city becomes their game board, and everyday objects are activated as social game pieces. Participants point at things, follow people, and physically connect with each other. They use checkerboard-tiled plazas as boards for giant games of Twister. The *MP3 Experiments* are a model for how a typically isolating experience—listening to headphones in public—can become the basis for a powerful interpersonal experience with strangers.

Participants in *MP3 Experiment 4* take photos of each other, following the instructions provided by their digital audio devices.

What made *Words Drawn in Water* a personal experience and the *MP3 Experiments* social? The difference is in the audio instructions. In both *Words Drawn on Water* and the *MP3 Experiments*, the audio track overlays unusual instructions and suggestions onto a familiar landscape. But Cardiff layered on strange and surprising narrative elements that confused and un-settled listeners. This confusion made visitors ask themselves: *Where am I? Is there really a bee in my ear? Why is she saying I'm in England?* As the audio piece continued, listeners followed specific instructions on where to step, but they were also immersed private worlds of strange, secret thoughts.

The *MP3 Experiments* added a layer of silliness and play, not story and mystery, to the instructional set. Unlike the step-by-step instructions in *Words Drawn on Water*, which made you feel as though you had to keep up or it might leave you behind, the *MP3 Experiments* were scripted to make participants feel comfortable, giving them lots of time to perform tasks and rewarding them energetically for doing so.

Deconstructing just the first few minutes of an *MP3 Experiments* audio piece reveals a lot about what makes this project so successful as a social experience. Here's a breakdown of the first five minutes of *MP3 Experiment 4* (2007):[29]

- 0:00–2:30: Music.
- 2:30–4:00: Steve, the omnipotent voice, introduces himself. He explains that you will have to follow his instructions to have "the most pleasant afternoon together." Steve asks participants to look around and see who else is participating. He asks participants take a deep breath.
- 4:00–4:30: Steve asks participants to stand up and wave to each other.
- 4:30–5:00: Steve asks participants to "play a pointing game," and to point to the tallest building they could see, the Statue of Liberty, and finally, Nicaragua. He pauses, then says, "Most of you are pretty good at geography."
- 5:00–5:30: Steve asks participants to point to the "ugliest cloud." Again he pauses, and says, "I agree. That cloud is pretty ugly."

These first few minutes were carefully designed to help participants get comfortable with the experience. The music allowed people to relax and get ready for the experience privately. Steve's first instructions—to look around and take a deep breath—were easy, inconspicuous, and non-threatening. When Steve finally asked participants to stand up, he asked three times if they were ready, and then said, "stand up now." During the pointing game,

29 You can download *MP3 Experiment 4* and listen for yourself [MP3] at http://www.participatorymuseum.org/ref4-29/

Steve offered encouragement and affirmation, complimenting participants on their geography skills and subjective assessment of clouds.

Steve gained participants' trust as a safe, friendly source of instructions, and participants followed his voice into stranger and stranger activities. They followed people, played freeze tag, took pictures of each other, and formed a giant dartboard. These unusual activities were made possible by an environment of safe progression, clear instruction, and emotional validation.

Are the *MP3 Experiments* superior to *Words Drawn in Water*? Not at all. The two audio pieces were optimized for different kinds of experiences, one social, the other personal. It's all in the instructions and how they were delivered.

Making Objects Shareable

Outside of cultural institutions, one of the most frequent ways people make objects social is by sharing them. People share objects every time they give each other gifts, share memories via photographs, or make mixes of favorite songs. Museums tend to be protective of their collections and restrict the extent to which visitors can physically, or even virtually, share their objects. But the social Web has made it easier to share objects and stories than ever before, and that's changing the way professionals think about sharing in cultural institutions.

Objects in online social networks like Flickr and YouTube are automatically associated with tools to share them in a variety of ways. Increasingly, even traditional content producers like movie studios and musicians want users to redistribute their content far and wide. In 2008, a team led by MIT media researcher Henry Jenkins published a white paper entitled, "If it Doesn't Spread, It's Dead,"[30] which argued that media artifacts have greatest impact when consumers are able to pass on, reuse, adapt, and remix them. The authors suggested that spreadability doesn't just help marketers expand their reach; it also supports users' "processes of meaning making, as people

---

30 Read the paper "If It Doesn't Spread, It's Dead" at http://www.participatorymuseum.org/ref4-30/

use tools at their disposal to explain the world around them." In other words, sharing content helps people learn.

Cultural institutions can make their objects more shareable in two ways: by initiating projects to share objects with visitors, and by creating policies that encourage visitors to share object experiences with each other.

Institutional Sharing

There are many designed ways, from exhibits to interactives to programs to performances, that cultural institutions share their objects with visitors. These sharing techniques are largely governed by two sometimes conflicting goals: offering high-quality object experiences to visitors and preserving collections safely. Museums must be able to ensure that objects will not be unreasonably damaged or endangered. Typically, this involves housing artifacts in cases, designing mediating technologies for visitor consumption, and storing and caring for objects out of public view when necessary.

Why is sharing objects important? At a conceptual level, the extent to which an institution shares its objects affects whether people see the institution as a publicly owned utility or a private collection. What the staff considers protecting and conserving, some visitors may see as hoarding. Museum mission statements often talk about the collections being in the public trust, but from the public's perspective, the objects are owned by the building that houses them. Visitors can't visit objects whenever they like. They can't take them home or get too close. Museums share their objects parsimoniously, at strict and rule-bound visiting hours, often for a fee.

Some of the enhanced ways that institutions share artifacts with visitors include:

- "Learning kits" of artifacts or replicas that are safe for visitors to paw through in educational programming and in the galleries
- Open storage facilities, which enable visitors to have access to a wider range of objects than those on display in the galleries
- Loan programs that allow special visitors (e.g. Native American groups) to use objects for spiritual or cultural practice

- Expanded hours, so that visitors can have access to objects on their own schedules
- Digitization projects, so that digital reproductions of objects (if not the physical objects themselves) can be accessed anytime, anywhere

Some institutions are experimenting with more radical approaches to sharing objects, particularly in the online landscape. Some share collection data and images openly on third-party social websites like Flickr or Wikipedia. Others build their own online platforms with custom functions and design that allow visitors to remix objects and spread them with social Web sharing tools. In some particularly radical cases, museums share their digital collection content and software coding openly with external programmers, who can then develop their own platforms and experiences around the digital media. The Brooklyn Museum and the Victoria & Albert Museum are leaders in this domain; both have made their collection databases openly available to outside programmers, who have used them to create their own online and mobile phone applications.[31]

In the physical realm, museums are often more careful about how they share their objects. Rather than making the actual artifacts available for use, some institutions share information or activities with visitors that are usually kept behind the scenes. For example, in 2009 the University College of London Museum and Collections hosted a two-week interactive exhibition called *Disposal?* that invited visitors to vote and comment on which of ten artifacts should be deaccessioned from the museum. The exhibition allowed staff members to "share" decision-making regarding objects with audiences, thus engaging visitors in the intriguing work of determining the value of the collection—and the act of collecting more broadly.[32]

---

31 For example, check out the Brooklyn Museum's online application gallery, which showcases the ways outside programmers use the museums' data to develop new software: http://www.participatorymuseum.org/ref4-31/

32 This exhibition also generated quite a lot of press relative to its size and duration. See http://www.participatorymuseum.org/ref4-32/ for links to media coverage.

CASE STUDY
SHARING ARTIFACTS AT THE GLASGOW OPEN MUSEUM

The Glasgow Open Museum stands out as an institution whose mission is to share artifacts with visitors for their own use.[33] The Open Museum started in 1989 as a project of the Glasgow Museum to "widen ownership of the city's collection." The Open Museum lends objects to visitors for their own collections and displays, provides expert advice on conservation and presentation of objects, and organizes community partnerships to help community groups create their own exhibitions. Through the early 1990s, the Open Museum reached out specifically to partner with marginalized groups like prisoners, mental health patients, and senior citizens. Community members produced exhibitions in their own hospitals, community centers, and at the Open Museum on controversial topics from homelessness to breast-feeding to food poverty.

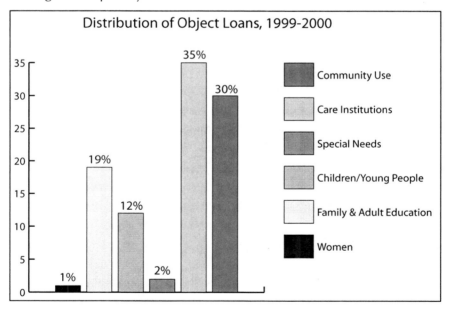

From 1999-2000, the Glasgow Open Museum shared over 800
objects with diverse community groups across the city.

---

33 To learn more about the Glasgow Open Museum's history and impact,
download *A Catalyst for Change: The Social Impact of the Open Museum* [PDF] at
http://www.participatorymuseum.org/ref4-33/

In its first ten years, the Open Museum's community partners created 884 exhibitions that were visited by hundreds of thousands of people.

In an extensive impact study completed in 2002, researchers identified three key impacts on participants: new opportunities for learning and growth, increased self-confidence, and changed perception of museums from "stuffy" places to being highly relevant to their own lives. They also determined that physical objects played a unique role in validating diverse cultural experiences, acting as catalysts for self-expression, and enhancing learning. Finally, the researchers commented that "the more focused the experience was on the needs of the individuals, the greater the impact." This was true both for participants and spectators. By inviting visitors to use what they needed from the institution, the Open Museum became a truly audience-centric place.

Institutional Policies on Sharing

The Glasgow Open Museum is an institution that shares its objects with visitors so that visitors can share them with each other. While its policies are radical by most museum standards, the basic premise applies to all sharing. When institutions allow visitors to share objects, visitors feel greater ownership over the experience and feel like the institution supports rather than hinders their enthusiasm about the content.

In museums, the most frequent way that visitors share objects with each other is through photographs. When visitors take photos in museums, few try to capture the essential essence of an object or create its most stunning likeness. Most visitors take photos to memorialize their experiences, add a personal imprint onto external artifacts, and share their memories with friends and families. When people share photos with each other, either directly via email or in a more distributed fashion via social networks, it's a way to express themselves, their affinity for certain institutions or objects, and simply to say, "I was here."

When museums prevent visitors from taking photos, the institutional message is, "you can't share your experience with your own tools here." While visitors generally understand the rationale behind no-flash policies, copyright-based no-photo policies can confuse and frustrate them. Photos are often permitted in one gallery but not another, and front-line staff members are not always able to answer visitors' questions about why photography is or isn't allowed. No-photo policies turn gallery staff into "enforcers" instead of supporters of visitors' experiences, and they diminish visitors' abilities to share their enthusiasm and experiences with others. As one frequent museum visitor put it:

> I like to think of museums as making history and art accessible to all; with photo restrictions, it can be an elite crowd. Imagine how a passion for art could be spread when someone, largely "ignorant" of art gets excited by a co-worker's pics and saves up and plans a trip to see a work, or works, that they would not otherwise see in their lifetime? And takes pics to send to their friends? Or someone who could never possibly afford to travel to great museums can live vicariously through a friend? This is making art accessible![34]

Photography policies are not easy to change, especially when it comes to institutions that rely heavily on loans or traveling exhibitions. But visitors who take photographs are people who actively want to share their cultural experience with friends and colleagues. These patrons want to promote the objects and institutions they visit, and photo policies are a key enabler—or restriction—to them doing so.

Gifting Objects and Other Ways to Share

Photos aren't the only way visitors can share object experiences with each other. Recommendation systems enable visitors to share their favorite objects with each other. Comment boards invite visitors to share comments and reflections with each other. Even pointing out an interesting object to a companion is a kind of sharing that enhances visitors' social experiences.

Memories, recommendations, comments, and photos are like gifts that people give to each other. How can cultural institutions explicitly support visitors sharing the "gifts" of their experiences, beyond sending them to the gift shop? In the mid-1990s, many bars and restaurants began to feature racks of free postcards promoting advertising messages. Imagine if, instead

---

34 You can read Roberta's full comment on my August 2009 blog post, "Museum Photo Policies Should Be as Open as Possible," at http://www. participatorymuseum.org/ref4-34/

of typical exhibition rack cards, institutions offered free postcards of objects in the galleries within and explicitly prompted visitors to think of a friend or family member who would enjoy a given object or exhibition. Visitors could pick their favorite postcards and mail off invitations to friends to visit the object on display right from the exhibition hall. Alternatively, visitors could use computer kiosks to produce simple e-cards or media pieces (photos, audio, video) to email to friends and family. The institution could provide standardized ways for visitors to share object experiences with others, either through low-tech devices like postcards or higher-tech digital interfaces.

These systems fall short when they become generically about "sharing experiences" and not about giving gifts to others. Some museums are experimenting with high-tech social platforms that invite visitors to send in photos and text messages to a central institutional account, which then broadcasts visitors' messages and images out to everyone. In 2008-9, visitors to the Mattress Factory in Pittsburgh could send a text message to a single number from anywhere in the museum. Those text messages were then displayed in real-time on a screen in the museum lobby. The goal was to share visitors' messages and photos with a larger audience.

But there's a problem with this approach. Many of these digital platforms experience low participation, even in institutions where visitors are text messaging and snapping photos all over the place. These platforms struggle because visitors don't have a clear idea of whom they are sharing their content with or why. When a visitor sends a message to her own friends or social network, she's motivated by her personal relationship with her friends, not a desire to generically share her experience. If these platforms emphasized the idea of giving and receiving gifts, rather than open sharing, they might have more success.

Gifting to Strangers

When well designed, social objects can create enjoyable opportunities for strangers to give each other gifts without requiring direct interpersonal contact. Consider an unlikely social object: the tollbooth. My friend Leo once had a thrilling experience in which a perfect stranger ahead of him in line at a tollbooth paid Leo's toll in addition to her own. It would be extremely strange to walk up to someone's car window and offer him $2.50 for the toll. He might be offended. He might be suspicious. But by giving this gift through the tollbooth operator, you shuttle the unsafe personal transaction through a safe transaction venue. It's semi-anonymous: the receiver can see the giver in the little blue Honda, but neither party is required to directly engage with the other.

The tollbooth enables personal giving between strangers and brings a third person (the tollbooth operator) into the experience. Arguably, three people who would never have met now get to share a nice experience and memory of generosity. And while the money is the gift, the object that mediates the social experience is the tollbooth itself.

Imagine if the Toll Authority decided that promoting social gifting was a goal they wanted to focus on. How would you redesign tollbooths to make them better social objects? Maybe you'd add a sign that tracks the number of gift tolls paid each day. Maybe there would be a discount or a special perk for people who pay for each other's tolls. There might even be a special high-risk lane for gifting, where each driver takes a gamble that she might either be a gifter or recipient depending on the lineup.

This sounds silly, but think about the potential benefits to the Toll Authority. Cars would move through lines more quickly because some would be pay for two. Rather than seeing toll operators as collection agents, drivers might see them as transmitters and facilitators of good will. People might take the toll road eagerly rather than avoiding it.

Could museum admission desks comparably be transformed into social objects, where visitors "gift" admission to each other? In many institutions, admission fees already do support other services, like free admission for school children, but that's rarely obvious to visitors. The Bronx Zoo tried to make this gift explicit in their *Congo Gorilla Forest*, which cost three dollars to enter. Computer kiosks near the exit invited visitors to explore different Congo-related conservation projects and select a project to receive their admission fee. In this way, the zoo transformed admission into a gift. This made visitors feel generous and changed their understanding of how their money was used by the zoo. But it also encouraged a diverse range of visitors to see themselves as donors and activists in support of worldwide conservation, a message that would be challenging to convey as effectively with a sign and a donation box.

Making Gifts Public

It's also possible to make gifting a community experience by publicizing gifts. I've seen bars and ice cream shops employ "gift boards" that publicly showcase gift certificate purchases with phrases like: "Nina gives Julia a hot fudge sundae" or "Ben gives Theo a double martini." When you come in to claim your gift, the message comes off the wall.

The public nature of these gift boards broadcasts the gifting experience to all visitors, making them more aware of opportunities both to give and receive. There are benefits for gift-givers, who look generous, and gift-getters, who are publicly adored. The boards encourage reciprocity and introduce a casual storyline to the store. Will Julia redeem her sundae? Why did Theo deserve that double martini? The venues position themselves as part of the emotional life of their patrons in a public way.

Gift boards are like donor walls, except that they celebrate transactions among visitors, not between visitors and institutions. They are egalitarian and dynamic. Imagine a board featuring "gifts" of museum admission, educational workshop fees, or items from the gift shop. Such a board would showcase visitors' ongoing interest in sharing cultural experiences in a way no donor wall could.

How can you treat your institution's objects as gifts? How can you share them generously and openly with visitors for their own purposes? When staff members can find ways to share institutional objects, they can empower visitors to see themselves as co-owners of and advocates for the institution overall.

You've reached the end of the design theory section of this book. Now that we've explored the diversity of participatory types and frameworks, it's time to turn to the practical question of how to design participatory projects that can succeed at your institution and help you achieve your goals. The second part of this book will help you plan, implement, evaluate, and manage participation in ways that best suit your institutional mission and culture.

CHAPTER 5

DEFINING
PARTICIPATION
AT YOUR
INSTITUTION

WHAT DOES IT TAKE for a cultural institution to become a place for participatory engagement? All participatory projects are based on three institutional values:

- Desire for the input and involvement of outside participants
- Trust in participants' abilities
- Responsiveness to participants' actions and contributions

When it comes to the "how" of participation, these values can be expressed in a wide variety of ways. Even when participation is focused on particular goals, there are many different approaches to designing effective projects that fulfill those goals. Consider the efforts of the fourteen museums engaged in the Immigration Sites of Conscience coalition. This coalition was formed in 2008 to stimulate conversation on immigration issues in the United States via participatory programs. Each museum took a different approach to "stimulating conversation:"

- The Arab American Museum in Detroit produced a contributory multimedia exhibition called Connecting Communities in which

visitors were encouraged to share their own immigration stories
and listen to others' via mobile phone.

- A consortium of five Chicago-based cultural museums hosted
community dialogues about the unique challenges and experiences of Cambodian, Polish, Swedish, and Japanese immigration
groups.[1]

- Angel Island State Park in San Francisco launched discussion-
oriented tours in which visitors grappled with complex issues of
immigration policy by exploring poetry carved on the walls of the
detention center by historic inmates.

- The Japanese American National Museum in Los Angeles offered
dialogue-based tours for high school students that encouraged
teenagers to discuss their reactions to cultural stereotypes and
discrimination.

There's no single approach to making a cultural institution more participatory. Each of these institutions initiated a project to stimulate conversation about immigration in a way that fit with its mission and resources. How
can you choose the model that will work best for your institution or project?
To do so, you need to understand the potential structures for participation,
and then find the approach that best supports your institutional mission and
goals.

Models for Participation

The first step in developing a participatory project is to consider the
range of ways visitors might participate with institutions. A participant who
writes her reaction to a performance on an index card is very different from
one who donates her own personal effects to be part of an exhibit. Both
these visitors are different from a third type who helps staff develop a new

---

1   This project was led by the Chicago Cultural Alliance and included the Field
Museum, the Cambodian American Heritage Museum & Killing Fields Memorial,
the Polish Museum of America, the Swedish American Museum Center, and the
Chicago Japanese American Historical Society.

program from scratch. How can we describe the ways visitors participate with formal institutions?

This was the question that Rick Bonney and a team of educators and science researchers at the Center for Advancement of Informal Science Education (CAISE) tackled in the Public Participation in Scientific Research (PPSR) project.[2] As far back as the 1880s, scientists have led "citizen science" projects in which amateurs are invited to participate in formal scientific research by volunteering to count birds, measure soil quality, or document non-native plant species.[3]

A birder participates in the Christmas Bird Watch, a citizen science project that has tracked the health of North American bird populations since 1900.

Despite its long history, few researchers studied the use and impact of citizen science until the 1980s. In 1983 Rick Bonney joined the staff at the Cornell Lab of Ornithology and co-founded its Citizen Science program, the

2   Download the PPSR report [PDF] at http://www.participatorymuseum.org/ref5-2/
3   Download biologist Sam Droege's highly readable overview of citizen science and its history [PDF] at http://www.participatorymuseum.org/ref5-3/

first program to professionalize the growing participatory practice. Over the course of several projects at the Lab, Bonney noted that different kinds of participation led to different outcomes for participants. In 2008, he led the PPSR team in a study to construct a typology of public participation to better understand the differences among project types.

The PPSR report defined three broad categories of public participation in scientific research: *contribution*, *collaboration*, and *co-creation*. These categories align roughly with the extent to which the public are involved in different stages of scientific research. In contributory projects, participants collect data in a scientist-controlled process. Scientists design the test questions, steer the data collection, and analyze the results. In collaborative projects, citizens collect data, but they also analyze results and draw conclusions in partnership with the scientists. In co-creative projects, the public develops the test questions, and scientists co-produce scientific regimens to address the community interest.

Most citizen science projects are contributory. These are the easiest projects for scientists to manage because they involve limited and specific participatory engagement. Contributors count birds, measure soil acidity, and perform other well-defined data collection activities. The PPSR report concluded that contributory citizen science projects are enormously successful at engaging the public with science content and activities but rarely connect participants to the entire scientific process.

Collaborative and co-creative projects help participants develop broader scientific research skills. Participants are actively engaged not just in scientific inquiry and observation but also in the analysis and development of research methodology. When participants analyze data themselves, their eagerness and ability to share scientific results with their own communities increases. The PPSR report also documented that co-created projects, when structured around a topic of community concern, like localized pollution, drew "concerned citizens into the scientific process who would not otherwise be involved with science-related activities." By applying scientific techniques to a community need, staff members were able to connect nontraditional audiences more meaningfully with science.

Like science labs, cultural institutions produce public-facing content under the guidance of authoritative experts. Therefore the three PPSR models for public participation can be applied directly to cultural institutions, with some slight changes in language:

- In contributory projects, visitors are solicited to provide limited and specified objects, actions, or ideas to an institutionally controlled process. Comment boards and story-sharing kiosks are both common platforms for contributory activities.

- In collaborative projects, visitors are invited to serve as active partners in the creation of institutional projects that are originated and ultimately controlled by the institution. *Top 40* (page 105) and *Click!* (page 115) were both collaborative projects in which visitors' choices shaped the design and content of resulting exhibitions.

- In co-creative projects, community members work together with institutional staff members from the beginning to define the project's goals and to generate the program or exhibit based on community interests. The Glasgow Open Museum (page 175) is an excellent example of a co-created institution. The staff partners with visitors to co-produce exhibits and programs based on community members' interests and the institution's collections.

I add a fourth model to the PPSR typology: *hosted*. Hosted projects are ones in which the institution turns over a portion of its facilities and/or resources to present programs developed and implemented by public groups or casual visitors. This happens in both scientific and cultural institutions. Institutions share space and/or tools with community groups with a wide range of interests, from amateur astronomers to knitters. Online, programmers may use cultural object registries or scientific data as the basis for their own research or products. Game enthusiasts may use the grounds of an institution as a giant game board for imaginative play. Hosted projects allow participants to use institutions to satisfy their own needs with minimal institutional involvement.

These participatory models are distinct, but many institutions incorporate elements from each of them. When staff members embrace visitor participation in earnest, they frequently move fluidly from one model to another, using different approaches for different projects and community relationships. For example, an art museum may host a late night program geared at creative professionals. At such events, the museum might invite attendees to contribute to community art projects. Staff might partner with outside artists in collaboration to present various components of the event, and if participants become deeply engaged, staff members may even invite them to lead their own projects or events in partnership with the museum, effectively co-creating new programs together.

Finding the Right Model for Your Institution

Contribution, collaboration, co-creation, hosted. No one model is better than the others. Nor should they even be seen as progressive steps towards a model of "maximal participation." Consider the difference between a project in which a museum sources exhibit material from visitors (contributory) and one in which the institution works with a small group of outsiders to develop an exhibit (collaborative). If the first project results in an exhibit made entirely of visitors' creations and voices and the second results in an exhibit that looks more like a "typical" exhibit, which project is more participatory? Which is more participatory: making art or doing research? Developing exhibits or using them to remix new media products?

There is no "best" type of participation in cultural institutions. The differences among participatory project types are highly correlated with the amount of ownership, control of process, and creative output given to institutional staff members and visitors. Not every project benefits from the same power structure. Institutional culture helps determine how much trust and responsibility the staff will grant to community members, and forcing an organization into an uncomfortable model rarely succeeds. Some contributory projects provide too few engaging experiences to attract any participation, and some co-created projects go far beyond what institutions desire or value in the outcomes they produce.

Which models of engagement will be most valuable for different projects or institutions? The chart on the following pages describes the differences among the models and can help you determine which participatory models will be most effective in specific scenarios. While there are outlier innovative projects that defy categorization, this chart displays the fundamental characteristics of each model.

Chapters 6 through 9 provide detailed examinations of each participatory model, demonstrating how they are structured, managed, and received by visitors. But first, the rest of this chapter explores how to find the model that will work best for particular institutional goals.

	Contributory	Collaborative	Co-Creative	Hosted
What kind of commitment does your institution have to community engagement?	We're commited to helping our visitors and members feel like participants with the institution.	We're commited to deep partnerships with some target communities.	We're committed to supporting the needs of target communities whose goals align with the institutional mission.	We're committed to inviting community members to feel comfortable using the institution for their own purposes.
How much control do you want over the participatory process and product?	A lot - we want participants to follow our rules of engagement and give us what we request.	Staff will control the process, but participants' actions will steer the direction and content of the final product.	Some, but participants' goals and preferred working styles are just as important as those of the staff.	Not much - as long as participants follow our rules, they can produce what they want.
How do you see the institution's relationship with participants during the project?	The institution requests content and the participants supply it, subject to institutional rules.	The institution sets the project concept and plan, and then staff members work closely with participants to make it happen.	The institution gives participants the tools to lead the project and then supports their activities and helps them move forward successfully.	The institution gives the participants rules and resources and then lets the participants do their own thing.
Who do you want to participate and what kind of commitment will you seek from participants?	We want to engage as many visitors as possible, engaging them briefly in the context of a museum or online visit.	We expect some people will opt in casually, but most will come with the explicit intention to participate.	We seek participants who are intentionally engaged and are dedicated to seeing the project all the way through.	We'd like to empower people who are ready to manage and implement their project on their own.

	Contributory	Collaborative	Co-Creative	Hosted
How much staff time will you commit to managing the project and working with participants?	We can manage it lightly, the way we'd maintain an interactive exhibit. But we ideally want to set it up and let it run.	We will manage the process, but we're going to set the rules of engagement based on our goals and capacity.	We will give much time as it takes to make sure participants are able to accomplish their goals.	As little as possible - we want to set it up and let it run on its own.
What kinds of skills do you want participants to gain from their activities during the project?	Creation of content, collection of data, or sharing of personal expression. Use of technological tools to support content creation and sharing.	Everything supported by contributory projects, plus the ability to analyze, curate, design, and deliver completed products.	Everything supported by collaborative projects, plus project conceptualization, goal-setting, and evaluation skills.	None that the institution will specifically impart, except perhaps around program promotion and audience engagement.
What goals do you have for how non-participating visitors will perceive the project?	The project will help visitors see themselves as potential participants and see the institution as interested in their active involvement.	The project will help visitors see the institution as a place dedicated to supporting and connecting with community.	The project will help visitors see the institution as a community-driven place. It will also bring in new audiences connected to the participants.	The project will attract new audiences who might not see the institution as a comfortable or appealing place for them.

Participation and Mission

Understanding the types of participatory engagement possible is the first step in designing participatory projects. The next step is to find the model that will best support specific mission-related goals. For example, when Shelley Bernstein talks about her award-winning work with social media at the Brooklyn Museum, she always couches it within the institution's fundamental mission as a community museum. Her team's technological efforts are inspired by Director Arnold Lehman's vision of the Brooklyn Museum as a place "based on accessibility, diversity, inclusion, and seeking out new ways to explore art so that everyone feels welcome and smart about what they're doing." Bernstein's team has focused on projects that promote this vision. For example, *Click!* (see page 115) encouraged a diverse community of photographers and visitors to feel included in creating and interpreting through both traditional and online interfaces. Arnold Lehman may not be attentive to the ins and outs of every technology initiative that comes down the pipe, but he trusts Bernstein's ability to deliver visitor experiences that enhance the overall value of the institution.

Working toward participation presents an ideal opportunity to examine your institution's mission statement. Often there are words or phrases that provide a strong justification for becoming more participatory. You may even be able to make the argument that in order to fully pursue its mission, the institution needs to become participatory in specific ways.

Consider the Minnesota Historical Society's mission statement:

> The Minnesota Historical Society connects people with history to help them gain perspective on their lives. The Society preserves the evidence of the past and tells the stories of Minnesota's people.

Look at the verbs in this mission statement. The institution *connects* people with history, *preserves* evidence, and *tells* stories. These goals are reflected in several participatory initiatives that invite Minnesotans to actively contribute to exhibitions and digital projects. These include:

- *MN150* - a permanent exhibition that connects visitors to the diverse voices of 150 community members who tell stories about the objects and events that define Minnesota

- *Placeography* - a wiki that gives people research and documentation tools to preserve and share the stories of their homes, neighborhoods, and favorite places[4]
- *Minnesota's Greatest Generation* - an ongoing project which invites people to collect, preserve, tell, and listen to the life stories of Minnesotans born from 1901 to 1924[5]

Each of these projects fulfills institutional goals to promote connections to history, preserve historical evidence, and tell the stories of Minnesota's people. Some of these initiatives required adopting new practices at the museum, but the projects were all conceptually grounded in the core values of the institution. Speaking the language of the institutional mission helps staff members and stakeholders understand the value of participatory projects and paves the way for experiments and innovation.

The Unique Educational Value of Participation

For institutions with educational missions, participatory techniques have the particular ability to help visitors develop specific skills related to creativity, collaboration, and innovation. These skills are often referred to as "21st century skills," "innovation skills," or "new media literacies."[6]

Educators and policy-makers define them as the skills necessary for people to be successful, productive citizens in a globally interconnected, multicultural world.

These skills include the ability to:
- Collaborate and interact with people from diverse backgrounds
- Generate creative ideas both alone and with others
- Access, evaluate, and interpret different information sources
- Analyze, adapt, and create media products

---

4   Visit the Placeography wiki at http://www.participatorymuseum.org/ref5-4/

5   Explore *Minnesota's Greatest Generation* at http://www.participatorymuseum.org/ref5-5/

6   There are many definitions of these skills. For complete lists and rubrics, consult: The Partnership for 21st Century Skills (http://www.participatorymuseum.org/ref5-6a/), the New Media Literacies research initiative (http://www.participatorymuseum.org/ref5-6b/), or the Innovation Skills Profile (http://www.participatorymuseum.org/ref5-6c/)

- Be self-directed learners
- Adapt to varied roles, job responsibilities, schedules, and contexts
- Act responsibly with the interests of the larger community in mind

Participatory projects are uniquely suited to help visitors cultivate these skills when they encourage visitors to:

- Create their own stories, objects, or media products
- Adapt and reuse institutional content to create new products and meaning
- Engage in community projects with other visitors from different backgrounds
- Take on responsibilities as volunteers, whether during a single visit or for a longer duration

Some institutions have adopted participatory learning skills as part of their commitment to overall visitor learning. For example, the Ontario Science Centre's *Weston Family Innovation Centre* was specifically designed to help visitors cultivate innovation skills in line with the Canadian government's Innovation Skills Profile. The *Innovation Centre* features participatory activities in which visitors can make their own objects to display and share with others, from low-tech constructions like shoes and found object sculptures to media products like stop-motion videos. In one area called the *Challenge Zone*, visitors work in groups using scrap materials to design potential solutions to real-world problems. These kinds of activities promote creative, collaborative forms of learning that are less available in the more traditional areas of the science center that focus on critical thinking and science content learning.

Participatory learning skills don't just apply to science centers. The Walters Art Museum in Baltimore, MD, has used the Institute for Museum and Library Services *21st Century Skills* report to help plan, fund, and evaluate educational activities with its Youth Advisory Council.[7] For example, in 2009, teenagers developed a publication called *Do's, Don't's, How-To's, Why Not's: A Zine For Teens About Museums And Art*. This co-creative

---

7   Download the IMLS *21st Century Skills* report [PDF] at http://www.participatorymuseum.org/ref5-7/

project showcased an alternative voice at the museum. It also helped the teens achieve target 21st century skills outcomes like critical thinking and problem solving, innovation, creativity, collaboration and communication, visual and media literacy, self-direction, productivity, accountability, leadership and responsibility. By tying the Teen Zine project to participatory learning goals, the Walters Art Museum was able to attract new funding and provide teenagers with desirable, innovative co-creative experiences.

There can be tensions between participatory skill building and content learning, even in institutions familiar with skill-based activities. In the summer of 2006, 2,400 visitors to the Exploratorium in San Francisco built *Nanoscape*, a giant ball-and-stick sculpture meant to represent atoms and molecules on the nanoscale. Visitors enthusiastically volunteered and learned a great deal about how to collaborate on a big project and put tiny pieces together, but they didn't necessarily learn about the nanoscience behind the project. Visitors were just as likely to describe what they were making as a "building" as they were to reference the atoms and tiny particles represented, and evaluators were dismayed at the lack of overall science learning that happened during the project.[8]

The Value of Giving Participants Real Work

When staff members are not able to articulate the unique learning value of participatory activities, it raises questions about the overall value of visitor participation. Learning participatory skills is just one part of the value of participatory activities. Many participatory projects invite visitors to do work that contributes content or research to institutions. These projects provide three kinds of value:

1. *Learning Value*. Visitors learn research or creative skills.
2. *Social Value*. Visitors feel more connected to the institution and more confident of their ability to contribute to the institution (or project).
3. *Work Value*. Visitors produce work that is useful to the institution.

---

8   See Erin Wilson's article, "Building *Nanoscape*," in *Visitor Voices in Museum Exhibitions*, ed. McLean and Pollock (2007): 145-147.

It's important to keep all three of these values in mind when designing participatory experiences. There are many cases where designers, quite appropriately, develop participatory experiences that offer only a small slice of "real" work—possibly too small to really be useful. Or in other cases the work is real but simplified, with more resources required to support participants than would be needed to do the work in-house. When learning is valued as an outcome, these simplifications make sense—they allow visitors to learn new skills while making a small or slow contribution to the institution. If participants' outputs are low or of variable value, a project can still be considered valuable for its learning and social outcomes.

Georgina Goodlander of the Luce Foundation Center at the Smithsonian American Art Museum reflected on this issue with regard to the *Fill the Gap* project, in which visitors selected and advocated for objects to fill vacant spots in the museum's study storage (see page 151). This proved a popular activity, but not one that saved staff any time or effort. Goodlander said,

> To do this staff had to first select a pool of objects for people to choose from. We posted a printed image of the gap, and people could play around with the different artwork choices (on laminated bits of paper) and select their choice. We also asked them to explain or justify their choice. The object with the most votes was then installed in the gap. This was hugely successful, with many people participating and commenting on how much fun it was to "be a curator." BUT it was no longer a real project and actually required quite a bit of work from us to set up—more work than it would be for us to just choose the artwork ourselves.

Goodlander's last sentence reflects an exclusive focus on participation for useful output. *Fill the Gap* is indeed a "real" participatory project, but it is one that provides more social and learning value than productive work. Visitors aren't curators or registrars. They don't have the expertise or the time to hunt through the entire collection for the items that will physically fit into a study storage location. Goodlander's approach—offering visitors a small set of objects from which to choose, and then focusing the activity on picking one and arguing for its inclusion—represents good design, not a fake experience. She appropriately identified the valuable visitor experience as arbitrating among objects and making an argument for a preferred one, and she designed a platform that supported those experiences.

The "true value" of a participatory project is not solely determined by the amount of time and money it takes staff to do the work offered to participants. It also includes the social value of building community relationships and the educational value of providing skill-building experiences for participants.

Consider the experience of cooking with a child. Under no circumstances is it easier or faster to bake a cake with an eight-year-old than to do it yourself. However, including the child builds your relationship with him, empowers him as a maker, and teaches him some basic cooking, scientific, and mathematical concepts. And it produces a cake for everyone to enjoy.

The Strategic Value of Participation

For some institutions participatory techniques aren't restricted to enhancing visitors' experiences. They can also be applied by boards, CEOs, and management teams to increase institutions' strategic value. Participatory projects can change an institution's image in the eyes of local communities, increase involvement in fundraising, and make new partnership opportunities possible. Particularly for institutions that are perceived as irrelevant to community or civic life, actively soliciting engagement and contributions from citizens can make a significant impact on the health and vitality of the organization.

CASE STUDY
USING PARTICIPATION TO REINVIGORATE THE CENTER OF SCIENCE AND INDUSTRY

Consider the story of the Center of Science and Industry (COSI) in Columbus, Ohio. COSI is an interactive science center that used participatory techniques to position itself with stakeholders, funders, and the public as an essential community hub of science and learning activity.

COSI's participatory strategy grew out of crisis. In 2004 voters refused to support a tax levy to support the institution, and the science center cut staff, closed off galleries, and struggled to stay open. In 2005 David Chesebrough came onboard as the new CEO to help turn the institution around. Reflecting on his early days at COSI, Chesebrough said:

> We had to readdress our value proposition and start raising serious money immediately. Historically, COSI had been really focused all on attendance, and everything was skewed in that direction. But I was out there in the community raising millions, and to do that, we had to be putting forward a community-focused value proposition, demonstrating that COSI was a valuable community asset and investment.

How did Chesebrough and his team demonstrate that COSI was a valuable community asset and investment? They positioned the institution as a community "center of science" and embarked on a broad slate of partnerships and projects to establish stronger ties with Columbus's academic research community, businesses, and schools. For example:

- COSI partnered with researchers from The Ohio State University (OSU) to provide visitors with access to scientists and the opportunity to engage in real research. The partners co-created the *Labs in Life* public galleries to give visitors the opportunity to interact with real scientists working on research projects related to physiology. Scientists present educational programs about their work, which is contextualized by exhibits related to their study areas.

- COSI hosted OSU researchers in child development and cognition who conducted research studies with young children and their parents in the *little kidspace®* gallery. This started informally, but it proved so successful that COSI dedicated a room within *little kidspace®* for the purpose of research. OSU's Center for Family Research (housed within COSI) has also used COSI exhibits effectively to assist in improving social dynamics for at-risk families.

- COSI rented 12,000 square feet of gallery space to the local public TV and radio station, WOSU, which began broadcasting and holding public programs at COSI in 2008. WOSU and COSI collaborated to host social media meetups, tech events, and other programs at the science center that brought together technologists, non-profit groups, and digital media enthusiasts. They have also hosted collaborative dialogue programs that invite community

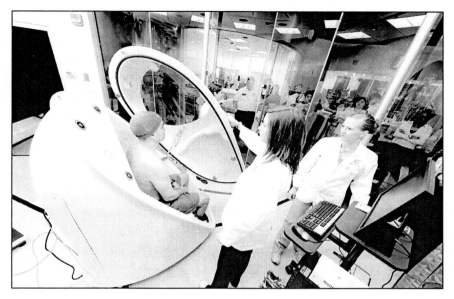

OSU researchers in the *Labs in Life* measure a subject's body fat percentage and lean muscle mass in the "BodPod" while visitors look on.

members to talk with scholars about contemporary issues related to science and religion.

- COSI collaborated with TechColumbus, a science and technology-based incubator for new businesses in town, to develop a new exhibition called *Innovation Showcase*. The exhibition features innovative work and people from local research and design companies and provides a platform for hosting events with the professional tech community.

Beyond these formal research, media, and business partnerships, Chesebrough encouraged COSI staff members at all levels to engage with visitors and Columbus residents directly in new relationships on the Web and at the museum. The science center hired a full-time Director of Community Relations director to support these efforts, and she focused specifically on engaging families and teenagers from communities that did not traditionally use the institution. Chesebrough expressed trust in and support for creative experimentation throughout the institution. Staff members responded by:

- Attending local science and technology meetups to represent COSI's support for technology learning and business growth
- Engaging visitors and members in extensive social media efforts, sharing everything from behind-the-scenes exhibit plans to a director's blog to opportunities for visitors to contribute programming and marketing ideas to the institution
- Incorporating community-created photos and videos into the institutional website
- Offering more science days and special programming for members, schools, and the public
- Introducing a very successful low-cost "family access membership" for families on government support
- Hosting more significant community events, such as the regional planning commission's Sustainability Summit and the launch and conclusion of the Governor's statewide educational conversation
- Working intensively for particular schools and school populations as a site for internships, work experiences, and learning

These activities have been incredibly successful, both in increasing general attendance and expanding the diversity of COSI visitors and participants. From 2004 to 2009 memberships increased from 11,000 to over 18,000, and as of the end of 2009 twenty percent of memberships were of the low-income "family access" type. Family access members renew at the same rates as general members, and their participation has brought COSI's visitor demographics roughly in line with those of the county in which it is situated.

COSI's new connections to community members didn't just motivate visits and memberships; they also brought in a cadre of enthusiastic donors and volunteers. From fiscal years 2004 to 2009 the COSI donor base of people giving $150 or more grew by 24%. People who had never participated with COSI before became connected in meaningful ways. Volunteers have provided everything from social media consulting to iPhone application development to help cleaning and painting the facility. Kelli Nowinsky, Public Relations and Social Media Manager, described one volunteer who connected with COSI early in their social media efforts:

A guy I met through Twitter asked me to meet in person. At first, I was skeptical because I thought he wanted to talk to me about the COSI website. When he expressed he just wanted to talk about ideas he had for COSI, we met for coffee. He pulled out this notebook with all these ideas and asked, "how can I help with the Innovation Showcase?" I was blown away. He did not want anything in return. Here I am sitting with this person who is a young professional without children, someone who would never have engaged with COSI before we got involved in social media. Now we are building a professional relationship and talk all the time about how he can help us in our social media efforts and help us reach out to the tech community.[9]

COSI used collaboration with new partners and energetic engagement with Columbus residents to turn around their position in the city. By 2009 COSI's admission, membership, and donor numbers had all increased, despite an economic downturn. High-level donors maintained and increased their commitments to the institution, and local politicians championed COSI as an essential community resource.

Rather than pursue a single participatory strategy, Chesebrough gave his staff support and encouragement to connect with the community in many different ways. Collectively they changed the value proposition of an institution that just a few years earlier was seen as "past its prime" and increasingly irrelevant to public life. Now the institution is relevant not only to its core family and school audiences but to a much wider audience of technologists, scientists, and young people.

When staff members are grounded in the institutional mission and feel supported by management, they are able to creatively and confidently explore participatory techniques in ways that benefit the institution, visitors, and themselves. The following four chapters provide detailed information about how cultural institutions structure and implement the four types of participatory projects introduced at the beginning of this chapter: contributory,

---

9   Read the February 2009 interview with Nowinsky, Chesebrough, and then-Web manager Kevin Pfefferle at http://www.participatorymuseum.org/ref5-9/

collaborative, co-creative, and hosted. We'll start in Chapter 6 with contributory projects, in which visitors participate by sharing their ideas, objects, or creations with cultural institutions.

CHAPTER 6

VISITORS AS CONTRIBUTORS

THE MOST COMMON WAY visitors participate with cultural institutions is through contribution. Visitors contribute to institutions by helping the staff test ideas or develop new projects. They contribute to each other by sharing their thoughts and creative work in public forums. Visitors contribute:

- Feedback in the form of verbal and written comments during visits and in focus groups
- Personal objects and creative works for crowd-sourced exhibits and collection projects
- Opinions and stories on comment boards, during tours, and in educational programs
- Memories and photographs in reflective spaces on the Web

Why invite visitors to share their stories and objects with the institution? Visitors' contributions personalize and diversify the voices and experiences presented in cultural institutions. They validate visitors' knowledge and abilities, while exposing audiences to content that could not be created by staff alone. When staff members ask visitors to contribute, it signals that the cultural institution is open to and eager for participation.[1]

Contributory projects are often the simplest for institutions to manage and for visitors to engage in as participants. Unlike collaborative and co-creative projects, which often accommodate only a small number of deeply committed and pre-selected participants, contributory activities can be offered to visitors of all types without much setup or participant coaching. These projects can function with minimal staff support; many are self-explanatory and self-maintaining. Contributory projects are also in many cases the only type of participatory experience in which visitors can seamlessly move from functioning as participants to audience and back again. Visitors can write a comment, post it on the wall, and immediately experience the excitement of seeing how they have contributed to the institution.

But contribution isn't just for quick and simple activities. Contributory projects can also offer visitors incredible creative agency: to write their own stories, make their own art, and share their own thoughts. Consider the Denver Community Museum, a small, temporary institution that presented short-term exhibitions sourced solely from visitor-contributed content.[2] The founder/director, Jaime Kopke, posed a monthly "community challenge" for participants to create or bring in objects related to a specified theme. For example, challenge number five, *Bottled Up!* invited people to:

> Fill a bottle with the memories of people and places from your life. Saved material can take any form - messages, objects, smells, sounds, photos - anything that shares your story. Multiple bottles welcome. Please decide if your bottle can be opened by visitors or if it should remain sealed.

The resulting exhibition displayed twenty-nine visitor-contributed exhibits: perfume bottles, pill bottles, wine bottles, and homemade vessels filled with evocative objects and images. Many participants designed their projects to be opened, allowing visitors to unfold secrets, take in smells, or discover hidden treasures. One young contributor was so excited that he

---

1   For an excellent list of the benefits of visitor contribution, consult Kathleen McLean and Wendy Pollock's introduction to *Visitor Voices in Museum Exhibitions*, ed. McLean and Pollock (2007).

2   Learn more about the Denver Community Museum in Jaime Kopke's December 2009 blog post, "Guest Post: the Denver Community Museum" at http://www.participatorymuseum.org/ref6-2/

returned to the museum every few days to rearrange his display of bottled toys and encourage visitors to play with his collection.

In addition to featuring pre-made visitor contributions, Kopke designed a simple interactive tree collage that hung on one gallery wall, holding open bottles with phrases like "First Love" and "Beliefs You Hold Sacred." Visitors could write a memory on a slip of paper and add it to a bottle if desired. Kopke explained: "There was never an exhibit where the visitor simply viewed and read. The shows always included something that you could touch, take...or most importantly leave behind."

The Denver Community Museum was a small institution with no budget or paid staff. By respecting visitors and their ability to contribute, Kopke was able to provide unique audience experiences in which everyone felt like a participant or potential participant.

Visitors to the Denver Community Museum enjoy "bottled up"
exhibits contributed by community members of all ages.

While few traditional institutions could be as completely contribution-driven as the Denver Community Museum, the same principle of respecting visitors and their contributions applies at even the largest institutions. In 2007, the Victoria & Albert Museum partnered with textile artist Sue Lawty to launch the *World Beach Project*, a contributory project with a very simple goal: to produce a global map of pieces of art made with stones on beaches.[3] The *World Beach Project* does not involve visitors coming to the Victoria & Albert Museum. It's a project that requires people to do four things: go to the beach (anywhere in the world), make a piece of art using stones, photograph it, and then send the photos to the museum via the Web.

The *World Beach Project* website showcases beach artworks made by hundreds of participants all over the world. The project succeeds by combining an encouraging tone with respect for visitors' unique contributions.

The *World Beach Project* website centers on a simple map that makes it easy for visitors to quickly browse beach artworks from all over the world.

---

3   This project is still ongoing as of this printing and can be accessed at http://www.participatorymuseum.org/ref6-3/

Friendly, prominent statements on the website like, "it is really easy to join in" and "I want to add my beach project to the map" encourage inspired spectators to contribute their own work. The project values participants' contributions by honoring the beach artworks as part of a commissioned work, accessioning them as collection pieces, and making them easy for visitors to explore.

Sue Lawty described the *World Beach Project* as "a global drawing project; a stone drawing project that would speak about time, place, geology and the base instinct of touch." Lawty encouraged participants to think of themselves as part of a community of artists and a geologically connected ecosystem. The *World Beach Project*, like the Denver Community Museum, did not provide opportunities for trivial participation. These projects respected visitors' creative abilities and provided engaging activities and platforms for their contributions.

Three Approaches to Contributory Projects

There are three basic institutional approaches to contributory projects:
1. *Necessary contribution*, in which the success of the project relies on visitors' active participation
2. *Supplemental contribution*, in which visitors' participation enhances an institutional project
3. *Educational contribution*, in which the act of contributing provides visitors with skills or experiences that are mission-relevant

The Denver Community Museum and the *World Beach Project* are examples of necessary contribution. These projects could not exist without visitors' active participation. In these projects, the goal of contribution is to generate a body of work that is useful and meaningful. Some necessary projects are helpful to staff because contributors generate data or research. Other necessary projects create new content for visitors to explore.

Participants often feel a high level of ownership and pride when their participation is tied to the project's success. This pride doesn't have to be individual; many contributory projects support a sense of shared ownership and community. One observer of the visitor-constructed *Nanoscape* sculptures at the Exploratorium (see page 195) appreciated the participatory approach "because anyone who comes could participate, and it makes people feel like they're a part of things."[4] No one contributor's individuality stood out in the final assemblage of balls and sticks, but the collective power of the group experience made it a powerful participatory display.

When a contributory project relies on visitors' contributions to succeed, it generates both high risk and high institutional investment. If participants don't act as requested, the project can quite publicly fail, and there have been cases of video contests with just a couple of entries, or comment boards with one or two lonely notes. But fear of failure often also motivates staff members to put more thought and commitment into project design, so they can feel confident that visitors' work will meet institutional needs.

For example, consider the experience of the exhibit developers at the Minnesota Historical Society who worked on the *MN150* project. *MN150* is a permanent exhibition of 150 topics that "transformed Minnesota." It opened in 2007 to celebrate the 150th anniversary of the state's founding.

The *MN150* team decided to crowdsource the topics for the exhibition, reasoning that "it didn't make sense" for a small group of developers and curators to decide which were the most important things to the residents of their large and varied state. Once they committed to this process, the team actively sought nominations from diverse residents by reaching out to leaders on Native American reservations, in small towns, and in immigrant communities. When an online call for topics brought in only a few nominations, staff members solicited people in other ways. They managed a booth at the Minnesota State Fair and hawked nomination forms cleverly designed as fans to encourage fairgoers to get out of the heat and contribute a topic. By the end of the nomination period, the staff had 2,760 nominations to sift through—more than enough to generate a high-quality exhibition that reflected the diverse opinions of Minnesotans.

Not every contributory project relies entirely on the participation of visitors. In supplemental contributory projects, the institution feels that

---

4   See Erin Wilson's article, "Building *Nanoscape*," in *Visitor Voices in Museum Exhibitions*, ed. McLean and Pollock (2007): 145-147.

.

The MN150 team encouraged people to contribute nominations to the exhibit at the state fair. The museum enticed people in with costumed historical interpreters, friendly staff, and an air-conditioned building.

visitors' contributions, while not necessary, add a unique and desirable flavor to a project. Comment boards and "make stations" where visitors contribute artistic creations, are common forms of supplemental contribution. In supplemental projects, the goal is typically to incorporate diverse voices, add a dynamic element to a static project, or to create a forum for visitors' thoughts or reactions.

When the London Science Museum displayed a temporary exhibition called *Playing with Science* about the history of science-related toys, the institution invited visitors to bring in their own toys on a few special weekends. Visitors' toys were temporarily accessioned into the collection and displayed in a few vitrines at the end of the exhibition. Contributors were photographed with their favorite toy and wrote short statements about them, such as, "I play with this toy and pretend to be out in space," or "I like making girls do boy parts because I am a tomboy."[5] These visitor contributions personalized the exhibition and helped noncontributing visitors connect to the objects on display by triggering their own toy memories. It also introduced a dynamic element to an otherwise static historical display, thus supporting a light and evolving conversation among visitors, the institution, and the objects themselves.

London Science Museum staff member Frankie Roberto contributed his own toy and story to *Playing with Science*'s participatory element.

Some people participate in supplemental contributory projects because they enjoy the momentary jolt of fame that comes from seeing their creation or comment on display. Others contribute to share a deeply felt sentiment or creative expression they feel driven to add to the evolving body of content. On many comment boards, sprinkled alongside the "John was here!" comments, you can read the impassioned arguments of visitors who loved, hated, or just wanted to discuss the exhibits on display. For example, the Pratt Museum's exhibition *Darkened Waters*, opened in 1989 in reaction to the Exxon Valdez oil spill, featured comment boards and books that quickly filled with debate and discussion among visitors. Visitors often responded to each other's comments or addressed the museum directly, feeling that even asynchronous conversation was valuable and necessary.[6]

If visitors become invested in dialogue about institutional content, it's important for staff members to respond to and take part in the discussion. Supplemental projects suffer when they feel like afterthoughts. When institutions don't need visitors' contributions, the staff may not be as attentive to

---

5   Browse more photos and statements from *Playing with Science* at http://www.participatorymuseum.org/ref6-5/
6   See Mike O'Meara's article, "*Darkened Waters*: Let the People Speak," in *Visitor Voices in Museum Exhibitions*, ed. McLean and Pollock (2007): 95-98.

or respectful of visitors' work. The best supplemental projects value visitors' unique self-expression. Unlike projects of necessity, in which institutions often introduce constraints to ensure consistency of contributions, supplemental projects thrive when visitors are given license—and encouragement—to be creative or share strong reactions.

Finally, there are educational contributory projects initiated by institutions that perceive the act of contribution primarily as a valuable learning experience. I expect these types of projects to increase as more institutions place emphasis on participatory learning skills and new media literacies.[7] Most of these projects aim to teach skill building rather than generate content.

Visitors who enjoy trying and learning new things are particularly drawn to educational contributory projects. Considering their emphasis on hands-on learning and skills attainment, it is not surprising that science centers and children's museums are most aggressively pursuing educational contribution. But participatory skill building can happen in history and art institutions as well. The Magnes Museum, a small Jewish art and history museum in Berkeley, CA, started the *Memory Lab* to invite visitors to contribute their own artifacts and stories to a digital archive of Jewish heritage.[8] While the emphasis is on "making memories," Director of Research and Collections Francesco Spagnolo emphasized the concept that participants learn how to use digital tools to preserve, organize, and care for their own heritage. This contributory project, which is cast as a personal experience, supports skill building and appreciation for the ongoing work of the institution.

The Magnes *Memory Lab* succeeds because it invites visitors to explore their own family heritage, not to generally learn the skills of digitization. People are more receptive to learning new skills when they can clearly see how those skills are relevant to their own lives.

---

7   See page 193 for more information about participatory learning skills and new media literacies.

8   Learn more about the *Memory Lab* at http://www.participatorymuseum.org/ref6-8/

Asking for Contributions

Contributory projects thrive on simplicity and specificity. Generic requests for visitors to "share their story" or "draw a picture" are not as successful as those that ask visitors to contribute particular items under clear constraints. When institutions offer visitors compelling and understandable opportunities to contribute, many will enthusiastically participate.

From the participant perspective, a good contributory project:

- Provides specific, clear opportunities for visitors to express themselves
- Scaffolds the contributory experience to make participation accessible regardless of prior knowledge
- Respects visitors' time and abilities
- Clearly demonstrates how visitors' contributions will be displayed, stored, or used

CASE STUDY
HOW THE VICTORIA & ALBERT MUSEUM ASKS FOR CONTRIBUTIONS

The Victoria & Albert Museum's *World Beach Project* has a particularly clear "ask" for visitors' contributions. The website gives visitors a brief overview of the process:

> The project happens in two stages, in two locations: first, at a beach where you choose the stones and make your pattern, recording the work-in-progress with some photographs along the way. Then later, at a computer, you can upload the photographs to this website to complete the project.[9]

This short statement is followed by step-by-step instructions that cover everything from finding a good beach to picking stones to sizing your photographs for submission to the site. The instructions provide encouragement for stymied artists, suggesting ways participants might sort or group beach stones to help plan their artworks. The instructions also assist less

---

9   Read the complete instructions for the *World Beach Project* at http://www. participatorymuseum.org/ref6-9/

technologically-savvy participants by providing specific information about how to transfer photographs from camera to computer.

In the final submission process, each contributor is required to submit her name, the location of the beach, the year of the creation, a photo of the finished artwork, and a brief statement about how the work was made. Contributors can also optionally upload two additional photos: one of the beach and one of the work in process. Because the instructions explain everything that will be asked of participants, people are not surprised by any of the requirements.

The Victoria & Albert Museum provides contributors with legal terms and conditions explaining that they grant the museum a non-exclusive license to their contributed content. For savvy people—especially artists—such statements are necessary to make ownership rights clear and to promote mutual trust between participants and institutions.

The *World Beach Project* only solicits information that is needed to participate. Participants don't have to register or share personal information to contribute. Email addresses are only used to correspond with contributors about their submissions. The staff respects the fact that people want to participate in the *World Beach Project* specifically and do not want to share their information.

When designing a contributory platform, it's easy to be tempted by the desire to ask for more information or content from visitors. These requests come at a significant cost. Every additional question the institution asks puts a burden on participants. Keep it as simple as possible, and respect the fact that not everyone wants to share their contact information with their contribution.

Modeling Desired Participant Behavior

The easiest way to make contributors' roles clear and appealing to would-be participants is through modeling. When a visitor sees a handwritten comment on a board, she understands that she too can put up her own comment. She takes cues from the length and tone of other comments. The models on display influence both her behavior and the likeliness of her participation.

Good modeling is not as simple as displaying representative contributions. The diversity, quality, and recency of the models, as well as the extent to which the platform appears "full" or "empty," significantly impact whether newcomers participate.

Modeling Diversity

The greater the diversity of contributions in terms of content, style, and participant demographics, the more likely an approaching visitor will feel invited to contribute. Many museums with video comment kiosks provide only professionally-produced model content featuring celebrities or content experts. This is not conducive to participation. These models may successfully attract spectators who want to watch videos of celebrities sharing their views, but the production values and the type of people displayed send a clear message to visitors that their own opinions are secondary to expert or celebrity perspectives.

If you want to encourage people of all ages and backgrounds to share their thoughts, you should deliberately reflect and celebrate contributions from a range of people. For example, you might mentally "slot in" a model contribution from a child, in another language, or expressing a divergent viewpoint. Remember that not everyone shares the same definition of "high-value contributions." Over-curating model content to feature only the contributions that please staff members will not motivate visitors with dissenting perspectives to participate.

In platforms like comment boards, where every new contribution is added to the model content, it's important that visitors feel like the board is physically open to their contributions. No one wants to act alone and be under the microscope, but participants also don't want to be lost in the crowd. We all intuitively know the difference between a conversation that feels open to our opinion and one that is already overcrowded with voices. Platforms that have explicit "slots" for content on display, such as comment boards or video kiosks that display grids of videos, can overwhelm and discourage continued participation when the slots appear to be all filled up.

One easy way to solve this problem is to give each new participant a clear position of privilege in the map of contributions to date. In exhibits that invite visitors to add their own personal memories via sticky notes onto maps or timelines, this position of privilege is self-evident. The newest layer of notes lies on top of older ones, giving participants confidence that their story will be read, at least for a while. In digital environments, or ones in which staff is in control of the presentation of contributions and model content, it is useful to provide visitors with an obvious "pathway" or slot for their contribution, so they can see where it will go visually and physically.

In physical environments in which visitors can display their own objects or creations, you may want to set a general rule for how much space will be kept open for new contributions. At the shoe-making station in the Ontario Science Centre's *Weston Family Innovation Centre*, the staff has settled on keeping one-third of the showcase space open for new visitors' handmade shoes at any time. Generally, a platform that has one-fourth to one-half of the space open provides a feeling of welcome and encourages visitors to share.

If you want to organize contributions using criteria other than recency, you can create explicit areas of a comment board or contributory platform for different kinds of participants. Labels with text like, "Where does your opinion fit into the conversation?" or "Place your creation near others that you feel are connected" can help visitors feel that there is a place for their unique participation, no matter how crowded the field.

Modeling Quality

While diverse models encourage visitors to participate, high-quality models inspire them to take contribution seriously. The most powerful model content is diverse, high-quality, and ideally, produced by "visitors like you." Superlative visitor creations are exciting and attractive, and people can identify with them more easily than they do with celebrity or staff-created content. Visitor-created models demonstrate how non-professionals can use the materials offered to create something of value.

High-quality model contributions can inspire and energize less-skilled visitors without making them feel inferior. For example, I am lousy at drawing, but like most people, I'm attracted to well-rendered sketches. When I see poorly-made drawings in a visitor-created exhibit, I'm never motivated to pick up crayons and start coloring. But when I see something really unusual, surprising, or appealing, I'm more likely to be intrigued by the experience overall, which may inspire me to participate as well.

Superlative visitor contributions make good models because they were created using the same tools available to every visitor. When institutions choose to feature celebrity or staff-produced model content, those contributions should be created using the same materials available to visitors. If visitors will write in crayon, staff members and celebrities should write in crayon.

This principle extends to entire exhibitions. In the best contributory displays, the tools available for contribution match those used by designers and curators elsewhere in the exhibition, so that visitors' contributions blend attractively into the overall display. This promotes respect and value for visitors' contributions. It also helps visitors naturally extend their emotional and intellectual experience of the exhibition to their contributions. Asking visitors to jump from a dimly lit, immersive display to a sterile comment book can be jarring. Inviting them to continue their experience in a well-designed contributory platform helps smooth the transition from spectating to participating.

This technique was very powerfully employed in a 2007 exhibition of Jack Kerouac's original typewritten manuscript for the beat masterpiece *On The Road* at the Lowell National Historical Park in Massachusetts. Alongside the iconic manuscript, the exhibition featured a talkback area in which visitors could contribute their own reflections. Instead of offering sticky notes and pens, the staff provided a desk with a typewriter (amazingly, donated by the Kerouac family) and an evocative quote from Kerouac: "Never say a commonplace thing." Visitors responded enthusiastically, generating over 12,000 messages at the typewriter in six months. Several wrote letters directly to Jack. Some wrote poems. The integrated design of the space invited visitors to extend their personal, emotional experience with the artifact to the comment station. This produced a powerful collection of visitor-contributed comments that enhanced the exhibition overall.

The visitor comment station for *On the Road* allowed visitors to stay in the emotional space of the exhibition while sharing their thoughts.

```
Dear Jack

        Thanks for being there that rainy night
in Greenwich Village at my basement apartment on Charles
Street next to the fire station with Howard Hart
and Bill Godden and Stella inher fur coat to keep
out the November cold and bringing the bottle of
scotch which I shouldn't have been drinking but
did anyway even though I was nine months pregnant
and about to deliver on the day of another John's
assassination in Texas abad the terrible days that
followed for the whole country and for me for
leaving one I loved the most but was too scared
to bring home just yet.

    Corinne
```

One of many touching visitor comments shared at the *On the Road* comment station.

Novice Modeling

Sometimes, the best way to encourage people to participate in new and potentially unfamiliar settings is by providing novice models. When staff members or professionals present themselves as amateurs, it helps people build confidence in their own abilities.

One of the best examples of novice modeling is the National Public Radio show *RadioLab*. *RadioLab* features two hosts, Robert Krulwich and Jad Abumrad, who explore broad science topics like "time" and "emergence" from a variety of scientific perspectives.[10] Commenting on their process at an event in 2008, Krulwich said:

> We don't know really what we're talking about at the beginning—we find out along the way. And we make that very clear. So we never pretend to anybody that we're scholars 'cause we're not. And we do represent ourselves as novices, which is a good thing. It is a good thing in a couple of ways. First, it means we can say, "what?!" honestly. And the second thing, "can you explain that again?" honestly. And then the third thing is, it allows us to challenge these people as though we were ordinary, curious folks.

---

10 Listen to *RadioLab* online at http://www.participatorymuseum.org/ref6-10/

We're trying to model a kind of conversation with important people, powerful people, but particularly knowledgeable people, where we say—YOU can go up to a person with a lot of knowledge and ask him "why?," ask him "how does he know that?" Tell him, "stop!" Ask him why he keeps going. And get away with it. And that's important.[11]

RadioLab isn't just a show where the hosts have conversations with scientists. It's a show where the hosts model a way for amateurs to have conversations with scientists and engage with experts rather than deferring to or ignoring them.

To do this kind of modeling, Krulwich and Abumrad actively portray themselves as novices. They make themselves sound naive so listeners don't have to feel that way. By humbling themselves, they create a powerful learning experience that promotes accessibility and audience participation.

Modeling Dynamic Participation

Visitors notice whether model content on contributory platforms is up-to-date. Recency of model content signals how much the staff cares for and tends to contributions. Imagine an exhibit that invites visitors to whisper a secret into a phone and then listen to secrets left by other visitors. If the secrets they hear are several months old, visitors may have less confidence that their own secrets will soon be made available to others.

When institutions promise, explicitly or implicitly, that visitors' contributions will be on display, visitors want immediate feedback that tells them when and where their work will appear. Whenever possible, they want it to be on display right away. If participants choose to contribute to a community discussion, they don't want to put their comments into a queue for processing—they want to see their words join the conversation immediately. Automatic display confirms that they contributed successfully, validates them as participants, and guarantees their ability to share their work with others.

Some projects motivate participation by displaying current contributions in compelling and desirable ways. For example, the United States Holocaust Memorial Museum's *From Memory to Action* exhibition features

---

11 Hear Krulwich and Abumrad talk about their approach in this segment (the quoted section occurs at minute 15): http://www.participatorymuseum.org/ref6-11/

a pledge station and display wall. Visitors can sit at the stations and scrawl their promises of actions they will take "to meet the challenge of genocide" on special digital paper with pens. The paper is perforated with one section about the exhibit and web presence, which visitors keep, and another section for the promise, which visitors leave at the museum.[12] Visitors drop their signed pledges into clear plexiglass cases that are beautifully lit. The paper "remembers" the location of pen marks on the pledge section, so visitors' handwritten promises are immediately, magically projected on a digital projection wall in front of the pledge kiosks.

Visitors make their handwritten pledges facing a projection screen which magically "rewrites" their promises digitally when they drop them in the slots.

This pledge wall is a beautiful demonstration of how the aesthetic and functional design of contributory platforms can be mutually beneficial. Why require visitors to hand-write their pledges rather than typing them in on a keyboard? It certainly would be easier for the museum to digitize and

12 In the original design, visitors were instructed to take their pledges home, but the staff quickly discovered visitors wanted to leave them at the museum. They adjusted the cards' design so visitors take home a bookmark and leave their pledges.

project visitors' entries if they were typed, and it wouldn't require so much expensive digital paper. But asking visitors to hand write a response and sign a pledge ritualizes and personalizes the experience. Adding their slips of paper to the physical, growing, and highly visible archive makes visitors part of a larger community of participants. Taking home the bookmarks reinforces their connection to the contributory act and inspires further learning.

The case full of signatures and the digital animations of the handwritten pledges provide a captivating and enticing spectator experience. The case full of visitors' signatures is reminiscent of the haunting pile of Holocaust prisoners' shoes in the permanent exhibition, providing a hopeful contrast to that devastating set of artifacts. The combination of the physical accumulation of the paper stubs and the changing, handwritten digital projection reflects the power of collective action and the importance of individual commitments.

There are far more visitors who spectate in *From Memory to Action* than actively contribute. Curator Bridget Conley-Zilkic noted that in its first eight months, about 10% of people who visited chose to make a pledge in the exhibit. However, about 25% of visitors picked up a pledge card. As Conley-Zilkic reflected, "There's an awkward moment where people want to think about it—they aren't necessarily immediately ready to share a pledge on such a serious topic." For these visitors, picking up a card is a way to express interest in the experience. Not everyone needs to contribute on the spot to participate.

Curating Contributions

There's a big difference between selecting a few contributions to model participation for visitors and putting all contributed content on display. When visitors' creations are the basis for exhibits, comment boards, or media pieces, the questions of whether and how to curate contributions comes up.

Curation is a design tool that sculpts the spectator experience of contributory projects. If institutions intend to curate visitors' contributions, the staff should have clear reasons and criteria for doing so.

There are two basic reasons to curate visitor-generated content:

1. To remove content that staff members perceive as inappropriate or offensive
2. To create a product that presents a focused set of contributions, such as an exhibition or a book

Removing Inappropriate Content

One of the most frequent concerns staff members voice about contributory platforms is the fear that visitors will create content that reflects poorly on the institution, either because it is hateful or inaccurate. Fundamentally, this concern is about loss of control. When staff members don't know what to expect from visitors, it's easy to imagine the worst. When staff members trust visitors' abilities to contribute, visitors most often respond by behaving respectfully.

On the Web, people who make offensive comments or terrorize other users are called "griefers." Fortunately, few museums suffer from participants who use contributory platforms to actively attack other visitors. Cultural institutions already have developed ways to deal with griefers of a different type—the ones who vandalize exhibits and disrupt other visitors' experiences. When it comes to people who want to vandalize the community spirit, the same techniques—proactive staff, model users, and encouragement of positive and respectful behavior—can prevail.

There are also many ways to block curse words in particular. One of the most creative of these was created by the interactive firm Ideum for a comment station in *The American Image* exhibition at the University of New Mexico museum. Ideum automatically replaced all curse words contributed with cute words like "love" and "puppies," which made inappropriate comments look silly, not offensive.

There are also intentional design decisions that can persuade visitors to behave well. At the Ontario Science Centre, the original version of the *Question of the Day* exhibit featured two digital kiosks on which visitors could make comments that were immediately displayed on overhead monitors. The staff quickly observed that young visitors used the kiosks to send off-color messages to each other rather than to comment on the exhibit question. They removed one kiosk, which ended the offensive conversations, but the remaining kiosk continued to draw off-topic content related to body parts. Then staff moved the kiosk to a more central location in front of the entrance to the women's bathroom. Once it was placed in the proximity of more visitors (and moms in particular!) the bad behavior on the kiosk dropped significantly.

Staff members need not be the only ones who moderate contributions. Visitors can also be involved as participants in identifying inappropriate comments. Many online contributory platforms allow users to "flag" content that is inappropriate. A "flagging" function allows visitors to express their concerns, and it lets staff focus on reviewing the content that is most likely to cause controversy rather than checking every item.

Some staff members are less concerned about curse words than inaccuracies. If a visitor writes a comment in a science museum about evolution being a myth, or misidentifies a Degas as a Van Gogh in an art institution, other visitors may be exposed to content that the institution does not officially sanction. This is not a new problem; it happens in cultural institutions all the time. Tour guides, parents, and friends give each other misinformation as they wander through galleries. The concern is that when this misinformation is presented in contributory exhibits, visitors may be confused about its source and incorrectly attribute it to the institution.

There are several ways to address inaccurate visitor contributions. Staff may choose to actively curate all submissions, checking them for accuracy before allowing them to be displayed. Other institutions take a "yes, then no" approach, moderating contributions after they have been posted or shared.

There are also design strategies that address the issue of accuracy by clearly identifying which contributions are produced by staff or institutional partners and which created by visitors. For example, on the Museum of Life and Science's *Dinosaur Trail* website, comments are color-coded by whether the author is a paleontologist (orange) or a visitor (yellow).[13] This subtle but easy-to-understand difference helps spectators evaluate the content presented.

---

13 Visit the *Dinosaur Trail* site at http://www.participatorymuseum.org/ref6-13/

Curating an Audience-Facing Display

There is a fundamental difference between contributory projects that promote community dialogue and sharing and those that produce a highly-curated product. If your goal is to validate visitors' voices or encourage conversation, the curatorial touch should be as light as possible. Spend your design time focused on how to display the contributions so they work well together rather than trying to select the best for display. The *Signtific* game is a good example of this (see page 111). Instead of developing a curatorial or monitoring system, the designers developed ways to explicitly require players to respond to each other and build arguments together, so that every new voice had a place in the growing conversation.

Even inconsequential visitor comments are important to include when your goal is visitor empowerment. When people write on each other's walls on Facebook, they are often just saying hi and asserting their affinity for the other person or institution. The same is true of the people who write, "Great museum!" in comment books in the lobby. These statements are a form of self-identification, and while they may not make very compelling content for audiences, the act of expression in a public forum is important to those who contribute their thoughts, however banal.

If your goal is to create a refined product for spectators, however, you may opt for a more stringent set of curatorial criteria. Phrases like "contribute to the exhibition" as opposed to "join the conversation" can help signal to visitors that their work may be curated.

There are many contributory art projects that only display a small percentage of contributions received. Frank Warren of *PostSecret* (see page 141) receives over a thousand postcards weekly from contributors all over the world, but he curates the postcards very tightly for public consumption, sharing only twenty per week on the *PostSecret* blog. *PostSecret* could easily devolve into a display of prurient, grotesque, and exaggerated secrets, but Warren's curatorial touch only puts cards with authentic, creative, diverse voices on display. Other artist-run projects, like the Museum of Broken Relationships,[14] which collects and displays objects and stories related to

---

14 Visit the virtual Museum of Broken Relationships at http://www.participatory-museum.org/ref6-14/

breakups, employ an invisible curatorial hand to maintain a consistently high-quality spectator experience, even as it receives unsolicited and unexhibited submissions on a continual basis.

Curation policies don't just impact how the staff uses visitors' contributions. They also serve as an important opportunity to demonstrate respect for participants and provide feedback. When visitors create something and then drop it into a box for staff review, they entrust their work into institutional hands. Visitors want to know how contributions will be evaluated, how long it might take, and whether they will be notified if their contribution is included in some audience-facing display. This doesn't need to be exhaustive. A sign that says, "Staff check these videos every week and select three to five to be shown on the monitor outside. We are always looking for the most creative, imaginative contributions to share" will help visitors understand the overall structure and criteria for contribution.

Very few institutions get back in touch with visitors to let them know that their content is being featured, but doing so makes good business sense. It's a personal, compelling reason for the institution to contact people who may not have visited since making their contribution, and it's likely to bring them back to show off their creation to friends and family.

Audience Response to Contributory Projects

There is a wide audience for contributory projects in cultural institutions. Participants, spectating visitors, stakeholders, and researchers may all use contributed content. When thinking about how to design platforms for contribution, it's important to consider not only what will motivate people to share their thoughts, but what will entice, inspire, and educate visitors who choose to read or observe others' contributions.

Making Contributory Projects Beautiful

One of the challenges of integrating contributory platforms into cultural institutions is the perception that comment boards and visitors' artistic creations are not as attractive to spectators as institutionally-designed material. However, it is possible to make even the most mundane visitor

contributions beautiful. In the late 2000s, manipulatable data visualizations became ubiquitous on the Web, and people enjoyed fiddling with
everything from data on baby names to crime statistics to the frequency of
different phrases in internet dating profiles. From an audience perspective,
playing with visitor-submitted data can be a comparably fun and attractive
way to explore vast sets of contributions while learning important analytical
skills. Even the simplest visualizations, such as the LED readouts above the
turnstiles in the Ontario Science Centre's *Facing Mars* exhibition (see page 87),
let audiences learn from, enjoy, and engage with visitor-submitted content.

CASE STUDY
MAKING VISITORS' COMMENTS AN ART EXPERIENCE AT THE RIJKSMUSEUM

In 2008, the Rijksmuseum in Amsterdam hosted Damien Hirst's piece
For the Love of God, and with it, a visitor feedback system that provided a
striking and attractive spectator experience. The artwork was a platinum-
cast skull encrusted with over 1100 carats of diamonds: a hype machine in
death's clothing. It was mounted in a dark room, surrounded by guards and
beautifully lit. Nearby, visitors who wished to provide feedback on the skull
could record videos in small private booths.

The *For the Love of God* website transformed the contributed videos
into an interactive online experience.[15] The videos were automatically chro-
makeyed (i.e., masked or cropped) so that each contributor appeared as
a floating head, which created an eerie, appealing visual consistency. The
heads drifted around an image of the skull, and spectators could sort the
videos by country of origin, gender, age, and some key concepts (love it,
hate it; think it's art, think it's hype). Click on a head and the video made by
that visitor popped up. After it played, it faded back into the floating mass.

The *For the Love of God* website was couched in the same self-con-
scious buzz that permeated the exhibit. A welcome screen informed visitors:
"Never before has a work of art provoked as much dialogue as Damien

---

15 Visit the *For the Love of God* website at http://www.participatorymuseum.org/
ref6-15/

For the Love of God
Damien Hirst

Online, visitors are part of the art. Their response
videos swirl around the skull, promoting the idea that
controversy and discourse surround the artwork.

Hirst's *For the Love of God*." Whether true or not, the website implied that
the contributed videos were a justification for this claim, a demonstration of
the rich dialogue supposedly surrounding the skull. In this way, the visitors'
videos were integrated into the larger artwork as part of the skull experience.
The audience experience of the feedback contributions was immersive, intriguing, and haunting—like that of the skull itself.

Visitor Reactions to Contributory Exhibitions

How does the experience of exploring visitor-contributed content dif-
fer from consuming standard exhibits or museum content? Just as a diverse
blend of contributions can motivate people to participate in contributory
platforms, audience members may feel more personally included in the
institution when they see "people like them" represented.

In 2006, the Art Gallery of Ontario (AGO) developed *In Your Face*,
an exhibition of 4x6 inch visitor-submitted self-portraits. Over 10,000 self-
portraits were submitted, and the portraits hung in an overwhelming and
beautiful mosaic, blanketing gallery walls from floor to ceiling. Toronto is

a very culturally diverse city, and Gillian McIntyre, coordinator of adult programs, noted, "The portraits noticeably reflected far more diversity of all sorts than is usually seen on AGO walls." She shared:

> On several occasions children in visiting school groups from West and East Indian communities enthusiastically pointed out people who looked like them on the walls, literally saying, "That looks like me" or "That's me with dreadlocks."[16]

The exhibition was incredibly popular, attracting significant crowds and media attention. Visitors saw themselves in the exhibition in a way they never had before. Another visitor even took the experience from personal to collective, commenting: "it's depicting the soul of a society."

MN150 had a similar effect on visitors, despite being a much more conservative installation. Unlike *In Your Face*, *MN150* was not a direct installation of visitor contributions. Instead, it displayed the distillation of 2,760 visitor nominations into 150 fairly consistently designed exhibits about the history of Minnesota. Each exhibit label included the text contributed in the original nomination form, as well as a photo of the nominee. But otherwise, with a few exceptions in cases where nominees provided objects, the exhibits were designed and produced by staff in a traditional process.

In summative evaluation of *MN150*, very few visitors commented on the user-generated process that created *MN150* but many saw the exhibition as both personally relevant and diverse in content. When asked "What do you think the museum is trying to show in the overall Minnesota 150 exhibit?" visitors frequently talked about the diversity of people and events represented in the exhibit, as well as their own state pride. They also related individual exhibits readily to their personal experiences, sharing memories from well-known places and events. One person commented that "her husband would love the exhibit. She would tell him, 'Here is your life.'"

Anecdotally, staff noted that the video talkback station in *MN150* was particularly active. The kiosk invited visitors to make their case for other topics that should have been included in the exhibition. The display of visitors' voices throughout the exhibition likely made audience members feel that

---

16 Read Gillian McIntyre's article, "*In Your Face*: The People's Portrait Project," in *Visitor Voices in Museum Exhibitions*, ed. McLean and Pollock (2007): 122-127.

there was more room for their own opinions than in a typical exhibition. The Art Gallery of Ontario's *In Your Face* exhibition had a similar effect, with many more visitors than was typical visiting a station where they could make their own portraits inspired by those on display. Exhibitions of visitor-contributed content can inspire new visitors to participate in related but not identical ways to the original contributors.

Alongside the exhibition of visitor-contributed portraits in *In Your Face*, there were popular activity stations where visitors could look in the mirror and draw their own self-portraits.

Does the Contributory Process Matter to Audiences?

Summative evaluation revealed that *MN150* visitors didn't express strong reaction to the contributory process that had created the exhibition. Yet their comments about the exhibition, and the social and participatory nature of the visitor experience, reflected the impact of that process. Visitors saw the exhibition as diverse, multi-vocal, and personal—all outcomes of an approach that celebrated the unique voices of 150 Minnesotans from across the state.

Audiences focus on the outcome, not the process that created it. Contributory processes generate outcomes that are different from those generated by staff alone. The staff could not have drawn the portraits shown in *In Your Face* that helped underrepresented visitors "see themselves" in the Art Gallery of Ontario. They could not have written the raw letters and poems that emerged from the typewriter in *On the Road*. They could not have created the silly labels that made the *Odditoreum* (see page 161) playful and fun.

Visitors are not only looking for the most authoritative information on a given topic. Visitor-contributed content is often more personal, more authentic, more spontaneous, more diverse, and more relevant to visitors' own experiences than institutionally designed labels and displays. Visitor-contributed content does not produce intrinsically better audience experiences than institutional-designed content. But many cultural professionals are unwilling or unable to produce content that is as raw, personal, and direct as that which visitors create. Hopefully, working with and seeing the positive impact of visitor-contributed content will give more institutions the confidence to transform the way they create and display content.

———

Contribution is a powerful model for institutions that have a specific time and place for visitors' participation. Some institutions want to engage with visitors in more extensive partnerships, inviting participants to help co-design new exhibits or projects. If you are looking for ways for people to contribute to your institution in more varied ways over a longer timeframe, you may want to consider shifting to a collaborative approach. That's the topic of Chapter 7, which describes the why and how of collaborating with visitors.

CHAPTER 7

COLLABORATING WITH VISITORS

IF CONTRIBUTORY PROJECTS ARE casual flings between participants and in-stitutions, collaborative projects are committed relationships. Collaborative projects are institutionally-driven partnerships in which staff members work with community partners to develop new programs, exhibitions, or offerings. Participants may be chosen for specific knowledge or skills, association with cultural groups of interest, age, or representation of the intended audience for the outputs of the project. In some collaborations, participants serve as advisors or consultants. Other times, participants are more like employees, working alongside staff to design and implement projects.

There are four main reasons that institutions engage in collaborative projects:

1. To consult with experts or community representatives to ensure the accuracy and authenticity of new exhibitions, programs, or publications
2. To test and develop new programs in partnership with intended users to improve the likelihood of their success

3. To provide educational opportunities for participants to design, create, and produce their own content or research
4. To help visitors feel like partners and co-owners of the content and programs of the institution

Effective collaborations are built on mutual trust, shared understanding of the project's goals, and clear designation of participant roles. Because collaborations often involve prolonged formal relationships between institutions and participants, institutions typically give participants more guidance than is provided in contributory projects. Staff members explicitly and exhaustively explain what roles the participants will be given, what expectations the institution has for the collaboration and its outcomes, and what benefits (education, publicity, remuneration) participants will receive. Many collaboration projects involve an application process, which serves as a vetting both for would-be participants' motivation and their ability to perform adequately in the collaboration. Participants often make long-term commitments to the project in exchange for institutionally-provided training.

In some collaborative projects, participants are paid or receive school credit for their efforts. Particularly when institutions collaborate with communities with whom there is no previous relationship, providing reasonable compensation helps participants appreciate the value of their work. Payment or school credit also makes participation accessible to people who would like to get involved but cannot afford to volunteer their time. For the most part, these external motivators work well. They professionalize the relationship between participants and staff members, encouraging all partners to do their best and be accountable to each other.

The litmus test of whether a collaborative project truly engages participants is not if they sign up; it's what happens after the project is over. A strong collaboration encourages participants to connect more deeply with the institution and to assign value to the project beyond the compensation offered. Participants may become involved in other areas of the institution or deepen their involvement with the collaborative project over time. A successful collaboration creates new relationships and opportunities that may span over many years.

ENGAGING TEENAGERS AS COLLABORATORS AT THE NATIONAL BUILDING MUSEUM

Investigating Where We Live is a longstanding, successful collaborative museum project. It is an annual four-week program at the National Building Museum in Washington D.C. in which thirty local teenagers work with museum staff to create a temporary exhibition of photographs and creative writing about a D.C. neighborhood. The program is coordinated and directed by education staff members, who select the neighborhood for the season, provide photography and writing instruction, and shepherd the project to completion. Teens join the group via an application process, and they are expected to participate in all twelve sessions of the program. They are not paid, but they do receive a digital camera and school community service credit for participating.[1]

In format, *Investigating Where We Live* functions like many museum camp programs. What distinguishes it as a collaboration is the fact that the teens create a partially self-directed exhibit for public display. The institution provides the framework—the space, the sessions, the instruction—but the content, design, and implementation of the exhibition are left up to the teenage participants.

Investigating Where We Live has been offered at the National Building Museum since 1996. Many graduates of the program come back in subsequent years to serve as volunteers, interns, or program staff. The blend of participants of different ages and levels of expertise and authority blurs the line between staff and student, and the result is a program that feels truly collaborative.

Consider James Brown, who first participated in the program as a student in 2007. In 2008 and 2009, he returned as a "teen assistant" to staff member Andrew Costanzo. On the 2009 project blog, Costanzo reflected:

> Of course, I have to mention my fantastic Teen Assistant, James Brown. This is the second time I have had the honor of working with James in

---

1   For a list of the goals of *Investigating Where We Live* and its benefits to participants, see: http://www.participatorymuseum.org/ref7-1/

Investigating Where We Live participants perform every step of exhibit development, from conducting initial interviews (top) to final installation of their artwork and writing (bottom).

this capacity. He dubbed us "Batman and Batman," because "there was no sidekick this time."[2]

Costanzo and Brown had become true partners in the program. This doesn't mean the teens completely control the program or can unilaterally take it in a new direction. As Brown wrote during the first week of the 2009 session:

> I must admit the training and first day the students arrived seemed like the rewind of a bad 80s movie. It was all the same as the year before and the year before that. Every exercise and activity mirrored those I had already done up until the point when people started to participate.[3]

Brown saw the program's structure as repetitive but valuable. He went on in his post to describe all the skills he'd honed over his time in the program and to call the program "the most fulfilling summer activity I have ever done." For Brown, *Investigating Where We Live* was an evolving educational experience, community project, and leadership opportunity.

Two Kinds of Collaboration

Collaborative projects fall into two broad categories:

- *Consultative* projects, in which institutions engage experts or community representatives to provide advice and guidance to staff members as they develop new exhibitions, programs, or publications
- *Co-development* projects, in which staff members work together with participants to produce new exhibitions and programs

The basic difference between consultative and co-development projects is the extent to which participants are involved in the implementation of collaborative ideas. Consultative participants help guide projects' development. Co-developers help create them.

---

2   Read Andrew Costanzo's August 2009 blog post, "Final Thoughts: U Street," at http://www.participatorymuseum.org/ref7-2/

3   Read James Brown's July 2009 blog post, "Groundhog Day," at http://www.participatorymuseum.org/ref7-3/

Consultative Collaboration

Cultural institutions have a long history of consultative collaboration via focus groups and formal advisory boards. Sometimes consultative collaboration is informal and short-term, as when visitors help test out interactive exhibit prototypes. Other projects require collaborators to engage with institutions on an ongoing basis, providing feedback, advice, and guidance as staff members develop new programs. Many larger museums recruit consultative advisory councils that are representative of special interest groups, such as teachers, teens, or members of local ethnic and racial communities.

In the business world, product design firms like IDEO and Adaptive Path have greatly enhanced the public profile of consultative collaboration, which they call user- or human-centered design. User-centered design advocates argue that consulting with intended users throughout the design process will result in products that are more appealing and understandable in the market. These firms don't engage users as collaborators to give users an educational experience; they do it to improve their firms' products.

In the book *The Design of Everyday Things* (1988), cognitive scientist Donald Norman demonstrated major differences between the ways that designers and users understand objects. Designers working on their own frequently make choices that make sense to them but confound intended users. When designers consult with end-users throughout the design process, they are more likely to develop something that works for everyone.

This is as true for cultural experiences as it is for consumer products. Take a tour of a cultural institution with a new visitor or watch someone try to access information about program offerings on a museum website, and you will quickly spot several differences between how professionals and patrons perceive and use institutional services. Particularly when designing wayfinding systems and informational material, consulting with a range of visitors helps generate outputs that work for diverse audiences.

User-centered design has emerged as a particularly useful technique when moving into new markets. As companies "go global," designers are being asked to design products for intended users from countries and backgrounds they may have never encountered. In foreign environments, consulting with intended end-users is often the most effective way to understand how a product will work or what other products might appeal to the new market.

Developing programs for nontraditional audiences is quite similar to developing products for foreign markets, and consultative groups can help cultural institutions find useful ways to connect with their communities. For example, Chapter 8 features the story of the co-created *Days of the Dead* program at the Oakland Museum of California (see page 275). This incredibly successful program was suggested by the museum's Latino Advisory Council, a consultative group that helps the museum connect to the particular needs and interests of Oakland's Latino community.

Consultative collaborations suffer when participants' roles are too vague. There's no point in having an advisory board or focus group if there aren't specific projects or problems for participants to address. Consulting collaborators should be given the power—and the responsibility—to provide actionable feedback and input to institutions. Clear goals and specific projects help both participants and staff members feel that collaboration is valuable.

Co-Development Collaboration

When participants function as contractors or employees, collaborations transition from consultation to co-development. *Investigating Where We Live* is a co-development project. Staff set up the project framework, then worked closely and collaboratively with their teenage partners to produce an exhibition.

Co-developed collaborative projects often involve weeks or months of engagement with participants. These projects require significant staff time, planning, and coordination. They typically involve small groups of participants working with dedicated employees.

Some co-development projects are focused more on participants' learning and skill building than on the final products they create. Because of their educational benefits, collaborative projects are frequently embedded into internship programs, teen employment programs, and learning programs for communities underrepresented at the institution.

While the learning value of collaborations may be high, focusing solely on providing participants with educational experiences is risky. Co-development collaborations often struggle when they only impact ten or twenty participants. When cultural institutions are under financial pressure, resource-intensive projects that serve such a small number of visitors are often the first programs eliminated.

Collaborations are most valuable for staff, participants, and visitors when they serve broader audiences. From the institutional perspective, it's easier to justify spending time and money on a small group project if participants produce something that can be experienced and enjoyed by many people. For participants, creating something for a wide audience makes their work more meaningful and connects them more closely to the institution. For audiences, the products of collaboration can present voices, experiences, and design choices that are different from the institutional norm.

Structuring Collaboration

There is no single methodology for coordinating collaborations. Finding the right process requires a clear institutional goal, as well as respect and understanding for participants' needs and abilities. Collaborative processes are highly culturally dependent. What works for one partnership might not work for another.

When developing a collaborative project, the best place to start is with a design challenge. A design challenge is an institutionally-developed question that helps guide decisions about who to engage as participants, how to structure project development, and what the collaboration will produce. Here are three sample design challenges:

- How can we tell the story of children's immigrant experiences in a way that is authentic, respectful, and compelling to immigrant and non-immigrant audiences?
- How can we give people with disabilities the tools to document and share their experiences in a way that supports their creative development, is sensitive to their privacy, and accessible to other audiences?

- How can we guide amateurs to successfully develop interactive exhibits for our music and technology gallery?

The more specific the design challenge, the easier it is to develop a process that is likely to address it. When collaborating with schoolchildren, staff members should develop a process that fits students' curricula and schedules. When collaborating with participants spread across geographic distances, Web-based communication tools may be the best way to facilitate participation. Defining the structure and scope of participation can help cultural institutions develop collaborative processes that work well for all involved.

CASE STUDY

COMMUNITY-BASED VIDEO AT THE VIETNAM MUSEUM OF ETHNOLOGY

In 2006, the Vietnam Museum of Ethnology (VME) opened an exhibition called *Subsidized Times (Thoi Bao Cap)* about everyday life in Hanoi under the strict post-war rationing policy from 1975-1986. The honest, critical exhibition included many contributed voices and artifacts, as well as documentary videos that were produced with Hanoi residents about their experiences. The video production was a collaboration among VME staff, Hanoi residents, and an outside community exhibit and video consultant, Wendy Erd. The design challenge was simple: "How can we share the stories of real people in Hanoi during the subsidized times so younger people can connect to and understand the challenges of their elders?"

To address this challenge, Erd worked with the VME staff to develop a collaborative process by which Hanoi residents would share their stories and work collectively to edit two documentary films. This was their process:

- VME staff members formed two three-person teams. Each team included two curator/researchers and a videographer. Each team would produce one documentary with a group of outside participants.
- VME staff teams selected outside participants to work with. One team solicited contributors from a previous project about the Old

Streets of Hanoi, who helped them find elders in the Old Streets who were interested in participating. The other team sought participants through friends and family. In general, staff reached out to people who had been adults during the subsidized period, though they also included a few younger people for a different perspective.

- VME staff teams met with the participants to introduce the seed idea and discuss the overall project concept and structure. The participants offered their feedback, shared stories of objects they connected to the time, and helped staff members identify "story-tellers" for video interviews. All participants were paid for working with the VME. This was a necessity for many participants, who could not afford to take time off work uncompensated.

- VME staff teams went to participants' homes and interviewed them individually. Rather than ask a fixed set of questions, Erd trained the staff to engage in responsive dialogue with participants, listening carefully and addressing what was important to them. Interviewers started with a few basic questions, including: "How did you overcome the difficulties of the Bao Cap?" and "What did you dream of at that time?" VME staff then followed the threads of individuals' stories and memories.

- VME staff members reviewed the tapes, looking for common themes and clips where participants spoke powerfully from the heart. They organized these clips into about two hours of content for each documentary.

- Participants came to the museum for a two-day session to provide feedback on the rough cuts and the structure of the films. The VME staff teams facilitated the discussion, asking participants to help determine the title of the film, where it should start, what themes were most important, and which clips should be included in each theme. Participants used logbooks to record notes and share them with the group. The VME staff members encouraged and listened to the participants but did not express their own perspectives.

Throughout the two days, staff would reassemble the clips and play them back, prompting more participant discussion.

- Based on the participant consultations, VME staff members assembled draft films that were reviewed by the participants for authenticity and final comments. The completed documentaries were presented in the exhibition. Staff members and participants also made presentations about the process and their experiences to the broader community of museum professionals, anthropologists, documentarians, filmmakers, and journalists.

A lighter moment during the two-day
collaborative editing session at the VME.

The two films and the overall exhibition had an incredible impact on participants, VME staff members, and wider audiences. Participants felt ownership and pride in their work. One participant, Ong Hoe, commented:

> Wendy and VME staff gave us people responsibility. We listened to others. Also the staff knew how to listen. I felt very open and proud. When people talk and others listen the speaker feels very confident. This encouraged me a lot. From Wendy and others wanting to listen led to the success of this project. The progress was reasonable from beginning to end and will give a strong feeling to the audience. Now I'm tired. But I feel useful to work in collaboration with VME.

Another participant, Ba Tho, simply said: "This film is the true story and true people of that time. I told the truth."

The VME's collaborative process respected participants' abilities and needs, treated them as meaningful partners, and generated a powerful result for all involved. After one of the two-day collaborative sessions, a VME staff researcher, Pham Minh Phuc, commented:

> We all live in the same community. All of us have listened to each other's ideas. The younger people could talk and be listened to also. This is the first time we have tried this way of making a video. It is strange for us too, so please forgive our learning moments. We want and appreciate your help and collaboration.

Visitors responded enthusiastically to *Subsidized Times* and its authentic stories of the era. The exhibition attracted huge crowds and was extended by six months to accommodate the demand. The authentic, personal stories of privation, hardship, and creativity helped young Vietnamese visitors understand their parents' and grandparents' experiences. A university student, Dinh Thi Dinh, commented: "I just cannot believe that a bar of Camay soap was a luxury at that time. This exhibit has inspired me to study harder to deserve the sacrifices of my parents and my grandparents."[4] Another young man who met Wendy Erd in Hanoi effused about the exhibition, showing her photos of it on his mobile phone and explaining that it helped him understand his mother and her experiences.

The collaboration with community members inspired the staff to continue integrating participatory approaches into subsequent community video projects. Starting in 2007, VME staff members and Erd collaborated across cultures with indigenous teams in Yunnan China in a multi-year project to produce six community-based videos. Their continued work in this direction is based on their responsive facilitation skills developed during the *Subsidized Times* exhibition.

---

4   Read the January 2007 Associated Press review of *Subsidized Times* at http://www.participatorymuseum.org/ref7-4/

Staff Roles in Collaborative Projects

There are four basic staff roles in collaborations. Staff members may function as:

1. Project directors, who manage the collaboration and keep the project on track
2. Community managers, who work closely with participants and advocate for their needs
3. Instructors, who provide training for participants
4. Client representatives, who represent institutional interests and requirements

While these roles are often blended, collaborations work best when they remain distinct. Participants have specific relationships with each of these staff roles, and these different relationships help make collaborations feel fair and equitable.

It's particularly important to separate out instructors and client representatives from other project staff. Instructors and client representatives are authority figures, not partners. It's much easier for project directors and community managers to collaborate with participants if they do not also have to play these authority roles.

Weaving instruction into a collaborative project requires careful planning. Collaboration requires equitable partnerships, whereas instruction often reinforces unbalanced power relationships between instructors and students. When you separate the instructors from the project directors, participants can connect with the project directors as partners or facilitators, not as teachers. Bringing in guest instructors, or employing past participants as instructors, can also help participants learn without feeling inferior.

It's also helpful to spread instruction throughout the duration the program, especially when working with young people. When the beginning of a program is focused on instruction, it sets up an expectation that the program will be "business as usual" with adults as authoritative leaders and students as followers. Front-loading instruction can also cause exhaustion in later weeks, especially in intensive programs where participants spend several

244 PART 2: PARTICIPATION IN PRACTICE

hours each day working on the project. Instructional sessions later in the program can serve as diverting breaks that help participants shift focus and gather additional skills to enhance their projects.

In optimal cases, most instruction is dictated by the needs of participants themselves. When working with participants on projects where they are designing exhibits, objects, or activities that draw on their own creative abilities, I use the initial stages to expose them to as many unique examples as possible rather than prescriptively offer a small set of tools or paths to take. I ask participants to write proposals for the type of projects they would like to create. Then, as a project director, I try to locate instructors or advisors who can specifically help participants learn how to use the tools they need to create their project, working from their particular levels of expertise. Particularly when working with young people and technology, it's extremely unlikely that everyone has the same knowledge of and interest in different tools. Students improve their skills more quickly and significantly when they receive specific instruction at their level with tools they consider essential to their work.

The client representative is the other staff role that is essential to keep separate. This client rep should be someone who has institutional authority over the direction of the project and may be different from the staff member who works with participants on an ongoing basis. The client rep helps hold participants accountable by giving specific feedback that may be more honest (and potentially uncomfortable) than that offered by other project staff. She also provides external motivation for participants and is the ultimate audience for their work.

Client representatives need not even be real. The 826 writing tutoring centers across the US provide popular field trip programs in storytelling and bookmaking. Student groups work together to write a book with the support of three staff volunteers—a writer, an illustrator, and a typist. These volunteers are community managers, and they work for a fictitious, tyrannical publisher who represents the client. The publisher is never seen but is portrayed by a staff member hidden in a closet who angrily pounds on the door and shouts out orders and demands. The beleaguered volunteers ask the students to help them write a book to satisfy the cranky publisher. This sets up an emotional bond between students and staff and helps the students stay motivated. The invisible publisher is a fictitious device used to create criteria, add drama, and help focus participants on what would otherwise be an overwhelmingly open creative project.

CASE STUDY
A COMPLICATED COLLABORATION AT THE TECH MUSEUM

Clear design challenges and delineated staff roles aren't just "nice to haves." Consider *The Tech Virtual Test Zone*, a project that demonstrates the essential value of clear structure and roles in collaborations.

The Tech Virtual Test Zone was a project of The Tech Museum in San Jose, CA. In the fall of 2007, I joined the staff of The Tech Museum to help lead an initiative called *The Tech Virtual*, of which the *Test Zone* was the pilot project. The design challenge was clear: to crowdsource exhibit development by collaborating with participants all over the world via online platforms. By inviting creative amateurs and content experts to share and prototype many exhibit ideas in parallel, we believed we could design and deploy more diverse, high-quality exhibits faster than had previously been possible. The goals for the pilot were to launch the collaborative platform, recruit participants, and build a prototype gallery in The Tech Museum based on their ideas within seven months.

The original plan for the *Test Zone* included all four staff roles. I was the project director, leading the collaborative exhibit development and fabrication of the real-world exhibits. Volunteers would serve as community managers, helping participants develop and prototype their exhibit ideas virtually. Tech Museum engineers and designers would serve as guest instructors, providing virtual workshops about interactive exhibit design. A curator would be hired to serve as the client representative, setting the criteria for what would be included and excluded from the final exhibition.

We set up a collaborative workshop in the virtual three-dimensional world of Second Life. Rather than overwhelm participants with a completely open-ended environment, I produced exhibit design templates and interactive walk-through tutorials to help participants learn the basics of exhibit design and structure their ideas in a viable direction. I trained other staff members in the basics of Second Life design tools so that they would be able to guide and assist participants. We set up a roster of virtual classes in exhibit design, marketed the opportunity throughout Second Life and to a broad audience of creative professionals, and quickly began collaborating with new partners.

Because Second Life is a social environment, users can talk to and work with each other in real time. We quickly discovered that interpersonal interaction, not tutorials or templates, was the key to motivating participants and encouraging them to develop their skills. We offered Second Life-based exhibit design classes twice a week, which blended virtual design skills with exhibit thinking. For invested participants, we hosted a weekly exhibit designers' meeting to discuss participants' projects, new developments in the *Test Zone* project overall, and community concerns. While these meetings only attracted a small percentage of the community (about 10-15 people per week, compared to about 100 in the workshop at any time), these participants tended to be the most motivated folks who often informally volunteered their time to greet new community members and help out wherever they could.

The use of Second Life as an exhibit development platform helped level the playing field between staff and participants. This may seem paradoxical, since Second Life is a complicated software platform. But many of *The Tech Virtual* participants were much more proficient in the Second Life environment than the museum staff. Second Life was a place where my authority as a museum exhibit designer came down a notch and we all became equal individuals bringing different design skills to the table. As participant Richard Milewski, commented,

> Second Life is an abstract enough environment that the somewhat intimidating prospect of attempting to collaborate with an institution such as The Tech was made to appear possible. *"After all, it's not real! It's just a cartoon on my computer screen and I could always just turn it off."* (Not really... but I told myself that more than once).[5]

5   Read Richard Milewski's entire comment on my June 2008 blog post, "Community Exhibit Development: Lessons Learned from The Tech Virtual," at http://www.participatorymuseum.org/ref7-5/

Participants frequently got together to brainstorm and build ideas
together in the virtual exhibit workshop in Second Life.

Later, when several of the virtual participants came to the opening
of the real world exhibition, we offered them a tour of the fabrication shop
where their exhibits were made. While a few people were enthusiastic,
several were strikingly overwhelmed and uncomfortable in the shop space.
It became immediately apparent to me that these were not people who
would have ever engaged with us as exhibit developers had it required them
coming to the actual museum or the staff design area. By meeting them on
"their own turf" in Second Life, we tipped the scales in favor of a positive
collaboration.

As the collaboration proceeded, three challenged arose. First, our staff
infrastructure collapsed. The Tech Museum never hired the curator who was
to serve as the client representative of the *Test Zone*. Senior executives also
decided it was a waste of time for engineers and designers to spend work
time as guest instructors in the virtual workshop and forbid their participation. That left me and several volunteers to manage the entire exhibition
project. I was frequently torn between my responsibilities as the de facto
client representative—to select the best exhibit ideas for creation—and my
role as the community manager—to support and cheer on participants. It

was impossible to be both the partner who helped participants learn and the authority figure who told them that their exhibit wasn't good enough to win. So I hid behind an imaginary panel of judges, invoking them when I needed to tell participants that "the judges didn't understand this part of your project," or, "the judges don't believe this would be feasible in the real world to fabricate." Using this device, it was possible to keep encouraging the participants throughout the process as their partner, not their evaluator.

The second challenge that arose was that the museum's leadership shifted the design challenge itself, making frequent changes to the budget, schedule, gallery location, and desired outcomes for the project. I scrambled to adjust the project accordingly, which was not always to the benefit of participants. While it's easy to say, "this is an experiment," it's difficult to build trusting relationships with people who are adversely affected by the changes that every experimental project undergoes. When we changed something, it wasn't an abstract project change. We were impacting real people's work. Fortunately, because we maintained honest and open communication with participants, most were willing to weather the changes and stick with the project. Much like the staff in the 826 tutoring program (see page 244), who use an imaginary authoritative publisher to establish rapport with students, I shared my own challenges and frustrations with the *Test Zone* participants, which helped us bond and deal with the chaotic process.

The third challenge that plagued the *Test Zone* collaboration was the fact that the entire project was a contest with cash prizes. At first, we thought a contest was a useful way to promote and accelerate the project. We offered a $5,000 award for each exhibit design that was translated to real life. Doing so helped us raise awareness very quickly. This was useful given the short time frame for completing the project. This cash prize also helped participants focus on producing finished prototypes. People didn't visit the virtual workshop to muse about exhibits; they came to build exhibits on a tight deadline for submission to the contest.

However, the contest prevented us from fostering meaningful collaboration among participants. People were unsure whether they should go it alone to try to win the whole prize or team up with others. We had several community discussions about how the competition discouraged collaboration. I fielded bizarre but understandable questions about whether participants should try to get involved with as many exhibits as possible to optimize chances of winning or produce only solo projects to maximize potential reward. The money sent a contradictory signal to all our talk about community.

The contest not only caused problems for collaboration among participants in the *Test Zone;* it also created ethical challenges for the staff. The staff found it challenging to align a clear, fair contest structure with the goal of developing seven interactive exhibits in seven months. In the beginning of the project, the museum director spoke about "copying" exhibits from Second Life to real life. The theory was that we would hold a contest with staged judging, and at each judging point, we would select fully completed virtual exhibits to "copy" to the real museum.

Our fabrication team quickly realized that this was unrealistic, both technically and conceptually. In general, we chose winning exhibits based on what seemed engaging, educational, and relevant to the exhibition theme. But we also chose based on practicalities of space and time and our professional instinct for what would succeed. In the case of an exhibit called *Musical Chairs,* our internal team of engineers was able to quickly identify the concept as a winner from a simple one-paragraph description of the concept. While Leanne Garvie, the participant who contributed that concept, did build a working virtual prototype in Second Life, it bore little similarity to the real-world version we designed in parallel at The Tech Museum. In the end, we gave $5,000 awards to each exhibit that was built in real life, but we also gave lesser prizes ($500 and $1,000) for outstanding virtual-only projects to acknowledge participants who contributed excellent work in good faith without winning.

We continued to include participants in the exhibition development after the virtual contest was over; however, at that point the staff asserted the upper hand in the collaborative relationship. The collaboration became easier for staff members when we moved to the fabrication phase because the staff knew how the fabrication process worked and where we could and couldn't integrate input from participants themselves. In cases where participants were local, they often visited to check on our progress and even

Jon Brouchoud (in background of bottom image) designed a
virtual music exhibit (top), which was translated into the popular
"Wall of Musical Buttons" exhibit in real life (bottom).

helped put their exhibits together. For those who were hundreds or thousands of miles away, I shared our real-world progress in virtual meetings, photos, calls, and emails.

Wherever possible, we asked participants to create or select content for exhibit artwork, audio, and video. All final exhibits featured a didactic label about the core educational content as well as a second label about the virtual designer and the collaborative process. Three exhibits featured original art and music by the virtual designers, and three relied heavily on the technical expertise of the virtual designers. The participants enabled our engineering and fabrication team to go beyond our in-house capabilities to tackle some exhibit components and content elements that we could not have produced in that short a timeframe.

A year later, many winning participants reflected effusively on their experience with the *Test Zone*. Several described how the project gave them pride in their work and opened up new cross-disciplinary opportunities. Jon Brouchoud, a Wisconsin-based architect who designed an exhibit on harmonics, commented:

> The Tech Virtual offered an opportunity to think outside of my own profession, and venture into other fields of interest (music) beyond just architectural practice - something I've always wanted to explore, but never had the chance. Additionally, the emphasis on cross-disciplinary collaboration opened doors to working with other team members who were each able to contribute their own unique knowledge and skill-set toward making an otherwise impossible dream become a reality.

Another participant, UK-based artist Pete Wardle, reflected:

> Having our work installed at the Tech gave me confidence to enter my work as submissions to other institutions. Since the exhibit at the Tech I've continued to build projects in Second Life and have recently returned from giving a talk at University of Nevada, Reno as part of their Prospectives09 conference (which I wouldn't have dreamed of prior to working with the Tech).

Overall, the *Test Zone* collaboration was an exciting yet frustrating one for staff and participants alike. In some ways, the chaotic nature of the project made us good collaborators because everyone was dependent on each other to complete the project in such a short time frame. However, the chaos did not foster a sustaining community of amateur exhibit developers.

There was no way for participants to rely on each other. Instead, they had to rely on me, the project director, as the source of changing information and criteria for success. This created an unhealthy community that revolved around one person who was forced to function as the community manager, project director, and client representative. After the *Test Zone* opened in real life, I ended my involvement with The Tech Museum. Unfortunately, the community did not survive after my departure. While *The Tech Virtual Test Zone* succeeded in producing a gallery of interactive exhibits designed with amateur collaborators worldwide, it did not lay the groundwork for an ongoing collaborative exhibit development process as The Tech hoped.

Is it possible to make this kind of collaboration work? Absolutely. Had we maintained distinct staff roles, pursued a consistent design challenge, and eliminated the contest, *The Tech Virtual* could have become a sustaining, viable approach to collaborative exhibit development. Here are a few techniques I learned from this project and have applied to subsequent collaborative initiatives:

- Find activities for participants that are meaningful and useful both for them and for the institution. The staff found participants' exhibit concepts incredibly diverse and useful, but their virtual prototypes rarely helped the exhibition design move forward. We could have prevented a lot of frustration for both staff members and participants if we had understood sooner what kinds of contributions would be most valuable.
- Let participants use the tools that they know, not just the ones the staff develops for them. It was a stroke of luck that we chose to use a software platform in which participants were more expert than staff. Their expertise made the collaboration more equitable by placing an unfamiliar activity in a comfortable context. Particularly when working with technology, supporting participants who use the tools they know or are interested in is more successful than training them to learn only your system.
- Don't rely solely on words to communicate with participants. Another surprise of Second Life was the benefit of working in an

environment that encouraged people to build virtual prototypes of their ideas. When you build something, it serves as a launch point for discussion about what's missing and where to go next. It allows people who aren't verbal to share their creative abilities, and it can make collaboration across language barriers possible.

- A strong collaboration requires both structure and mutual trust. *The Tech Virtual* participants worked incredibly hard to meet the shifting demands of the institution. While participants were able to deal with a certain amount of flux, every change caused new confusion, frustration, and fears to pop up. Everyone felt most confident and positive when we were working together towards a clear and well-defined goal.

Collaborating on Research Projects

For some cultural institutions, it is easier to involve visitors as collaborators on research projects than on creative projects like exhibition or program development. While collaborative exhibition projects support creative skill building and story sharing, research collaborations support other skills like visual literacy, critical thinking, and analysis of diverse information sources. Creative collaborations are often personally focused, with participants reflecting on and sharing their own personal knowledge and experience. Research collaborations, on the other hand, are institutionally focused, with participants working with and adding to institutional knowledge. When well-designed, research collaborations help participants feel more connected to and invested in the institution as a whole.

In collaborative research projects, participants typically collect data, analyze it, and interpret results alongside institutional partners. Staff members design research collaborations to support participant learning and engagement while at the same time generating high-quality research. In the best collaborative projects these goals are coincident, but it's not always easy to construct a research project that exposes participants to a diversity of skills and experiences while maintaining consistent results.

CASE STUDY
CONDUCTING RESEARCH WITH VISITORS AT THE UNITED STATES HOLOCAUST MEMORIAL MUSEUM

In early 2008, the United States Holocaust Memorial Museum launched a pilot collaborative research project called *Children of the Lodz Ghetto*.[6] The project started with a single artifact: a school album from the Lodz Ghetto, signed by more than 13,000 children in 1941. The research project is a "worldwide volunteer effort" to reconstruct the experiences of those children during the Holocaust. Using a subset of the online research databases used by professional Holocaust researchers, participants try to find out what happened to individuals in the album by running a variety of searches on different spellings of names of children across many geographic locations, concentration camps, and government registries. The database queries are sorted into timeframes (ghetto, labor camps, concentration camps, liberation) so that users can progressively add information about individuals' location and status throughout the 1940s. Eventually, the goal is to have a record of each child's story, starting from those 13,000 signatures from 1941.

For the institution, the *Children of the Lodz Ghetto* research project provides valuable information about the children in the album. As the project website says, "Now the museum needs your help." This help comes at an incredible (but acceptable) cost. Staff members vet every entry in the research project. In the first year of the pilot, one-third of user-contributed submissions were validated as accurate or potentially accurate. The rest were invalid. However, despite the fact that staff researchers could have done this research more quickly and accurately on their own, the learning and social value of the project was deemed high enough to make the project worthwhile from an institutional perspective. Staff researchers engaged in ongoing discussion with participants and helped them learn how to be researchers themselves. As project director David Klevan put it:

> I hesitate to refer to any data as "bad" because each time a learner submits "bad" data, they receive feedback that about the submitted data

---

6   The *Children of the Lodz Ghetto* project is still in progress as of this printing and can be accessed at http://www.participatorymuseum.org/ref7-6/

that hopefully helps them to learn more about the history and become a better researcher.

In the first 18 months of the pilot, the museum engaged approximately 150 university students and teachers as participants and evaluated their experience both for usability and impact. The educational experience for pilot participants in terms of research skill-building and content learning was very high. Additionally, performing research themselves increased the participants' emotional engagement and perspective on the Holocaust. Many commented that they now had tangible, specific people and incidents to connect to the horror of the time.

One of the most popular design features of the pilot research portal was the emphasis on collaborative research. The portal was set up to encourage users to help each other, review each other's work, and work together to trace the paths of individual children. Participants noted how much they enjoyed and learned from reviewing each other's research and receiving feedback from staff members and other participants alike. In an evaluation, one participant commented:

> Having their help made this project less stressful and made it feel like we were working as a team. Much of the time, our peers allowed our research to continue without any dead ends. When we were stuck, it was comforting to know that the United States Holocaust Museum and our peers had our backs.

Museum staff members are continuing to adjust the project as time goes on, and once it is open to the public (expected mid-2010), they hope to encourage a community of self-motivated, more skilled researchers to sustain the project on their own. The staff vetting is the unscalable part of this project, and if the project gets flooded with bad data, it may not be able to grow easily. But Klevan believes that the research can improve in quality and the community can effectively self-police entries if participants stay involved and the institution can find ways to reward them for improving their research skills. Because the project was built to support and integrate peer review and active collaboration on individual research efforts, it has the potential to get better the more people use it.

Collaborating with Casual Visitors

What if, in the course of a normal visit, visitors could collaborate with the cultural institution to co-create new knowledge about exhibits and programs on display? Integrating collaboration into visitor experiences makes participation available to anyone, anytime. Because on-the-floor experiences are explicitly audience-facing, these collaborative projects tend to be designed with both spectators and participants in mind. Contributory platforms often promote a virtuous cycle in which participants are enticed out of passive spectating into action and then model that experience for others. On-the-floor collaborative platforms can have the same effect. These kinds of collaborative projects can be fruitful for visitors and institutions alike, as long as they can be sustainably managed as they evolve over time.

On the Web, Wikipedia is a good example of this kind of evolving, "live" collaborative platform. At any time, non-contributing users can access and use the content presented while authors and editors continue to improve it. The collaborative workspace is a click away from the audience-facing content—close enough to observe and join in on the process, but separate enough to keep the spectator experience coherent and attractive. The ideal collaborative cultural experience is comparable: appealing to visitors, with a thin and permeable division between spectating and actively collaborating.

Collaborating on Internal Processes

Sometimes bringing collaboration onto the floor is as easy as bringing your process out into the open. When the Ontario Science Centre was developing the *Weston Family Innovation Centre*, they went through an extensive and prolonged prototyping phase. They developed a technique called Rapid Idea Generation (RIG) in which staff teams would physically build ideas for exhibits, programs, and strategic initiatives out of junk in a few hours. The RIG started as an internal process. The team would occasionally show off the final prototypes on the floor in casual consultation with visitors about the ideas. Eventually, the staff began to integrate visitors into their RIG teams, and eventually, hold public RIGs on the museum floor in public space. The RIGs were highly collaborative, bringing together executives, designers, front-line staff, shop staff, and visitors to design things in an open-ended, team-based format. By bringing the development process onto the floor, staff members became more comfortable with one of the core ideas behind the *Weston Family Innovation Centre*: the concept that visitors would be encouraged to design and create things all the time. This also allowed staff members to share their work with visitors in a format that was structured, creative, and highly enjoyable.

CASE STUDY

REAL-TIME VISITOR COLLABORATION AT THE UNIVERSITY OF WASHINGTON

Imagine designing a gallery with the goal of inviting casual visitors to collaborate with each other. What would it look like? In 2009, when working as an adjunct professor at the University of Washington, I challenged a group of graduate students to design an exhibition that would get strangers talking to each other. They produced an exhibition in the student center called *Advice: Give It, Get It, Flip It, F**k It* that invited visitors to collaborate with each other to give and receive advice. *Advice* was only open for one weekend, but during that time, we observed and measured many ways that visitors to the University of Washington student center collaborated with each other and with staff members to produce a large volume of interpersonal content.[7]

Advice offered four main experiences—two facilitated, two unfacilitated. The facilitated experiences were an advice booth, at which visitors could receive real-time advice from other people (both visitors and staff),[8] and a button-making station, where a staff member helped visitors create buttons featuring personalized adages. The two unfacilitated experiences involved visitors writing their own pieces of advice on sticky notes and walls and answering each other's questions asynchronously.

While many of the activities offered were contributory, *Advice* can be characterized as collaborative because the contributions steered the content

---

7   For more details and an evaluation report on *Advice*, visit http://www.partici-patorymuseum.org/ref7-7/

8   See page 104 for more detail on the advice booth (and a picture).

of the entire exhibition. Visitors didn't hand in their contributions to be pro-
cessed and then presented. Instead, visitors worked with staff members to
add new content, reorganize it, and prioritize what was meaningful to them.

At any time, there were two staff members in *Advice*. The staff members were not there to guide the experience, but to give visitors a friendly,
encouraging introduction to the participatory elements of the exhibition.
For example, at the button-making station, staff members played a simple
Madlibs-style game with visitors to create a new, often silly piece of advice.[9]
Staff would ask visitors for two words and then work them into a traditional
piece of advice, yielding buttons that read, "A frog in the hand is worth
two in the pickle" or "Don't count your monkeys before they bicycle." The
facilitators collaborated with visitors, talking with them, listening to them,
and playing with them.

While the facilitated experiences pulled many spectators out of their
solitude and into participation, the unfacilitated sticky note walls were the
places where visitor-to-visitor collaboration really thrived. The setup was
simple: the staff came up with a
few seed questions, like "How
do you heal a broken heart?,"
and put them up on signs behind glass. Then, they offered
sticky notes in different sizes
and colors, as well as pens and
markers, for people to write
responses. The engagement
with the sticky note walls was
very high. Random passers-by
got hooked and spent twenty
minutes carefully reading each
note, writing responses, creating chains of conversation,
and spinning off questions and

In general, visitors to *Advice* wrote
questions on large sticky notes and used
smaller ones to give advice to each other.

---

9   Madlibs is a game in which players write silly stories by filling new words into
blanks in a pre-existing narrative.

pieces of advice. The sticky notes hooked maintenance staff, students, athletes, men, and women—it spanned the range of people passing through.

There were 230 responses to the nine staff-created seed questions, and in a more free-form area, visitors submitted 28 of their own questions, which yielded 147 responses. Some of the advice was incredibly specific; for example, one person wrote a note that asked, "Should a 17 year old who is going to college in the fall have a curfew this summer?" That note received nine follow-ups, including a response from another parent in the same situation. Some visitors stood and copied pieces of advice (especially classes to take and books to read) carefully into personal notebooks.

It might seem surprising that people would take the time to write questions on sticky notes when there was no guarantee that someone would respond and very low likelihood that a response would come in real-time. Collaboration was not guaranteed, especially in a low traffic hallway in an odd area of the UW student center. But the impulse to participate was high and the threshold for doing so was very low. The sticky notes and pens were right there. The whole exhibit modeled the potential for someone to respond to your query, and as it grew, the sense that you would be responded to and validated grew as well. We saw many people come back again and again to look at the sticky notes, point out new developments, laugh, and add new ideas to the wall.

While the sticky note walls were the most popular, *Advice* offered many ways to talk back: the notes, a bathroom wall, a comment book, a call-in voicemail box, and various online interfaces. Each of these interfaces took pressure off the others as a visitor participation outlet, and the overall result was a coherent, diverse mix of on-topic visitor contributions. My favorite example of this was the "bathroom wall" component, in which visitors could scrawl with marker on what appeared to be a bathroom stall door. At first, it wasn't apparent why this was necessary. If visitors could write on sticky notes anywhere in the exhibit, why did they also need a bathroom wall?

But the bathroom wall turned out to be a brilliant exhibit element. It was a release valve that let people write crude things and draw silly pictures. The bathroom wall was "anything goes" by design. While the content on it was not as directed and compelling as that on the sticky notes, it served a valuable purpose as a relief valve. There was not a single off-topic or inappropriate submission on the sticky note walls. They were totally focused on the questions and answers at hand. I think the bathroom wall made this possible by being an alternative for those who wanted to be a little less focused and just have fun with markers.

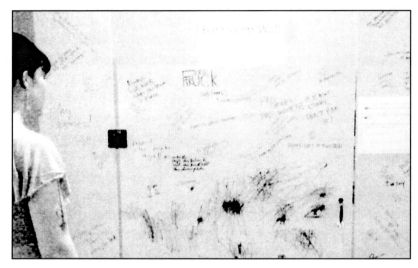

The "bathroom wall" gave visitors a place to screw around and let off creative steam. They clearly understood that the bathroom wall and the sticky note walls were for two very different kinds of participation.

By designing a collaborative platform into the exhibition, the *Advice* staff members were able to reduce their ongoing management role to organizing the sticky notes in appealing ways and highlighting visitor content they perceived as particularly compelling. While this was a small experimental project, it is a model for institutions that wish to pursue collaborative floor experiences that are highly distributed, available and appealing to visitors, and low impact from a resources perspective.

Audience Response to Collaborative Projects

Like audiences for contributory projects, visitors to collaboratively-produced exhibitions or programs may not be aware of or particularly interested in the unique design process that generated their experience. While the labels in *The Tech Virtual Test Zone* that explained the collaborative process were interesting to some adult visitors, most people focused on using the interactive exhibits as they would elsewhere in The Tech Museum. In the case of the *Test Zone*, the collaborative process was explicitly developed to produce exhibits comparable to those in the rest of the institution, so this outcome is not surprising.

When collaborative processes produce outcomes that are different from the norm, however, the impact is often quite significant. Like contributory projects, collaborative projects can incorporate new voices that can make exhibitions and programs feel more authentic, personal, and relevant. For example, many young visitors to the Vietnam Museum of Ethnology's *Subsidized Times* exhibition said it helped them connect personally with the elders in their own families who had lived through the period of privation. Collaborating participants are also more likely to take ownership of the projects they work on and to share their enthusiasm about the exhibitions with their friends and neighbors, potentially bringing new visitors to the institution.

When visitors are invited to actively collaborate in the context of their own visit, as in exhibitions like *Advice* or *Top 40* (see page 106), they frequently demonstrate high levels of social engagement and repeat visitation. *Top 40*, the Worcester Museum exhibition that ranked paintings based on visitor votes, drew record numbers of repeat visitors, many of whom who came back weekly to see how community actions impacted and altered the relative rankings of the paintings. Similarly, because the content in the *Advice* exhibition kept growing as more people added sticky notes to the walls, many visitors came back to see what questions had been answered and what new questions were open for their input. Even the *Click!* exhibition at the Brooklyn Museum (see page 115), which showcased a collaborative process but did not provide new opportunities for participation, generated a high rate of repeat visitation and discussion among visitors who explored and debated the photographs that collaborators had selected for inclusion in the show.

Finally, collaborative processes affect the ways that staff members at cultural institutions perceive visitors and community members. When staff members see visitors as partners instead of consumers, they start treating people differently both in the design of projects and in casual interactions. Asking, "What do you think?" shifts from being a throwaway question to a sincere request. Staff members who work on collaborative projects frequently gain new skills in facilitation and responsive dialogue. These new skills and attitudes change the way that staff members ask visitors questions, manage educational programs, and conceptualize new exhibits. All of this helps foster a sense of ownership and inclusion in the institution.

When staff members form collaborative relationships with community members, they often gain new respect for participants' abilities, interests, and desires. At some institutions, this can lead to projects that are initiated and conceptualized not only *for* participants but also *with* and *by* them. When institutions partner with visitors to co-develop projects based on community members' ideas, they enter into co-creative relationships. Co-creation is the subject of Chapter 8, which explores ways for staff members and participants to develop institutional projects to achieve both community and institutional goals.

CHAPTER  8

CO-CREATING WITH VISITORS

CO-CREATIVE PROJECTS ORIGINATE in partnership with participants rather than based solely on institutional goals. A community group may approach the museum seeking assistance to make a project possible, or the institution may invite outside participants to propose and work with staff on a project of mutual benefit. Rather than the institution declaring, "we want to do an exhibit on potato farmers, please come and help us make it happen," staff members ask, "potato farmers, do you have an idea for an exhibit you'd like to make with us?" Or the potato farmers approach the museum on their own accord. While co-creative and collaborative processes are often quite similar, co-creative projects start with community as well as institutional needs.

There are three main reasons that cultural institutions engage in co-creative projects:

1. To give voice and be responsive to the needs and interests of local community members
2. To provide a place for community engagement and dialogue
3. To help participants develop skills that will support their own individual and community goals

The directors of co-creative projects often see their institutions as community-based organizations in service to the needs of visitors, rather than as providers of services the institution perceives as valuable. Co-creative projects are "demand-driven" in the most rigorous sense of the term, and they often require institutional goals to take a backseat to community goals. For example, the Glasgow Open Museum (see page 175) is a co-creative institution whose mission is to provide community members with access to artifacts for use in visitors' own exhibits, programs, and events. Its founder, Julian Spaulding, envisioned it as an institution that would "deliver what people wanted rather than what the museum thought they wanted or thought they ought to want."[1]

Co-creative projects progress very similarly to collaborative projects, but they confer more power to participants. Staff members and community partners work closely to achieve their shared goals. The project development process is often co-determined by the preferences and working styles of participants. The result is a project that is truly co-owned by institutional and community partners.

CASE STUDY
CO-CREATION AS A WAY OF LIFE AT THE WING LUKE ASIAN MUSEUM

The Wing Luke Asian Museum in Seattle, WA, has a well-documented, longstanding commitment to co-creative exhibition development. Their community process is based on a dedication to empowering community members to tell the stories that are most meaningful to them, and community members are engaged in every step of exhibition development. The Wing Luke has been recognized for its achievements in participatory exhibition development, but it has also received honors for producing exemplary audience-facing exhibition products. In 2002, the community-directed exhibition *If Tired Hands Could Talk: Stories of Asian Pacific American Garment Workers*, which featured first-person narratives collected and designed

---

1   Download *A Catalyst for Change: The Social Impact of the Open Museum* [PDF] at http://www.participatorymuseum.org/ref8-1/

with a team of fifteen garment workers, was named best exhibition by the Western Museums Association. This is an institution that knows how to use a co-creative process to create high quality products.

The Wing Luke Asian Museum includes this 100-year-old preserved import-export store. The TV in the middle of the exhibit features the stories of Jimmy Mar, former owner-operator of this local business.

Former Director Ron Chew's unusual background as a journalist and community activist led him to initiate a unique exhibition model that focuses on oral history and local issues instead of curatorial or authoritative content. As Chew put it in 2005:

> There has always been an assumption that the work that we do should be guided by the community here and now. There is an assumption that the museum is a portal for reflection for the outside world rather than a fortress of knowledge that people enter. There has been an assumption that change and the development of the relationships that we need to do our work will take a long time. We are not about stuff and projects but about relationships and stories that rise up from the community. The

story is more important than the stuff. The museum is more a place of dialogue than stated facts.[2]

The result is an institution that has become "a people's museum" in the words of Velma Veloria, the 11th District state representative. As Velma put it:

> Ron has given me a lot of pride in being Filipino. He's put forward the history and contributions of our people. We're no longer just a bunch of these people who went to the canneries every summer . . . we helped build this country.[3]

For Veloria and others, the Wing Luke Asian Museum is an essential community institution, and its co-creative exhibition model is at the heart of that sense of belonging and ownership.

The Wing Luke community process is simple to understand and hard to implement. Their handbook reads like a Zen koan: "The work is labor intensive. The work requires flexibility. We willingly relinquish control."[4] The staff puts top priority on relationships with the community, and exhibition projects involve extensive and sometimes contentious deliberation as community members from diverse backgrounds come together with staff to turn their stories into visitor experiences.

The process begins with an open exhibition proposal model. Anyone can propose an exhibition, and proposals are reviewed yearly based on topic, significance, and relevance to the museum's mission. Staff members and community advisors pick the projects to pursue and launch a two-to-three year development process. The project team is composed of three groups:

1. A Core Advisory Committee of 12-15 community members with specific and diverse connections to the topic at hand, who lead the project development

2. Staff, who facilitate the process as technical advisors, project administrators, and community managers

3. More informally engaged community members, who participate as contributors and collaborators to the project

---

2   This quote from Chew was published by the Community Arts Network at http://www.participatorymuseum.org/ref8-2/

3   Ibid.

4   The Wing Luke Community-based Exhibition Model handbook is available both in print and at http://www.participatorymuseum.org/ref8-4/

The exhibit development process is facilitated by staff but steered by the Core Advisory Committee (CAC). The content, timing, and decision-making process for each project changes based on the dynamics and needs of the particular community with whom each project is developed. The CAC is "the primary decision-making body within the Exhibit Team, and are charged with developing the main messages, themes, content and form of the exhibition and its related components."[5] A community member, not a museum staff member, leads the CAC.

Once the overall concept is defined, the CAC recruits other members of the community to contribute artifacts or stories, perform research, and provide outreach programming for the exhibition. Meanwhile, the staff provides support in design, research, and community facilitation. Staff members often manage interpersonal relationships alongside shifting project schedules.

Museum staff members lead design and fabrication, with CAC members offering input and curatorial direction over artifact selection, multimedia story creation, and general design to ensure it remains in line with exhibition goals. CAC members are invited to drop by at any point during fabrication and installation and are occasionally asked to help install particular artifacts or elements. There are special opening events for all participating community members, and participants are solicited both formally and informally for evaluation on the exhibitions. In addition, community members often develop and lead educational programs alongside volunteers and staff members during the run of each exhibition.

Because the co-creative process is the only way that exhibitions are developed at the Wing Luke Asian Museum, the audience experience is not differentiated from that of other types of exhibits or programs. The audience is considered in exhibition design insofar as the co-creation process is set up to deliver a product that is meaningful and relevant to a range of diverse communities. The museum performs summative evaluations of all exhibitions, measuring audience numbers and impact as well as growth and impact of new community connections.

Because the Wing Luke's co-creative exhibition model is so tightly integrated with the overall goals and strategies of the institution, the staff also

---

5   Ibid.

evaluates the extent to which the museum as a whole is a successful community place. The museum is very specific in stating its indicators of success:

> We observe significant community participation in museum programs.
>
> Community members return time and time again.
>
> People learn and are moved through their participation in museum programs.
>
> People see something of themselves in our exhibits and event.
>
> People become members of the museum.
>
> People contribute artifacts and stories to our exhibits.
>
> The community supports the museum's new capital campaign.
>
> Constituents are comfortable providing both positive and negative feedback.[6]

The museum's internal hiring and training practices also reflect their overall focus on community engagement. The Wing Luke Asian Museum hires people for relationship-building skills as well as content expertise. They put a priority on staff continuity, diversity, and cultivation of young staff as future leaders. The staff is trained extensively in dialogue and community-response techniques to help them carry out the museum's mission. At the Wing Luke Asian Museum, co-creation and community partnership is a way of life, infiltrating all its efforts, from exhibition design to board recruitment to fundraising.

Designing Platforms for Co-Creation

While some institutions like the Wing Luke Asian Museum are wholly co-creative, many traditional institutions with broader missions incorporate co-creative programs into their offerings. Successful co-creation projects rely on two principles:

1. Staff members and participants respect each other's goals and interests in pursuing the project. They should create a set of shared

---

6   These indicators were published by the Community Arts Network at http://www.participatorymuseum.org/ref8-6/

CO-CREATING WITH VISITORS   269

guidelines for what is and isn't acceptable and expected over the duration of the project.

2. Staff members should not harbor pre-conceived ideas about the outcome of the project. They should be willing to let the project go in the direction that is of greatest value to participants, within the scope of the project guidelines.

Successful co-creative projects scaffold participation to help participants achieve their goals without prescribing the outcome. This kind of scaffolding requires a careful balancing act between structure and flexibility. It starts with a simple question: "How can staff give amateurs the skills and tools needed to accomplish shared goals?"

At the Wing Luke Asian Museum, staff members provide the training, support, and structure to enable community members to make high-quality exhibits. But this question can be applied to simpler projects as well. Imagine taking a co-creative approach to museum tours. How could the staff give visitors the skills and tools needed to lead their own tours? They could:

- Provide visitors with maps and encourage them to mark their favorite places as they explore the exhibits
- Ask visitors to assign a theme or title to a collection of their favorite places
- Post the maps and titles in a central location along with the times when visitors will be available to give the tours they have devised
- Make available interpretative literature or staff consultations to give tour guides reference materials for their tours

A group of game designers who call themselves *antiboredom* used this technique to devise a popular co-creative platform called *SFZero* that allows amateurs to design their own games.[7] The *antiboredom* team got their start in Chicago designing complicated puzzle games. They knew people enjoyed playing their games, but they realized that the real fun, at least for them, was in making up the puzzles and game challenges. So they decided to develop a game that let people make their own games, and *SFZero* was born.

---

7   You can play *SFZero* at http://www.participatorymuseum.org/ref8-7/

SFZero is a "collaborative production" game in which people perform creative tasks in an urban environment. The players design the tasks, perform them, and keep score by assigning points to others' documentation of their task fulfillment. The players are also the audience for each other's tasks and their attempts to complete them. Tasks tend to be short, evocative, and a bit transgressive, such as "distract the mailman," "reverse shoplifting (insert an object into a store)," or "create a permanent and visible neighborhood tattoo." Some tasks are personal, like "make a sound portrait of yourself," while others encourage people to explore new places or learn new skills.

The *antiboredom* team does not design the individual game tasks. Instead, the staff manages the community website on which players propose new tasks and share stories about the ones they have completed. This allows the *antiboredom* team to focus on encouraging new players, providing guidelines, and improving the tools that support the game. Staff members provide the scaffolding that empowers players to co-create their gaming experience.

In response to the task: "Install a door in a public place," a group of *SFZero* players constructed *Doorhenge* in Golden Gate Park. The artwork stayed up for two months, aided by occasional cleanup and reconstruction by dozens of *SFZero* players.

Challenge and Compromise

Co-creation projects run into trouble when participants' goals are not aligned with institutional goals, or when staff members are not fully aware of participants' goals at the outset. When community members come forward with an idea for a project, the discussion often quickly jumps to the how of participation without a full investigation of the why. Visitors and staff members often have very different ideas about how cultural institutions work and what they do. If someone comes in saying he wants to make an exhibit based on his community's experiences, it's important to find out what that means to that individual and whether his goals are truly aligned with institutional goals.

CASE STUDY
ALIGNING CO-CREATORS' GOALS IN WIKIPEDIA LOVES ART

Wikipedia Loves Art is a good example of a co-creative project in which institutions and participants struggled to understand each other's goals. It was a short-term co-creation project that first took place in February 2009. It started with a request from a group of New York Wikimedians (members of the Wikipedia community) to the Brooklyn Museum. The Wikimedians asked if the museum would coordinate a project in which people could photograph copyright-free artworks in cultural institutions to illustrate Wikipedia articles. The museum agreed and brought fifteen institutions from the US and UK on board to participate.

The museums asked Wikimedians to provide the institutions with lists of thematic topics that required illustration. Museums used these thematic lists to develop scavenger hunt lists to distribute to participants so that they might find art objects to illustrate Wikipedia topics like "Roman architecture" or "mask." Participants were asked to photograph objects and their accession numbers so staff members could identify and describe the objects properly. The museums developed careful rules about what could and couldn't be photographed, and how participants could upload their images to Flickr for use by the project.

The Wikimedians' and museums' goals were not as aligned as they originally thought. Museums saw this project as an opportunity to engage local photographers to think creatively about how artworks might represent different topics. In contrast, the Wikimedians' goal was to make cultural content digitally available online using as open a licensing structure as possible. The museums cared about participants connecting with artworks and identifying them properly, whereas the Wikimedians cared more about participants sharing images under open legal licenses.

From the institutional perspective, the best way to deliver good participant experiences was to limit contributions through the Flickr uploading system. Institutional representatives were concerned about losing control of images of their collections, and they wanted to make sure the images were linked to the correct information about each object. But many Wikimedians were confused or frustrated by what they perceived as arbitrary institutional constraints in the submission format. Some people invented their own rogue ways to upload museum images outside of the project framework. This caused concern for museum representatives, who saw these actions as causing confusion and potentially violating intellectual property agreements.

Using accession numbers to identify the objects also created a massive and unexpected amount of work for institutional staff. One hundred and two photographers at fifteen different institutions submitted over 13,000 photographs, documenting about 6,200 pieces of art. While these participants had done the hard work of capturing the images, it was up to the institutions to validate, tag, caption, and prepare them for Wikipedia's use. This was a Herculean effort, and some staff members were unable to verify the majority of the images captured at their institutions. At the Brooklyn Museum, data processor Erin Sweeney used a ten-step process for determining whether an image was a valid contribution. After determining validity, Sweeney added tags to the images to identify the objects with which they were associated, the number of points the team received for the images, and more.[8] Eventually, all the work was completed, but when the dust settled, the overall effort by institutions involved in *Wikipedia Loves Art* was so great that many saw it as an unsustainable collaboration.

Fortunately, the short time frame for *Wikipedia Loves Art* helped institutions see it as an experiment and quickly learn from its challenges. In June of 2009, Dutch Wikimedians worked with forty-five institutions in the Netherlands to produce *Wikipedia Loves Art / NL*, which took a new

---

8   Read Sweeney's April 2009 blog post, "Wikipedia Loves Art: Lessons Learned Part 4: The Stats" at http://www.participatorymuseum.org/ref8-8/

approach to the project. Rather than starting with a list of themes provided by Wikimedians and inviting visitors to shoot the objects that they felt fit the topics, the Dutch Wikimedians asked the museums to provide a list of specific objects that participants could photograph. This compromise achieved three things:

1. The museums knew exactly what would be photographed and could more tightly control the experience. At some institutions, staff members set up specific dates for photography and escorted photographers through the galleries.

2. The Wikimedians knew that all the images would be legal for use from a copyright perspective. There was no concern about museums needing to verify that an object on the list was legal for use.

3. The participants received a numbered list of objects to photograph and could tag their images with these identification numbers instead of with accession numbers. This significantly reduced the number of object identification errors and reduced the staff time required to review the images submitted.

The redesigned project was a success, with 292 participants contributing 5,447 photographs. The project was also fundamentally different from the original version. The Dutch project successfully served the needs of both the museums and the Wikimedians. It offered participating photographers less creative agency, but it also created less attendant confusion. While photographers could not freely choose what to shoot, some institutions opened up collections that are not typically available to the public for this project. Participants thus had an important role in providing public access—albeit digitally—to these artworks. As one Dutch participant, Yola de Lusenet, commented:

> I joined because I feel very strongly that museums should make images freely available. So I consider it a success that images of works by Van Gogh and Bosch can now be used by everyone legally (a series of very interesting contemporary works from the private collection of a bank have come out into the open too).[9]

9   Read de Lusenet's entire comment on my January 2010 blog post, "Is Wikipedia Loves Art Getting Better?" at http://www.participatorymuseum.org/ref8-9/

By simplifying and constraining the project, *Wikipedia Loves Art / NL* sustainably engaged art institutions, Wikimedians, and photographers in co-creation. *Wikipedia Loves Art* events are continuing to be planned and implemented at museums around the world. The co-creative partnerships will continue to evolve as museums and free culture advocates work together to define how to open up cultural content to a wider digital audience.

Co-Creation and Institutional Culture

More than any other type of visitor participation, co-creative projects challenge institutional perceptions of ownership and control of content. Co-creative projects require "radical trust" in community members' abilities to perform complex tasks, collaborate with each other, and respect institutional rules and priorities. To execute a successful co-creation project, staff members must not only trust the competencies and motivations of participants but deeply desire their input and leadership.

There are several museums where co-creation occurs in pockets, and these pockets tend to reside in education departments. Education staff members are more likely to be hired in part for their ability to be responsive to and collaborate with community partners and program participants. Educational programs traditionally focus on deep engagement with content, and co-creation fits into that overall mission. Unfortunately, these programs run the risk of isolation, and some education departments can become "participatory ghettos" within larger, more traditional institutions.

What happens when staff members across a cultural institution have different perspectives on how much trust to put in community participants? Consider the story of the St. Louis Science Center's *Youth Exploring Science* program *(YES)*. *YES* is a community-based program in which 250 underserved teenagers, recruited from community partner organizations, are employed by the science center to participate in science learning, professional development, and service back to the community. Adult employees of the *YES* program work in partnership with students, and while they definitely provide some formal instruction, they do so in a co-creative environment that is frequently teen-led. For example, in the *Learning Places* project (funded by the National Science Foundation), *YES* teens designed, installed, and staffed interactive science exhibits and activities for local community children's organizations.

YES teens are empowered to manage their program's digital presence by publishing content on several public social networking sites. Because the *YES* staff has a co-creative approach to relationships with *YES* participants, there are fairly loose guidelines for what teens may post, and participants share everything from reflections on their science learning to photos of themselves dancing.

In the context of *YES*, these activities are both appropriate and desirable because they promote technology skills and help *YES* participants feel ownership of their program. But *YES* staff members have clashed with the marketing department of the St. Louis Science Center about their online presence. From the marketing perspective, *YES* teens are not the most appropriate spokespeople for the institution across the social Web. The *YES* website has not been integrated into the overall Science Center website, and accessing it via the museum's website requires some concerted effort. While the *YES* program powerfully fulfills the museum's mission "to stimulate interest in and understanding of science and technology throughout the community," it is not presented as a flagship to audiences that are not already in the know.

These kinds of conflicts are common in institutions that do not have a unified vision of their relationships with constituent communities. Institutions that are just beginning participatory projects of any type should expect to confront these kinds of challenges. In the best cases, the staff can use them as an opportunity for internal dialogue about what the institution's eventual strategic policy on participation will be.

CASE STUDY

CO-CREATION INSPIRES REINVENTION AT THE OAKLAND MUSEUM OF CALIFORNIA

At the Oakland Museum of California, a co-creative project in the education department became a vehicle for institutional change. The Oakland

Museum has a long history as a community-focused institution, reaching back to its roots as a radically democratic museum in the late 1960s and 1970s. In the 1980s and 1990s, however, audiences plateaued, and in 2005, the museum began a major redesign process (to be completed in 2012) with the goal to reinvent the institution as a model institution based on strong community engagement. The museum had ambitious goals for increasing visitation, and specifically, for increasing the number of local visitors and visitors who are demographically representative of the museum's highly diverse neighborhood. The staff also wanted visitors to see the Oakland Museum as a home for diverse voices—including their own.

To accomplish these goals, the museum took inspiration from a long-standing co-creative project: the *Days of the Dead* exhibition. *Days of the Dead* embodies many of the goals and outcomes that the staff has for institutional reinvention. It is a program that involves diverse community members as participants and draws a large, enthusiastic, and multi-cultural audience.

Days of the Dead is a community exhibition and celebration that the museum's education department has run annually since 1994. Education staff members partner with local artists, community members, and outside curators as guest curators, and these guests assemble diverse artists, school groups, and community members to build shrines, or ofrendas, as offerings to the dead. The shrines are mounted in a dedicated exhibition space within the museum, and they range from funny to heart-wrenching to political in tone. The exhibition typically is open for two months surrounding the Day of the Dead (November 2) and features regular gallery talks and

Staff member Evelyn Orantes and youth intern Blanca Garcia created this traditional ofrenda at the entrance to the 2003 *Days of the Dead* exhibition, *Global Elegies: Art and Ofrendas for the Dead.*

tours by participating artists. The museum hosts a community celebration on a weekend-day before the Day of the Dead, a free event that includes crafts and demonstrations, live music and dance performances, a market, and a ceremonial procession into the museum gardens.

Days of the Dead was conceived by the institution's Latino Advisory Council. The staff had approached this consultative group of community leaders and asked what they could do to connect with a broader Latino audience. The Council suggested a Day of the Dead program. Day of the Dead is one of the most important traditions in Latino Mexican culture, one with the potential to bring diverse communities together for shared healing. Why, asked the Latino Advisory Council, couldn't the Oakland Museum become the home for Day of the Dead in San Francisco's East Bay, where many Latinos live?

Days of the Dead and the community celebration are enormously successful programs. The museum teems with local visitors speaking many different languages. On the day of the celebration, 3,000 to 5,000 people come to participate, and close to 7,000 visitors tour the exhibition annually, mostly in student groups. It's the only exhibition at the Oakland Museum that requires a waiting list for bookings.

While *Days of the Dead* does attract many Latino and Mexican visitors, it also attracts other nontraditional audiences to the Oakland Museum because it relates to a universal human experience. The exhibition enjoys high visitation from health industry groups, support groups for families with relatives in hospice, groups of terminally ill patients, people dealing with grief, and grief counselors. The student audience isn't uniform either; Headstart facilitators bring preschoolers to learn about art, elementary and high school students come to connect with cultural heritage, and university Spanish and ethnic studies classes visit as well. Project director Evelyn Orantes commented:

> The topic of death transcends culture or ethnicity. It's something we all grapple with. And here is an educational institution providing you a safe way to gather tools to grieve. The exhibition has a real intimacy that you get right away—about your mom who died, or your child. The instant level of intimacy from the subject adds this whole other closeness between the museum, participant, and the viewer. It's a program

that makes people feel like this is their place, their museum, and there's a sense of ownership.

The Oakland Museum's experience with *Days of the Dead* helped staff members articulate what was and wasn't possible across other galleries during the transformation. The *Days of the Dead* co-creative process, like that at the Wing Luke Asian Museum, is highly deliberative and time intensive. While some redesigned galleries at the Oakland Museum will include fully co-creative projects, most visitor participation will be contributory or collaborative in nature. Visitors will be able to share their own immigration stories, discuss art with each other through interactive journals, and add their own images and stories to collages on display. The galleries will also feature many exhibits and media pieces that have been collaboratively produced with Californians from diverse backgrounds. The staff is also engaging visitors to help prototype new exhibit components in all galleries (including those like art in which visitor testing is not traditionally part of exhibit development).

Days of the Dead significantly impacted the conversation at the Oakland Museum about what it would take for the institution to achieve its goals. The transformation of the institution has not been easy, and many staff members have had to confront their own biases and fears about visitor participation. Reflecting on the community-driven way *Days of the Dead* is developed, executed, and received by visitors, Orantes said:

> In some ways, it's almost like having a community center in the museum. And I hesitate to put *Days of the Dead* in that box because it will be devalued. People will say that the artists that we bring on aren't "artists," they are "community artists." This is a program that challenges the basic ideas about how art is displayed. We take an egalitarian approach, merging artists, community members, and school groups, so you will often see the work of an established artist right next to an installation of glitter-covered macaroni. And I think some museum people don't know what to do with it.

Days of the Dead's co-creative format is a radical departure from the way things are typically done in a traditional museum. As part of the Oakland Museum's redesign, Orantes and her colleagues in the education department have been working collaboratively with curators, researchers, and designers to share their knowledge about visitor needs and designing participatory projects. As museum director Lori Fogarty noted, "This is an institutional capacity-building effort. It takes a very different kind of skill set and staff roles to engage with visitors in these ways." By sharing their experience, the staff members who manage *Days of the Dead* are helping make the whole museum a welcoming place for visitor participation.

Co-creative projects allow cultural institutions to form partnerships that are responsive to the needs and interests of their audiences. Of course, visitors walk into museums with their own needs and interests every day. When staff members are attentive to and interested in accommodating these needs, they can design programs to invite visitors to use the space for their own reasons without entering extensive co-creative partnerships. These projects fall into the hosted model for participation, which is the topic of Chapter 9.

CHAPTER 9

HOSTING PARTICIPANTS

HOSTED PROJECTS, in which the institution turns over a gallery or a program to community partners, are common vehicles for visitor participation. Hosting happens frequently in the context of formal partnerships: institutions regularly host traveling exhibits, artists-in-residence, independent tour operators, and special functions. This chapter does not focus on these formal relationships with vetted professionals but rather on situations where the institution is used or repurposed by amateur groups and casual visitors.

There are four broad reasons that institutions may choose to pursue hosting models for participation:

1. To encourage the public to be comfortable using the institution for a wide range of reasons
2. To encourage visitors to creatively adapt and use the institution and its content
3. To provide a space for diverse perspectives, exhibits, and performances that staff members are unable or unwilling to present
4. To attract new audiences who may not see the institution as a place for their own interests

Unlike other participatory models, in which the institution needs to somehow motivate and convince visitors to participate, hosting requires no coercion—just an open platform in which visitors can do what they like. But in most cases it's not that simple. Complications arise when institutional and participant perspectives about what is valuable diverge. Hosting is only a useful technique when institutions have clear reasons why they want to provide a particular opportunity to visitors. In the same vein, when forbidding visitors to use the facility in certain ways (for example, to take photographs or to have loud conversations), staff should understand the potentially negative impact these limitations may have on visitors' relationship with the institution.

Consider the concept of "loud hours." Some museums and libraries have instituted loud hours to provide opportunities for visitors to talk more freely than they would at other times. Loud hours help some visitors feel more comfortable in cultural institutions by explicitly permitting them to communicate at the volume that is natural for them. In art museums, staff can use loud hours to encourage visitors to talk about the art, promoting social learning experiences that some visitors might feel uncomfortable engaging in under normal conditions.

Loud hours may be distracting and frustrating to patrons and staff members who value museums and libraries as quiet places. For an institution to confidently offer loud hours, staff members have to feel that the benefits outweigh the negatives. The institution needs to evaluate loud hours not just for the potential to generate noise, but also for the extent to which the program can support social learning and help engage new audiences. Loud hours might be more effective at promoting social engagement if the environment provides specific prompts for visitors to respond to and discuss. Loud hours might be most effective at attracting new audiences if offered at specific times of day or outside traditional open hours.

Hosting strategies can be used to implement simple programs, but they can also be used for institution-wide efforts. Hosting can be a strategic way to demonstrate an institution's commitment to a particular topic or audience. By hosting a large-scale event or offering space to community partners from other organizations, cultural institutions can demonstrate their unique ability to serve as a "town squares" for public engagement.[1] When you can articulate the goals behind a hosting strategy, you will be more likely to design it in a way that best serves institutional goals and visitors' needs.

Hosting to Promote Casual Use and Revenue Generation

Loud hours are an example of a hosting strategy that is focused primarily on encouraging visitors to feel at home in cultural institutions. Basic design considerations, such as the amount of comfortable seating, hours of availability, ticket prices, dining facilities, and services for guests with disabilities all impact the extent to which visitors feel comfortable and well-hosted in a cultural institution.

Most cultural institutions are comfortable hosting visitors for social experiences—for example, providing a nice setting for a date or a family outing. Many museums have started counting visits to gift shops and restaurants in their overall visitor counts, arguing that shoppers and café patrons are visitors even if they don't attend exhibitions or programs. Similarly, many institutions aggressively market themselves as venues for special functions, weddings, and birthday parties. While most museums have some restrictions about who can rent the facility or for what purposes (for example, forbidding raves or political fundraisers), facility rental has become a significant way to cover operating costs. Hosting visitors for meals, functions, or gift-shop purchases is typically considered positive, since these activities generate revenue and connect the institution to visitors' personal lives, however loosely.

When it comes to non-revenue-generating casual uses of cultural institutions, the situation can get complicated. Consider the question of providing free wireless access to the Web (Wi-Fi). Wi-Fi has become a core offering at libraries, where it helps fulfill institutional missions to provide citizens with open access to information. At museums, the question of whether to provide Wi-Fi is less clear. Some institutions see Wi-Fi as a basic provision that helps visitors learn in the museum with their own devices. Others want to encourage people to spend time in the museum casually,

---

1   For an example of an institution that uses hosting to connect with nontraditional audiences around the topic of climate change, see the case study on The Wild Center on page 14.

even if they are using the Web for uses unrelated to institutional content.

The Wi-Fi debate is indicative of the cultural biases inherent in determining what makes an institution a good host. Suzanne Fischer, curator of technology at the Henry Ford Museum, has called Wi-Fi "a necessary service to visitors, like bathrooms."[2] But the staff could just as easily argue that visitors have access to the Web elsewhere in their lives and do not need it at the museum. A subset of visitors may consider Wi-Fi to be a necessity, just as other visitors would consider strollers or vegetarian options in the cafeteria to be essential. When staff members decide which casual activities to encourage, they dictate what subsets of people will be most comfortable visiting the institution.

A banner outside the Indianapolis Museum of Art advertises Wi-Fi as one of the free amenities of the institution.

Hosting to Encourage Creative Adaptation

Some visitors use cultural institutions as settings for their own creative expression or social experiences. These can be positive learning experiences that produce useful and attractive outcomes that advertise the institution. But they can also generate outcomes that violate copyright or make staff members and other visitors uncomfortable. While it might be charming to see a pastor leading a tour of a natural history museum for congregants, the staff might be disturbed if he reinterprets the displays to put forward a creationist perspective.

Again, this comes back to the balancing act between institutional and participant needs. Participants who use institutions for their own creative purposes focus on serving themselves and their own constituencies, and have only secondary interest in the institution and its broader audiences. Hosted participants are likely to regard audiences very differently from the way the institution sees them, and those differences may be a delight (when

---

2   See http://www.participatorymuseum.org/ref9-2/

they make new audiences comfortable in the venue) or a mess (when they alienate or confuse other visitors).

For example, the blog *Jumping in Art Museums* features photographs of people leaping in museum galleries.[3] Washington D.C.-based artist Alison Reimus started the blog to express her desire to "jump for joy" when engaging with art. Reimus encourages others to share their joy as well, and the blog features photos of art jumpers all over the world.

The audience for the *Jumping in Art Museums* blog includes other art enthusiasts who are probably frequent museum visitors. But not all people who come to museums expect to see people jumping, or want to jump themselves. Some visitors, like the blog's followers, are probably delighted by the jumping. Some institutions, like the Belgian FotoMuseum, were so taken by the idea that the staff took professional shots of visitors jumping. But staff members and security guards at some other institutions have been annoyed or concerned by the actions of these jumpers.

Visitors and staff members jumping at the FotoMuseum in Antwerp, Belgium.

When creative adaptation is mission-relevant, staff will often provide formal sanction and infrastructure to support it. For example, in 2009 staff members at SFMOMA noticed that some visitors like to sketch the art in the galleries. So, the staff started hosting informal sketching hours in the lobby. The staff didn't provide drawing instruction or programmatic content, but they did provide approval and social support for sketching, explicitly welcoming and celebrating an activity they hoped to encourage.

To make reasonable decisions about what kind of creative activities are appropriate to host, staff members need to be able to separate their

3   Visit the *Jumping in Art Museums* blog at http://www.participatorymuseum.org/ref9-3/

personal reactions and preferences from the needs of the institution and its visitors. It is reasonable for staff members to intervene if they think that participants are making an environment unfriendly to other audiences or unsafe for objects on display. But it is unreasonable to object to activities that staff members simply don't like or are uncomfortable with because of their own cultural preferences.

When guidelines for behavior aren't clear, it causes confusion and frustration for both visitors and staff. I once wandered through an art museum with my father and an audio recording device, intending to record our conversation for a podcast about how visitors talk about exhibits. We were interrupted immediately by a gallery attendant who asked us to stop but could not give us a reason why. We went to the main desk, where we inquired about the policy and were instructed to wait for a response from the Manager of Public Relations. Twenty minutes later, she told us that we could record ourselves, but we could not record any sounds emanating from the artworks (which might be copyrighted), nor could we interview other visitors (no reason given).

We felt that our desire to create an audio piece at the museum was unsupported, so we left. No wonder people apply the term "rogue" to podcasts and tours led by individuals who are not museum staff.[4] In many institutions, even if these activities are not explicitly against the rules, they violate unwritten rules about how visitors can and should use the facility.

Hosting Outside Program Offerings

Cultural institutions are often more comfortable with creative adaptation of their facilities and content when they partner directly with artists, local hobbyist groups, or other community partners to develop offerings that are relevant to the institutional mission. Some art or cultural institutions host craft sales in December to promote local artists while connecting to holiday shopping. The Boston Children's Museum hosts a weekly farmer's market, which reflects an institutional value around healthy eating.

---

4   To hear excerpts from a particularly delightful rogue museum podcast, check out Vital 5 Productions' Portland Art Museum Unauthorized Audio Tour at http://www.participatorymuseum.org/ref9-4/

These creative partnerships are most useful when outside participants can provide services or experiences that the institution is unable to offer itself. For example, a science museum might not have the resources to run its own citizen science projects but would be happy to provide space to support local amateur scientists who are looking for a home base for their experiments.

Art museums have moved aggressively into the hosted arena when it comes to educational programming. In Denver, San Francisco, and Seattle, among other cities, art museums host large-scale monthly parties geared towards young professionals, often featuring collaborative art-making activities that are run by outside groups. Such activities include communal knitting, social games, and screen-printing. The Denver Art Museum's *Untitled* program also features "detours" led by non-art professionals—from Jungian psychologists to zookeepers—who share their observations and reactions to the art on display. The late-night *Remix* program at the Seattle Art Museum includes a similar tour component led by guest guides called "My Favorite Things."

These programs frequently offer the same kinds of experiences provided by unsolicited creative adaptations, like rogue art museum podcasts, but they allow institutions to vet creative partners before the event. Soliciting visitors and outside artists directly can also increase participation. People are more likely to engage enthusiastically in creative reuse of cultural institutions when they are specifically invited and encouraged to do so.

Hosting New Audiences

Hosted participation can help institutions connect with people who don't naturally see cultural institutions as relevant to their own lives and interests. For these audiences, hosted projects are most successful when they demonstrate the institution's ability to add value to an activity these visitors already enjoy. For example, many museums host "lates" that attract young adults to dance, flirt, and party in the galleries. These events are intended to help new audiences see the museum as a fun venue for a social experience.

These kinds of programs can be controversial for the institution. Some traditionalists do not see the benefit of spending resources on programming that is radically different from their usual offerings. But just as multilingual labels help foreign visitors feel comfortable and confident in museum galleries, social events can help young adult audiences feel comfortable in the museum setting.

A similar argument can be made for a popular type of hosted program in public libraries: game nights. Many American libraries host game nights, geared toward kids and teens, in which visitors use library computers and gaming consoles to play multi-player online and digital games. During these programs, librarians encourage kids to use the library in non-traditional ways—playing games, running around, eating pizza, yelling. Librarian Toby Greenwalt hosted family game nights at his library in Skokie, Illinois in 2008 and set up feedback stations for kids to share their thoughts. Kids made comments like, "This night is the best night at the library ever. I had so much fun." and "this place is AWESOME!!!!!!!!!!"[5]

Is this hosted program mission-relevant, or does it give kids a false sense of what the library is about? The librarians who run these programs argue that gaming in the library is on-mission when it comes to institutional goals that address community outreach and engagement, as well as their commitment to providing access to media content. The Skokie Public Library's vision statement reads:

> Skokie Public Library is essential to a vibrant and diverse community where individuals of all ages and families freely engage in lifelong learning and discovery, and enjoyment of popular culture and the arts. Residents have many opportunities to become well-informed, with their intellectual freedom and privacy protected, to benefit from cultural diversity, and to actively participate in the life of the community.[6]

Game nights support the sense that the library is a vibrant community space dedicated to family discovery, enjoyment, and learning. From the perspective of the institutional vision, game nights are just as mission-relevant as other hosted programs, like classical music lunch hours or community group meetings.

---

5   Read Greenwalt's June 2008 blog post, "User Comments from Game Night," at http://www.participatorymuseum.org/ref9-5/
6   Learn more about the Skokie Public Library vision and mission at http://www.participatorymuseum.org/ref9-6/

Hosting new audiences in this way helps people understand how their identity goals might be fulfilled at the institution. When a library fulfills a kid's goal to challenge herself and be social, she starts to see the library as a positive and useful place that she can contextualize into her recreational choices. She may begin to look more broadly at what else it offers. As librarian Marian Hose wrote about her own experience hosting a game night: "The kids had great fun and we saw plenty of fresh faces in the library. Anyone who did not have a library card already was signed up for one and many of the new kids have come back again the use the library 'for real.'"[7]

Not all of the kids who come to game night (or to other hosted library programs) return to use the traditional resources and functions of the library. That's fine. The Skokie Public Library's vision statement doesn't make any value judgments about the right kind of "lifelong learning and discovery" experiences for its patrons. If the staff members truly embody this vision, they can feel positively about patrons who only use the library for limited mission-related purposes—whether to play games, participate in meetings, or read.

The question of which hosted programs are worth pursuing becomes more complicated when hosted programs grow larger and more expensive. What's the value of engaging new communities if it requires a lot of time and money? That's the question the Ontario Science Centre grappled with in the next case study.

CASE STUDY

ASSESSING THE VALUE OF HOSTING THE 888 TORONTO MEET-UP

On August 8, 2008, the Ontario Science Centre (OSC) hosted a meet-up called *888* for international YouTube users. *888* was expensive to host, complex in its outcomes, and provoked many questions about the true value and cost of engaging new audiences.

---

7   See comment number 7 on Aaron Schmidt's November 2005 blog post, "Another Successful DDR Night," at http://www.participatorymuseum.org/ref9-7/

888 emerged as an event idea from the OSC's successful forays into online video sharing. The OSC had a high profile on YouTube and other video-sharing sites, and their videos—mostly short, staff-produced excerpts from demonstrations and outside speaker presentations—received millions of views on YouTube. The designer in charge of video production and sharing, Kathy Nicholaichuk, had become deeply involved with the YouTube community, and she expressed an interest in taking the OSC's involvement further. She worked with staff members from the events, programs, and visitor experience teams to conceptualize a meet-up that would accomplish three goals:

1. Demonstrate the OSC's commitment to the YouTube community
2. Bring creative, energetic, young videographers to the Science Centre
3. Produce video content that would benefit the institution and the meet-up participants

Nicholaichuk and other YouTube enthusiasts promoted *888* via YouTube and other social media tools. Many YouTube users created videos in which they effused about the Ontario Science Centre before ever setting foot inside. About 460 people showed up for the actual event—the largest YouTube meet-up held to date. The event was a massive party in the Science Centre, featuring talent shows, open exhibit galleries, food and drink, and lots of cameras.

While participants came from all over the world, a survey conducted at the kickoff party indicated that more than 75 percent were local to Toronto or from Canada.[8] About half were under 19, and another quarter were 20 to 25 years old. More than one-third had never visited the OSC, and the majority attended with friends or family. Over 1,000 videos were made at the event, and the OSC received 2 million impressions from print, radio, and TV coverage. The videos themselves received millions of views and tens of thousands of comments on YouTube.

---

8   For more information on the attendees and impact of *888*, see Kevin Von Appen, Kathy Nichoaichuk, and Karen Hager's 2009 paper, "WeTube: Getting Physical with a Virtual Community at the Ontario Science Centre," available at http://www.participatorymuseum.org/ref9-8/

These numbers were impressive. The OSC has a commitment to promoting innovation, and like most science centers, it struggles to attract older teens and young adults (their core audiences are families and school-age audiences). As Associate Director of Daily Experience Operations Kevin Von Appen noted, "[Teens] explore technology and they innovate. Those are exactly the kind of skills, attitudes, and behaviors we're trying to grow in our visitors." *888* clearly portrayed the OSC to young adults, and their own social networks of friends and followers, as a cool place to hang out and an attractive context for social experiences.

The vast majority of videos made and shared from the meet-up were social in nature, focusing solely on participants' excitement at meeting each other, partying, flirting, and hanging out. While many videos did feature or mention the OSC as the location for the social activity, there were only a handful of videos in which *888* participants actually used exhibits or tried to communicate about science in some way. Everyone had a good time and no one did anything offensive, but the activities shown in the videos are not representative of typical OSC visitor experiences, nor do they communicate the venue experience accurately to potential visitors. On one level, this is to be expected; the OSC hosted the YouTube community so it could have its own YouTube experience. But on another level it's problematic because large numbers of YouTube spectators continue to be introduced online to the OSC as a venue for a party, not as an educational facility.

In other words, 460 young people produced 1,000 videos of themselves having a great time at the Science Centre. And the question remains: what is that worth?

From the participant perspective, the experience was incredibly valuable. Several participants made comments like, "The best time of my life!!... I will never forget it." The meet-up was well designed to support YouTube users' needs, and those users felt fully able to enjoy the venue for their own social and creative purposes.

From the institutional perspective, the results were mixed. The OSC spent about US $74 per participant (mostly on labor) to promote and host the event. The staff had hoped that more participants would use the meet-up as an opportunity to engage with the exhibits and produce videos reflecting experiences that were educational in nature. But the event also brought local young adults to the science center who otherwise weren't visiting, and it may have encouraged some local YouTube users to see the OSC in a new light.

While the OSC team considered *888* to be a valuable experiment, they elected not to host an identical 999 meet-up in 2009. Von Appen commented:

> Repeating it didn't make sense as a next step. We had entered or engaged with something that was changing really quickly at the right moment in the right way, and we got the results we got. And now it's time to be thoughtful about what comes next. We're still looking for ways to make it easier, make it local, make it repeatable, make it deeper.

The *888* participants are the kinds of people that the OSC wants to attract through its innovation-focused exhibits and open-ended programs. Thus *888* was a starting point that established the Ontario Science Centre as a relevant and appealing venue for teen and young adult experiences. The question is how to transform a popular hosted event like this one into one that aligns more successfully with institutional goals.

Hosting as a Launch Point for Deeper Engagement

Events like *888* often feel discontinuous with the other programs cultural institutions offer. How can a successful hosted experience lead to broader engagement with institutional programs?

The first step is to be explicit about other programs that are relevant to participants' interests. Only a small number of people who show up for a party or event will gravitate towards wandering through exhibits or picking up program brochures. It's okay to offer participants at hosted events targeted activities that connect to other institutional offerings. The Denver Art Museum's *Untitled* program isn't just a party—the staff also provides activities that encourage participants to connect with the art in the galleries. Similarly, you could imagine a future YouTube meet-up at a science center or museum in which staff would provide specific challenges for participants to make videos related to the exhibits on display.

If your institution wants to engage hosted participants more deeply, start with an activity or experience that the audience already enjoys in your venue. If people use your museum as a place to take photos, ask if they'd consider playing paparazzi at an upcoming event. If they use your museum as a place to work, suggest a quiet spot or an exhibit that's particularly good for inspiration. If they come with friends and give their own well-informed tours, invite them to volunteer as guides for school groups or other visitors. If they make out in a dark exhibit...well, some activities you might not want to encourage.

CASE STUDY
HOSTING TEENAGERS AT THE EXPERIENCE MUSIC PROJECT AND SCIENCE FICTION MUSEUM

In 2009, I started working with the Experience Music Project and Science Fiction Museum (EMPSFM) in Seattle on a project to enhance teen engagement with the museum. Like the Oakland Museum and the *Days of the Dead* (see page 275), EMPSFM has a flagship program that embodies the best of their engagement with teenage audiences. This program, called *Sound Off!*, is a battle of the bands for musicians aged 13 to 21. Each fall, youth bands submit applications, and twelve are selected to participate in a series of four semifinal concerts in the spring. These twelve bands receive mentoring from industry professionals, lots of press attention, and the opportunity to perform in front of hundreds of screaming fans at the museum.

In my first meeting with EMPSFM staff members, they commented that *Sound Off!* is an amazing program, but they felt the teens who participate and attend the semifinals only see the museum as a venue for a cool rock concert. They were concerned that teens didn't see the museum as a place with other appealing or worthwhile experiences. The staff wanted to find ways to capitalize on teens' love of *Sound Off!* to get them more engaged throughout the institution. This is a multi-year process with the goal to develop programs that are teen-led and which expand the museum's teen audience beyond those who participate in *Sound Off!*

Rather than designing a new program and figuring out how to motivate teens to engage with it, we started with the teens who love *Sound Off!*

and inferred other kinds of experiences that might appeal to them. Because these teens see the museum as the host of an enjoyable live music experience during *Sound Off!*, we decided to use their preexisting interest in live music performed by local bands as the starting point for other museum experiences. EMPSFM is engaging the *Sound Off!* audience more deeply with the institution in four ways:

1. Online, staff members opened a social network where *Sound Off!* enthusiasts and bands can connect with each other and learn about other live music shows and venues in the Pacific Northwest. This online community attracts teen musicians and their fans, as well as young band managers and promoters who want to announce their gigs. We worked with teens who were already engaged with *Sound Off!* as youth advisory board members and former competitors to promote and produce content for the online community. The goal is that, over a three-year timeframe, the online community will transition from being managed by staff to being managed by youth advisory board members and *Sound Off!* participants.

2. On the educational program side, the staff drew clearer lines among the different music-making and performance-oriented educational programs at the museum, so teens could more effectively pursue paths to and from the *Sound Off!* experience. The museum offers several educational programs, including camps and intensive workshops, to help young musicians improve their musical and performance skills. Many bands who enter the *Sound Off!* competition are unaware of these other opportunities. The vast majority of bands who enter the *Sound Off!* competition do not make it to the semifinals concerts, and they frequently end their participation with the museum for the year if they are not selected. The staff is working to explicitly advertise the opportunity for competitors to engage with courses and camps that may help them improve their chances in the competition for the following year.

3. In the museum galleries, the staff is integrating multimedia content from *Sound Off!* semifinalists and winners into exhibitions, so that the bands' fans can pursue their interest in these bands as part of a museum visit. The museum is integrating *Sound Off!* bands into pre-existing oral history projects and media exhibits focused on contemporary artists, and the staff are considering options that would allow teenage visitors to access and produce additional audio and visual content via mobile phone.

4. *Sound Off!* itself is becoming more participatory. Over three years, audience members will gradually be invited to help judge the competition, to design T-shirts and graphics for the program, and to serve as journalists reporting on the entrants and the performances.

Hosting Exhibitions in Community Galleries

Not all hosted projects are event-based. One of the most frequent ways that cultural institutions invite people to share their own artworks, stories, and collections is through community galleries, in which individuals or community groups produce their own exhibitions. Unlike the Wing Luke Asian Museum's co-creative exhibition development model (see page 264), community galleries are typically set up so that outside participants manage all aspects of content development, exhibit design, and fabrication themselves, within some broad guidelines set by the institution. Community members propose exhibitions in an application process, and the museum selects proposals to be implemented. The community members are responsible for developing and implementing their proposed exhibitions with minimal staff support.

Successful community gallery projects feature several logistical elements:

- The exhibitions are time-limited. A fixed term allows institutions to support many rotating voices while mitigating the adverse effects of a poorly executed community project.

- Participants receive a stipend for their work. This is usually a fixed amount for materials and development costs. If institutions want to engage less privileged community members, they may offer more significant compensation to cover time spent working on the project.
- Institutions provide basic schedules and frameworks for developing the exhibitions. Staff members typically meet with participants at fixed points in the process to respond to questions and help exhibitors stay on track.
- Beyond formal meetings, staff members are available to a limited extent to help participants with design and technical issues. Having an expert to talk with helps bolster participants' confidence and develop their skills towards a higher-quality result. Unlike co-creative projects, in community gallery projects, the staff typically tries to limit—not extend—time consulting with participants.
- Participants are encouraged to develop marketing materials to promote their exhibits. This motivates participants to bring in their own audiences, who may be potentially new to the institution, rather than relying solely on the institution's traditional visitors.
- Participants are encouraged to offer educational programs or tours during the run of their exhibit. Many community exhibits come to life when presented by the people who are passionate about the stories on display.

While community exhibitions often reflect topics of keen interest to niche audiences, the quality is not always at the level of the rest of the museum's professionally produced exhibitions, nor are they likely to conform to institutional style guides. The results may appear inconsistent with other staff-managed galleries.

Community galleries are frequently designed to require as little staff involvement as possible, not to produce the best exhibitions possible. At the Detroit Historical Society, Director of Exhibitions and Programs Tracy Irwin has noted that while their community gallery allows the institution to reflect the unique and diverse stories of Detroit's citizens, the quality of design varies widely. Graphic panels may be over laden with tiny text, or exhibitors may place objects and labels at heights that are not accessible to everyone.

A text-laden timeline in an exhibition on Detroit's Chinatown in
the Community Gallery at the Detroit Historical Society.

While the museum staff has the knowledge and experience to avoid dubious
design choices in their own galleries, the community gallery is designed by
partner groups, who have been given the freedom to design the exhibit as
they see fit.

This hands-off approach overvalues the open-ended creativity of participants and undervalues the utility of scaffolding and creative constraints.
While not all institutions can afford the time required to make community
galleries more co-creative, there are some simple things that staff members
can do to improve the overall experience of community galleries for participants and audiences alike. They can:

- Provide tutorials or workshops on exhibit design
- Require community groups to include an artist or designer on
  their team
- Hold brainstorming sessions focused on creative forms of interpretation or interactivity
- Ask community partners to participate in evaluation of existing
  exhibits, to help them reflect on what does and doesn't work
- Encourage community partners to prototype exhibits, or to incorporate visitor evaluation into their planning

- Incorporate creative challenges into exhibition solicitations that encourage specific interpretative styles and themes

While community galleries are typically used to invite participants to create content unrelated to that displayed in other parts of the institution, hosting can also be used to invite outsiders to reflect on the role of the institution itself. In 2007, the Museu Picasso in Barcelona partnered with a local design university, Eina School of Design and Art, to set up an unusual community exhibition produced by illustration students.

The students' professor challenged them to produce images that reflected an aspect of life at the museum. Twenty-six illustrators spent three months at the museum, watching how people used the gift shop, the bathrooms, and the galleries. In 2009, their resulting exhibition, *Rethinking Picasso (Repensar el Picasso)*, was mounted in a small gallery. It featured a unique take on the institution and its functions.[9] The participants incorporated everything from the bathroom cleaning protocols to the guards' circuits, to the scam artists hawking cheap souvenirs outside the museum.

By inviting artists to "rethink" the museum, the Museu Picasso ended up encouraging the illustrators to engage deeply with its many functions and idiosyncrasies. The result was an attractive exhibition presenting outsiders' perspectives on the most intimate workings of the museum.

---

9   View more images from Rethinking Picasso and download the exhibit catalog at http://www.participatorymuseum.org/ref9-9/

Illustrator Oze Tajada focused on street vendors offering fakes outside the Museu Picasso in his piece, *Wanted Picasso*.

These last four chapters explored design techniques for developing contributory, collaborative, co-creative, and hosted projects. If your institution embarks on a participatory project of any type, how will you be able to confidently assert that it will enable you to accomplish your goals? To answer this question, we turn next to Chapter 10, which presents techniques for evaluating participatory projects and assessing their impact.

CHAPTER

EVALUATING PARTICIPATORY PROJECTS

L ACK OF GOOD EVALUATION of participatory projects is probably the greatest contributing factor to their slow acceptance and use in the museum field. Evaluation can help you measure the impact of past projects and advocate for future initiatives. It helps you articulate and share what worked and what didn't. Particularly in an emerging field of practice, evaluation can help professionals learn from and support each other's progress.

While participatory projects do not require fundamentally different evaluation techniques from other types of projects, there are four considerations that make participatory projects unique when it comes to their assessment:

1. *Participatory projects are about both process and product.* Participatory projects require people to *do* something for them to work, which means evaluation must focus on participant behavior and the impact of participatory actions. It is not useful to merely catalog the participatory platforms institutions offer—the number of comment boards, participatory exhibit elements, or dialogue

programs provided. Evaluators must measure what participants *do* and describe what happens as a result of participation. Participatory outcomes may be external, like increased incidence of conversation among visitors, and internal, such as development of new skills or enhanced relationships.

2. *Participatory projects are not just for participants.* It is important to define goals and assess outcomes not only for participants, but for staff members and non-participating audiences as well. For each project, you should be able to articulate goals for the participants who actively collaborate with the institution, for the staff members who manage the process, and for the audience that consumes the participatory product.

3. *Participatory projects often benefit from incremental and adaptive measurement techniques.* Many participatory projects are process-based. If you are going to work with community members for three years to design a new program, it's not useful to wait until the end of the three years to evaluate the overall project. Incremental assessment can help complex projects stay aligned to their ultimate goals while making the project work for everyone involved.

4. *Sometimes, it is beneficial to make the evaluative process participatory in itself.* When projects are co-designed by institutions with community members, it makes sense to involve those participants in the development and implementation of project evaluations. This is particularly true for co-creative and hosted projects in which participants have a high level of responsibility for the direction of the project.

Evaluating Impact

Evaluating the impact of participatory projects requires three steps:[1]
1. Stating your goals
2. Defining behaviors and outcomes that reflect those goals
3. Measuring or assessing the incidence and impact of the outcomes via observable indicators

Goals drive outcomes that are measured via indicators. These three steps are not unique to evaluating participatory projects, but participatory projects frequently involve goals and outcomes that are different from those used to evaluate traditional museum projects.

Recall the wide-ranging indicators the Wing Luke Asian Museum uses to evaluate the extent to which it achieves its community mission (see page 264). When it comes to participants, the staff assesses the extent to which "people contribute artifacts and stories to our exhibits."[2] With regard to audience members, staff track whether "constituents are comfortable providing both positive and negative feedback" and "community members return time and time again." Institutionally, they evaluate employees' "relationship skills" and the extent to which "young people rise to leadership." And with regard to broader institutional impact, they even look at the extent to which "community responsive exhibits become more widespread in museums." These outcomes and indicators may be atypical, but they are all measurable. For example, the metric around both positive and negative visitor comments is one that reflects their specific interest in supporting dialogue, not just receiving compliments. Many museums review comments from visitors, but few judge their success by the presence of negative as well as positive ones.

---

1   For a comprehensive approach to outcome and impact measurement, you may want to download the British government report on Social ROI at http://www.participatorymuseum.org/ref10-1a/ For specific frameworks for impact assessment related to informal science projects, consult the NSF Frameworks for Evaluation Impact of Informal Science Education Projects (PDF): http://www.participatorymuseum.org/ref10-1b/

2   Read the full list of indicators of success for the Wing Luke Asian Museum at http://www.participatorymuseum.org/ref10-2/

Step 1: Articulating Participatory Goals

The first step to evaluating participatory projects is to agree on a clear list of goals. Particularly when it comes to new and unfamiliar projects, staff members may have different ideas about what success looks like. One person may focus on sustained engagement with the institution over time, whereas another might prioritize visitor creativity. Clear participatory goals can help everyone share the same vision for the project or the institution.

Goals for engagement do not have to be specific to individual projects; they can also be generalized to participatory efforts throughout the institution. For example, at the Museum of Life and Science (MLS), Beck Tench created a honeycomb diagram to display the seven core goals MLS was trying to achieve across their forays into social participation: to educate, give a sense of place, establish transparency, promote science as a way of knowing, foster dialogue, build relationships, and encourage sharing. This diagram gave staff members at MLS a shared language for contextualizing the goals they might apply to participatory projects.

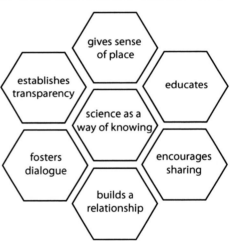

This simple diagram helps MLS staff members evaluate potential programs against institutional goals.

The diagram became a planning tool. For proposed social media experiments, Tench and other MLS staff members shaded the cells of the honeycomb to identify which goals they felt that project would target. This helped them prioritize their ideas and be aware of potential imbalances in their offerings. Later, staff teams used the diagrams to reflect on the extent to which the goals they expected to achieve were met in implementation.

The honeycomb diagram is a simple framework that MLS staff members can apply against a range of projects at different points in their planning and implementation. It is accessible to team members of all levels of evaluation experience and expertise, including visitors and community participants. This makes it easy for everyone to use and understand.

Step 2: Defining Participatory Outcomes

Shared goals provide a common vocabulary to help staff members talk about their aspirations. Outcomes are the behaviors that the staff perceives as indicative of goals being met. Outcomes and outputs are two different things. For example, consider the participatory goal for an institution to become a "safe space for difficult conversations." The starting point for many museums with this goal would be to host exhibits or programs on provocative topics likely to stir up "difficult conversations." But offering an exhibition about AIDS or a panel discussion about racism neither ensures dialogue nor the perception of a safe space. An exhibition is an output, but it does not guarantee the desired outcomes.

What are the outcomes associated with a "safe space for difficult conversations?" Such a space would:

- Attract and welcome people with differing points of view on contentious issues
- Provide explicit opportunities for dialogue among participants on tough issues
- Facilitate dialogue in a way that makes participants feel confident and comfortable expressing themselves
- Make people feel both challenged and supported by the experience

Each of these is an outcome that can be measured. For example, imagine a comment board in an exhibition intended to be a "safe space for difficult conversations." Staff members could code:

- The range of divergent perspectives demonstrated in the comments
- The tone of the comments (personal vs. abstract, respectful vs. destructive)
- The extent to which visitors responded to each other's comments

Researchers could also conduct follow-up interviews to ask visitors whether they contributed to the comment board, how they felt about the comments on display, their level of comfort in sharing their own beliefs, the extent to which their perspective was altered by the experience of expressing their own ideas and/or reading others, and whether they would seek out such an experience in the future.

Developing Meaningful Measurement Tools

Once staff members know what goals they are trying to achieve and what outcomes reflect those goals, they can develop evaluative tools to assess the incidence of the outcomes. This is often the most challenging part of evaluation design, and it requires thinking creatively about what behaviors or indicators are associated with desired outcomes.

The New Economics Foundation has defined four qualities of effective evaluative indicators: action-oriented, important, measurable, and simple.[3] Imagine developing indicators to reflect this goal for an educational program: "visitors will have deeper relationships with the staff." What measurable indicators would provide valuable information about relationships between staff members and visitors? How could assessment help staff members develop new strategies or practices to improve incidence of the outcome in future projects?

To assess this outcome, you might consider the following indicators:

- Whether staff members and participants could identify each other by name at different stages during and after the program
- The volume and type of correspondence (email, phone, social networks) among participants and staff outside of program time
- Whether staff members and participants stayed in touch at fixed time intervals after the program was over

These indicators might help determine what kinds of behaviors are most effective at promoting "deeper relationships" and encourage the staff to adjust their actions accordingly. For example, some educators (like the volleyball teacher described on page 33) find it particularly valuable to learn students' names and begin using them from the first session. These kinds of

---

3   This list came from the excellent InterAct report on *Evaluating Participatory, Deliberative, and Co-operative Ways of Working*, which you can download [PDF] at http://www.participatorymuseum.org/ref10-3/

discoveries can help staff members focus on what's important to achieve their goals.

CASE STUDY

ENGAGING FRONT-LINE STAFF AS RESEARCHERS AT THE MUSEUM OF SCIENCE AND INDUSTRY TAMPA

When indicators are simple to measure and act on, staff members and participants at all levels of research expertise can get involved in evaluation. For example, at the Museum of Science and Industry in Tampa (MOSI), front-line staff members were engaged as researchers in the multi-year REFLECTS project. The goal of REFLECTS was to train educators to be able to scaffold family visitor experiences in ways that would encourage "active engagement" (as opposed to passive disinterest). To make it possible for front-line educators to effectively recognize when visitors were and were not actively engaged in their experience, the research team developed a list of eleven visitor behaviors that they felt indicated active engagement, including: visitors making comments about the exhibit, asking and answering each other's questions, making connections to prior experiences, and encouraging each other's behaviors.

Educators made video and audio recordings of their interactions with families and then went back later to code the recordings for those eleven indicators. The REFLECTS team didn't judge the content of the cues (i.e. whether a visitor asked a personal question or a science-focused one), just tallied their incidence. And then educators headed back out on the floor to adjust their behavior and try again.

At the 2009 Association of Science and Technology Centers conference, MOSI staff members showed video of themselves engaging with visitors before and after working in the REFLECTS program, and the difference was impressive. The educators didn't communicate more or better content in the "after" videos. Instead, they did a better job supporting visitors' personal connection to the exhibits, rather than trying, often unsuccessfully, to coerce visitors into engagement.

The REFLECTS research served three audiences: visitors, front-line staff, and the institution. For visitors, it improved the quality of staff interactions.

For the front-line staff, it provided empowerment and professional development opportunities. For the institution, it made front-line interactions with
visitors more effective. The primary researcher, Judith Lombana, had observed that museums spend a lot of time engaging with visitors in ways that
do not improve engagement or learning. This is a business problem. As she
put it: "waste occurs with activities or resources that some particular guest
does not want." By finding action-oriented, important, simple measures for
active engagement, the REFLECTS team was able to create an evaluation
strategy that succeeded on multiple levels.

Evaluation Questions Specific to Participation

Because participatory practices are still fairly new to cultural institutions, there are few comprehensive examples of evaluation techniques
and instruments specific to participatory projects. Traditional evaluation
techniques, like observation, tracking, surveys, interviews, and longitudinal
studies are all useful tools for assessing participatory projects. However,
because participatory projects often involve behaviors that are not part of
the traditional visitor experience, it's important to make sure that evaluation
instruments will capture and measure the distinct experiences offered.

If your institution's standard summative evaluation of an exhibition or
program is about the extent to which visitors have learned specific content
elements, switching to an evaluative tool that allows the staff to assess the
extent to which visitors have exercised creative, dialogic, or collaborative
functions can be quite a leap.

To design successful evaluative tools for participatory projects:

- Review the specific skills and values that participatory experiences support (see page 193) to determine which kinds of indicators
  might reflect your project's goals
- Take a 360 degree approach, looking at goals, outcomes, and
  indicators for staff members, participants, and non-participating
  visitors
- Consult with participants and project staff members to find out
  what outcomes and indicators they think are most important to
  measure

Here are some specialized questions to consider that pertain specifically to the participant, staff, and visitor experience of participatory projects.

Questions about participants:
- If participation is voluntary, what is the profile of visitors who choose to participate actively? What is the profile of visitors who choose not to participate?
- If there are many forms of voluntary participation, can you identify the differences among visitors who choose to create, to critique, to collect, and to spectate?
- How does the number or type of model content affect visitors' inclination to participate?
- Do participants describe their relationship to the institution and/ or to staff in ways that are distinct from the ways other visitors describe their relationship?
- Do participants demonstrate new levels of ownership, trust, and/ or understanding of institutions and their processes during or after participation?
- Do participants demonstrate new skills, attitudes, behaviors, and/ or values during or after participation?
- Do participants seek out more opportunities to engage with the institution or to engage in participatory projects?

Questions about staff:
- How do participatory processes affect staff members' self-confidence and sense of value to the institution?
- Do staff members demonstrate new skills, attitudes, behaviors, and/or values during or after participation?
- Do staff members describe their relationships to colleagues and or visitors as altered by participation?
- Do staff members describe their roles differently during or after participation?
- How do staff members perceive the products of participation?

- Do staff members seek out more opportunities to engage in participatory projects?

Questions about non-participating visitors who watch or consume the products of participation (exhibits, programs, publications):

- Do visitors describe products created via participatory processes differently from those created via traditional processes? Do they express comparative opinions about these products?
- If participation is open and voluntary, do visitors understand the opportunity to participate?
- Why do visitors choose not to participate? What would make them interested in doing so?

Because participation is diverse, no single set of questions or evaluative technique is automatically best suited to its study. There are researchers in motivational psychology, community development, civic engagement, and human-computer interaction whose work can inform participatory projects in museums.[4] By partnering with researchers from other fields, museum evaluators can join participatory, collaborative learning communities to the mutual benefit of all parties.

CASE STUDY
STUDYING THE CONVERSATIONS ON SCIENCE BUZZ

Imagine a project that invites visitors to engage in dialogue around institutional content. How would you study and measure their discussions to determine whether users were just chatting or really engaging around the content of interest?

In 2007, the Institute of Museum and Library Services (IMLS) funded a research project called *Take Two* to address this question. *Take Two* brought together researchers in the fields of rhetoric, museum studies, and science education to describe the impact of a participatory project called *Science Buzz* that invited visitors to engage in dialogue on the Web about science.

---

4   For a comprehensive resource bank of research and case studies related to public participation (with a focus on civic participation), see http://www.participatorymuseum.org/ref10-4/

Science Buzz is an award-winning online social network managed by the Science Museum of Minnesota.[5] It is a multi-author community website and exhibit that invites museum staff members and outside participants to write, share, and comment on articles related to contemporary science news and issues. *Science Buzz* also includes physical museum kiosks located in several science centers throughout the US, but the *Take Two* study focused on the online discourse.

Science Buzz is a complicated beast. From 2006 to 2008, staff members and visitors posted and commented on over 1,500 topics, and the blog enjoyed high traffic from an international audience. While the museum had conducted internal formative evaluation on the design and use of Science Buzz,[6] the staff was interested in conducting research on how users interacted with each other on the website and what impact it had on their learning.

That's where *Take Two* came in. Because Science Buzz is a dialogue project, it made sense to work with researchers from the field of rhetoric. Jeff Grabill, a Michigan State University professor who focuses on how people use writing in digital environments, led the research. The Take Two team focused their study on four questions:

1. What is the nature of the community that interacts through Science Buzz?
2. What is the nature of the on-line interaction?
3. Do these on-line interactions support knowledge building for this user community?
4. Do on-line interactions support inquiry, learning, and change within the museum – i.e., what is the impact on museum practice?[7]

The first two questions are descriptive and focus on better understanding the user profile and the dialogic ways that people engage with each other on the website. The last two are about impact outcomes both for participants

5 Visit the *Science Buzz* website at http://www.participatorymuseum.org/ref10-5/

6 Download the formative evaluation of *Science Buzz* at http://www.participatorymuseum.org/ref10-6/

7 You can learn more about the study from Jeff Grabill, Stacey Pigg, and Katie Wittenauer's 2009 paper, "Take Two: A Study of the Co-Creation of Knowledge on Museum 2.0 Sites," available at http://www.participatorymuseum.org/ref10-7/

and for the staff. Since the researchers were examining historic blog posts, they did not have access to non-participating audience members. They did not study the impact on those who consume the content on *Science Buzz* but do not contribute content to the site themselves.

To evaluate the knowledge building impact of *Science Buzz*, the researchers coded individual statements in blog posts and comments for twenty percent of posts with fifteen comments or more, grouping them into four categories: "building an argument," "exploring new ideas," "building a writer's identity," and "building a community identity." Staff members associated each statement with one of these four categories using a comprehensive set of descriptive indicators (see table on page 313). By coding individual statements, researchers were able to spot patterns in argumentation used on the site that represented different forms of individual and or interpersonal knowledge building. For the representative sample used, the researchers found the following overall distribution of statement types:

- Building an argument - 60%
- Building a writer's identity - 25%
- Building community identity - 11.4%
- Exploring new ideas - 1.8%

This data demonstrated that Science Buzz users were definitely using the blog to make arguments about science, but not necessarily to construct knowledge communally. For this reason, the *Take Two* team shifted its research in the third year of the study, away from "co-construction of knowledge" and toward a broader examination of "learning."

They used the National Academies of Science's 2009 *Learning Strands in Informal Environments (LSIE)* report as the basis for the development of new indicators with which to code *Science Buzz* conversations.[8] The *LSIE* report presented six "strands" of science learning, including elements like identity-building, argumentation, and reflection that were clearly visible in *Science Buzz* discourse. As of January 2010, this research is still ongoing. Dr. Kirsten Ellenbogen, Director of Evaluation and Research in Learning at the Science Museum of Minnesota, commented:

8   Read or purchase the LSIE report at http://www.participatorymuseum.org/ref10-8/

Building an Argument	Exploring New Ideas	Building a Writer's Identity	Building a Community Identity
■ Claim ■ Citation of authority ■ Citation of evidence ■ Other argument	■ Introduction of a new idea ■ Improvement of the idea of another ■ Use of stasis	■ Articulation of a role ■ Invocation of place ■ Invocation of education ■ Invocation of status ■ Use of values ■ Use of affect ■ Use of technology to achieve a purpose	■ Construction of a connection between ideas/people ■ Articulation of a shared role ■ Articulation of a shared experience ■ Invitation

The *Take Two* research team coded comments on Science
Buzz based on the incidence of these indicators.

The LSIE report stated that science argumentation is rare in museum exhibits, and it suggested that informal environments were a long way from providing the necessary instruction to support scientific argumentation.[9] But Science Buzz is a natural dialogue setting, and we felt like we were seeing scientific argumentation and debate happening all over the site. The Take Two research gave us evidence to support that.

By partnering with researchers in the field of rhetoric, the *Science Buzz* team was better able to understand and describe the nature and potential impact of conversation on the website. The research also revealed new questions for study both on *Science Buzz* and other online dialogue sites. One of the findings of *Take Two* was that identity-building statements are often intertwined with scientific arguments, and it is important to understand who a person is as well as what they say. This may sound obvious, but as

---

9   See pages 145, 151, and 162 of the LSIE report for the discussion about the potential for scientific argumentation in museum settings.

Grabill noted, rhetoriticians frequently separate what they consider rational statements from affective or "identity work" statements, which are considered less important to argumentation. While the first phase of the research focused entirely on types of statements made in discrete, anonymized comments, the second phase included examination of the particular role of staff participants in promoting learning. In future research of *Science Buzz*, it's possible to go even further, examining how individual users' interactions with the site over time impact their learning, self-concept, and contribution to the community.

Part of the challenge of the *Take Two* project was simply developing the analytic tools to study a familiar question (science knowledge-building) in a new environment (online social network). The team focused on mission-driven questions, found reasonable tools to answer those questions, rigorously applied those tools, and published the results. Hopefully many future teams will approach research on visitor participation with a comparable level of rigor, creativity, and interest in sharing lessons learned with the field.

Incremental and Adaptive Participatory Techniques

While formal evaluation is typically separated into discrete stages—front-end, formative, remedial, summative—participatory projects often benefit from more iterative approaches to assessment. One of the positive aspects of participatory projects is that they don't have to be fully designed before launch. Participatory projects are often released bit by bit, evolving in response to what participants do. This can be messy and can involve changing design techniques or experimental strategies along the way, which, as noted in the stories of *The Tech Virtual* and *Wikipedia Loves Art*, can either alleviate or increase participant frustration. While changes may be frustrating and confusing, they are often essential to keep an experimental project going in the right direction.

Adaptive evaluation techniques are particularly natural and common to the Web for two reasons. First, collecting data about user behavior is fairly easy. There are many free analytical tools that allow Web managers to capture real-time statistics about who visits which pages and how they use them. These tools automate data collection, so staff members can focus on working with the results rather than generating them.

Second, most Web designers, particularly those working on social websites, expect their work to evolve over time. Most Web 2.0 sites are in "perpetual beta," which means that they are released before completion and remain a work-in-progress—sometimes for years. This allows designers to be responsive to observed user behaviors, altering the platform to encourage certain actions and minimize or eliminate others.

Adaptive evaluation can help designers and managers see where they are and aren't hitting their goals and adjust their efforts accordingly. For example, the Powerhouse Museum children's website features a popular section called "Make & Do" which offers resources for family craft activities.[10] Each craft activity takes about two weeks of staff time to prepare, so the team decided to use Web analytics to determine which activities were most popular and use those as a guide for what to offer next.

In the site's first two years, Web analytics showed that the most popular craft activity by far was *Make a King's Crown*, which provides templates and instructions to cut out your own royal headgear. At first, the staff responded by producing similar online craft resources, providing templates for wizards' hats, jester hats, samurai helmets, and masks. Then, the Web team dug a little deeper into the Web metrics and realized that the vast majority of the visitors

Make a crown fit for a king.

While the *Make a King's Crown* page received high traffic, only 9% of the visitors were Australians, compared to 54% from the US and 14% from the UK.

to the *King's Crown* page were based outside Australia. When they looked at the geographic detail for the Make & Do section, they found that gardening and Easter-related activities were far more popular with Australian and Sydney residents than various forms of hat making. Because the Powerhouse is a majority state-funded museum (and because the children's website was intended to primarily provide pre- and post-visit experiences), their

10 Visit the Make & Do website at: http://www.participatorymuseum.org/ref10-10/

priority is local audiences. They decided to redirect future craft resources away from headgear and towards activities that were of more value and interest to Australians from New South Wales.[11]

Adaptive evaluation can be applied to physical venues and visitor experiences, but it's not easy. Cultural institutions tend to lack both the Web's automated analytic tools and flexible growth pattern. If the educational program and exhibition schedule is set months or even years in advance, it is unlikely that staff members will be able to shift gears based on visitor input. This is one of the reasons that remedial evaluation can be so painful in museums; even if staff members would like to make changes to improve the visitor experience based on observed problems, it's hard to find the money or time to do so. Many staff members can also get focused on "seeing it through" and may be concerned about tainting data by making changes in mid-stream. Encouraging adaptive evaluation requires cultivating a culture of experimentation.

When it comes to physical platforms for participation, it's not necessary to design the perfect system behind the scenes. Release it unfinished, see what visitors do, and adjust accordingly. If projects are truly designed to "get better the more people use them," then there's a built-in expectation that they will grow and change over their public life. Staff members can be part of that growth and change through adaptive evaluation.

Continual evaluation can also provide a useful feedback loop that generates new design insights that can ultimately lead to better visitor experiences. Consider the humble comment board. If there is one in your institution, consider changing the material provided for visitors to write on or with and see how it affects the content and volume of comments produced. Change the prompt questions, add a mechanism by which visitors can easily write "response cards" to each other, or experiment with different strategies for staff curation/comment management. By making small changes to the project during operation, you can quickly see what kinds of approaches impact the experience and how.

---

11 For more information, consult Sebastian Chan's January 2010 blog post, "Let's Make More Crowns, or the Danger of Not Looking Closely at Your Web Metrics," at http://www.participatorymuseum.org/ref10-11/

Involving Participants in Evaluation

One of the underlying values of participatory projects is respect for participants' opinions and input. Because project ownership is often shared among staff members and participants, it makes sense to integrate participants into evaluation as well as design and implementation. This doesn't mean evaluating participant experiences, which is part of most institutional evaluative strategies. It means working with participants to plan, execute, and distribute the evaluation of the project.

Adaptive projects often include casual ways for participants to offer their feedback on projects at any time, either by communicating with project staff members or sharing their thoughts in community meetings or forums. Particularly when participants feel invested in a project, either as contributors or as full co-creative partners, they want to do what they can to help improve and sustain the project's growth. Participants may notice indicators that are not readily apparent to project staff, and they can offer valuable input on the most effective ways to measure and collect data related to their experiences.

For example, the St. Louis Science Center's *Learning Places* project, in which teenagers designed science exhibits for local community centers, was evaluated in two ways: by an external evaluator and by internal video interviews with the teenage participants.[12] The external evaluation focused on the teens' understanding and retention of science, technology, engineering, and mathematics concepts, whereas the participants' interviews focused on the project's impact on teens' educational and career choices. These different evaluative techniques reflected two different sets of measurement goals and priorities. While the funder (the National Science Foundation) was interested in how *Learning Places* promoted science learning, the teen participants and the project staff were interested in how the program impacted personal and professional development.

Involving community members in the design and implementation of evaluative techniques is not easy. Participatory evaluation requires additional resources. For many institutions, it may be too expensive to sustain

---

12 See the *Learning Places* teen videos at http://www.participatorymuseum.org/ref10-12/

participatory partnerships through the research stage, or participants may not be able to continue their involvement beyond the co-design project.

Participatory evaluation is also challenging because it requires a radical shift in thinking about the audience for the research and how it will be used. At least in the museum field, researchers and practitioners are still working out how visitor studies can be most useful to actually impact how institutions function. It's an even further step to suggest that not only should visitors' reactions and experiences partly guide professional practice, but that their goals should drive research just as much as institutional goals. This can be particularly challenging when working with an outside funder with specific research expectations that may not be relevant to the goals and interests of participants.

How can you decide whether to involve participants in evaluation? Just as there are multiple models for ways to engage community members in participatory projects, there are several ways to involve them in evaluation. The LITMUS project in South London separated evaluation of community projects into three basic models: top-down, cooperative, and bottom-up.[13] Top-down evaluation is a traditional assessment strategy in which senior managers or external evaluators plan and manage evaluation. External evaluators also lead cooperative evaluation, but in this model, evaluators serve as guides, working with participants and project staff to develop assessment techniques and to collect and analyze data. In bottom-up models, external evaluators still facilitate the evaluation process, but their work is directed by participants and project staff to address their interests rather than institutionally driven measures of success.

Choosing the most effective way to engage participants in evaluation depends on several factors, including:

- *Participant motivation.* Are participants interested and willing to participate in evaluation?
- *Participant availability.* Are participants able to continue to contribute to the evaluation of projects after they are completed? Can the institution compensate them for their time in some way?

---

13 Read more about the LITMUS project in Section 5 of *Evaluating Participatory, Deliberative, and Co-operative Ways of Working*, available for download [PDF] at http://www.participatorymuseum.org/ref10-13/

- *Participant ability.* Are participants sufficiently skilled and trusted in the community to help lead a fair evaluation of the project? Are the assessment indicators simple enough for amateur evaluators to measure them?
- *Relevance.* Are the evaluative goals and measures relevant to participants' experience? Can they gain something from participating in evaluation? Will they be able to take new action based on their involvement?
- *Transparency.* Is the institution willing to open up evaluative processes to outside involvement? Will participants be able to distribute and use the results of the evaluation for their own purposes?

If the answer to many of these questions is "yes," it might be appropriate to pursue cooperative or bottom-up evaluation instead of a traditional study. If the answer is mostly "no," staff members can improve the potential for participatory evaluation in the future by improving the incidence of these indicators. For example, staff members might make traditional internal evaluations available for public use to enhance transparency, or they might work with participants to develop some questions for evaluation without including them in the entire process.

While it can be complex to execute, participatory evaluation encourages staff members to design measurement techniques that are actually useful—tools that they can use to improve the work for next time. When participants are invested in acting as researchers, they hold staff members accountable to the findings. Especially in long-standing partnerships—for example, consultative advisory boards—both the staff and community members should feel that research is helping enhance the project overall. Otherwise, why spend all that time on evaluation? In this way, participatory techniques can help make evaluation more beneficial to how cultural institutions function—not just in participatory projects, but across the board.

We've now looked at a range of techniques for planning, implementing, and evaluating participatory projects. In Chapter 11, we'll focus inward and look at how institutional culture can impact which kinds of projects are most likely to succeed at different organizations. Sustaining participation isn't just a matter of motivating visitors; it also requires developing management strategies that help staff members feel supported and enthusiastic about being involved.

CHAPTER 11

MANAGING & SUSTAINING PARTICIPATION

REMEMBER THE TAGGING BOOK DROPS that were introduced in Chapter 1 as an elegant way to let people add their opinions to library books (page 6)? As I finished writing this book, I decided to solicit a photo to illustrate that story. A Dutch friend agreed to take pictures of the book drops. A month before the book went to press, this email arrived in my inbox (emphasis added):

> I am afraid I have got bad news for you... This afternoon I went to the library in Haarlem Oost to take your pictures. When I arrived there, I noticed that they used 'normal' returning shelves instead of the tagging system. I asked one of the employees and it turned out that they quit using the system some time ago. Of course I asked her why. **She explained that it more or less was a victim of its own success.** First of all, particular shelves were overloaded in a short period of time (to be frank, I don't see the problem here, but to her it was a big problem, so I guess it influenced their working processes).
>
> **Next to that, people were using the system so seriously that it took them a lot of time per book to decide where to place it.** That caused some logistic problems in the (small) building, especially as they have some peak times. That meant that people often had to wait for other

people to return their books - and then once they reached the front, they too needed time to decide where to place their books. There was an alternative system next to the tagging system to improve the flow, but people did not want to be rude and waited patiently on their turn—so the alternative did not work.

The woman I spoke to regrets that they do not use the tagging system anymore. **She said that it gave them a good understanding of what the people in the neighborhood like to read.** She said that they are determined to introduce the system again when they have a good solution on the logistic problem, but unfortunately she could not give me a concrete term for that.

What happened here? The library introduced a participatory project that proved wildly successful. Visitors liked the activity, and it helped the staff learn more about the usage of the collection. But the book drops failed because they disrupted staff expectations and behavior. The system introduced new challenges for staff—to manage return shelves differently and to deal with queues. Rather than adapt to these challenges, they removed the system.

This doesn't mean that the librarians at Haarlem Oost were lazy or unsympathetic to patrons' interests. They were part of an institutional culture that was not effectively set up to integrate and sustain a project that introduced new logistical challenges. They lacked the ability—and possibly the agency—to make the system work reasonably within their standard practices, and so the project became untenable.

Participatory projects can only succeed when they are aligned with institutional culture. No matter how mission-aligned or innovative an idea is, it must feel manageable for staff members to embrace it wholeheartedly. Building institutions that are more participatory involves educating, supporting, and responding to staff questions and concerns. It also requires a different approach to staffing, budgeting, and operating projects. This chapter provides a blueprint for developing management structures that can support and sustain participation, so institutional leaders, staff members, and stakeholders can confidently and successfully engage with visitors as participants.

Participation and Institutional Culture

In 2008, a group of researchers associated with the Online Computer Library Center (OCLC) published a report called *Beyond the Silos of the LAMs: Collaboration Among Libraries, Archives, and Museums* that reviewed the implementation and outcome of several collaborative projects. The authors noted three frequent reasons why some projects failed to get started or completed successfully:

> The idea was not of great enough importance.
>
> The idea was premature.
>
> The idea was too overwhelming.[1]

The first of these is a question of mission relevance, but the second and third relate to institutional culture. Promoting participation in a traditional cultural institution is not always easy. Engaging with visitors as collaborators and partners requires staff members to reinterpret their roles and responsibilities. This can be threatening or uncomfortable for professionals who are unsure how their skills will be valued in the new environment. To successfully initiate a participatory project, staff need to be able to directly address the value, mission relevance, and potential of participation—both for institutions as a whole and for individual staff members.

There are five common issues that arise when pitching or planning a participatory project:

1. *Some cultural professionals perceive participatory experiences as an unappealing fad.* Some people see social networking and related activities as over-hyped, trivial entertainment that will hopefully blow over soon. This perception is exacerbated when well-meaning professionals advocate for engaging on the social Web and in participatory activities because "everyone else is doing it," using threats of impending irrelevance to prod people into action. While these admonitions may have some truth to them, scare tactics often lead skeptics to become more entrenched in

---

1   Download and read the *Beyond the Silos of the LAMs* report by Diane Zorich, Gunter Waibel, and Ricky Erway [PDF] at http://www.participatorymuseum.org/ref11-1/

their opposition. Focusing on mission relevance will help these people see the potential value of participation beyond the hype.

2. *Participatory projects are threatening to institutions because they involve a partial ceding of control.* While some other innovative endeavors, like technology investment, have heavy financial risks associated with them, participatory projects need not be expensive to develop or maintain. Instead, they are disruptive to the ways that museum staff members and trustees perceive the image, stature, and content of the institution. To successfully initiate a participatory project, you must be willing to engaging stakeholders in dialogue about the ways participation might diffuse or distort institutional brand and content. Discussing the positive and negative outcomes of visitor participation can help staff members air their concerns and explore new perspectives.

3. *Participatory projects fundamentally change the relationships between the institution and visitors.* If staff members see visitors as a hazy mass of consumers, it will take a lot of work to assert the value of integrating visitors' voices and experiences into museum content experiences. Additionally, if staff members are not permitted to be personal and open with visitors, they may not be able to facilitate dialogue or manage community projects successfully. To successfully encourage participation, there must be some level of mutual trust and genuine interest among staff members and visitors alike.

4. *Participatory projects introduce new visitor experiences that cannot be evaluated using traditional museum assessment techniques alone.* When talking about the goals of participatory projects, you may find yourself talking about visitor behavior and outcomes that are new to many cultural institutions. Outcomes like empowerment and community dialogue don't fit into traditional assessment tools used by institutions and funders, which tend to measure outputs rather than impact. Be prepared to educate both managers and funders about alternative ways to frame the goals and outcomes of participatory projects, and to include evaluative

tool development as part of the project development process and budget.

5. *Participatory projects require more staff time and budget allocated for operation than for development.* While many cultural institution projects generate products—programs, events, exhibitions, performances—that are released in a completed state and are maintained for a fixed amount of time, participatory projects are released in an "initial" state and then evolve and grow over time. For example, an exhibition that includes heavy visitor contribution on the floor is not "done" until the exhibition closes, and content and design staff members who might have otherwise moved onto other projects after opening may need to continue to manage the project throughout its public run. Make sure your budget and staffing plans match the reality of participatory needs over the course of your project.

Addressing these five concerns should demonstrate how participatory projects are viable at your institution. The next step is to tailor the project's development to staff culture. Every institution has different strengths and weaknesses that impact which projects are most likely to succeed. If staff members are wedded to long editorial review processes for developing public-facing content, community blogs or on-the-floor contributory projects might not succeed. But that same slow-moving institution might be highly amenable to personalized floor experiences or more long-term community partnerships. Just as each project must fit mission and programmatic goals, it must also be designed to function with pre-existing work patterns in mind.

For example, when the Minnesota Historical Society embarked on the design of the crowdsourced *MN150* exhibition, the design team found a way to incorporate visitors' voices while honoring staff desires to retain control of the overall project. The staff invited citizens to nominate topics for the exhibition, but not much more than that. They didn't let visitors vote or join in on the topic selection process. They even planned a parallel "Plan B" content development process in case the public nominations didn't bear fruit (which they did). Once the nominations rained in, senior exhibit developer Kate Roberts reflected:

> We locked ourselves in this room with the nominations. We as a team then winnowed based on our criteria—geographic distribution, diversity of experience, topical distribution, chronological distribution, evidence of sparking real change, origination in Minnesota, exhibit readiness, and quality of nomination. We did it with a lot of talking.

A few months later, they emerged with a list of 150 topics and a plan for the exhibition. This project enabled exhibit developers, curators, and designers to start encouraging visitor participation without feeling overwhelmed or uncomfortable.

The *MN150* staff and advisor team, deep in deliberation about the topics to be included in the exhibition. At this point, they were vetting a list of 400 nominations that they had sent out to historians, subject experts, and educators for review.

Every institution has some programs or practices about which they are highly protective. It's important to start with projects that feel safe and open to participation, even if the ultimate goal is to make changes across the institution. For example, while working with a very traditional museum that was trying to start experimenting with participatory engagement with visitors,

I proposed a wide range of starting points. We quickly realized that while engaging visitors in dialogue on the Web was acceptable to the staff, giving visitors sticky notes to "mark up" the museum with their questions was not. Though the sticky notes would have taken a fraction of the resources required for the online experiments, curators had two concerns: that the notes would visually degrade the exhibits, and that visitors might ask and answer questions incorrectly, thereby disseminating inaccurate information within the museum. They felt this way despite the fact that the museum had very low visitation and many more people were likely to see the websites than the sticky notes.

In this kind of situation, starting with a tactic that is comfortable for staff can get the conversation moving in a participatory direction. But it's important to keep pushing the conversation into areas that are less comfortable. At the museum in question, starting on the Web helped staff members feel comfortable, but it also let them separate themselves from participation. They felt like participation was happening "somewhere else" and not on the hallowed ground of the galleries. Our discussions revealed how dedicated they were to creating and controlling the visitor experience in the galleries, and it became clear that it would take concerted effort and a clear strategic vision to move toward engaging in more substantive participatory projects onsite.

Participation Starts with Staff

The best place to start introducing participatory techniques in a cultural institution is internally with staff members and volunteers. If staff members do not feel comfortable supporting or leading participatory projects, these initiatives are unlikely to go far. Like visitors, employees need scaffolding and encouragement to try new things. By educating and including them in the development of participatory projects, you can help staff members feel comfortable and confident with these new endeavors. A participatory institution isn't just one that is responsive to and interested in visitors' contributions; it is also one that eagerly and effectively integrates contributions from the staff and stakeholders across the institution.

For example, when the Museum of Life and Science (MLS) in North Carolina started working with social media in a substantive way in 2007, it took a holistic approach that encouraged staff members across the institution to get involved. The MLS hired Beck Tench as Director of Web Experience to lead their efforts. Tench approached individual staff members and stakeholders to see how participatory technologies might support their departmental goals, and she set up small experiments across the institution to help staff experiment with online social engagement and technology.

Horticulture staff members were interested in connecting with people around the unique specimens in the MLS's plant collection. With Tench's help, they started the *Flickr Plant Project*. A horticultural staff member uploads a single image of a rare plant to Flickr once a week along with information about that plant, and then encourages other individuals on Flickr to share their own images and comments of the same plant. Over the first six months of the project, staff uploaded twenty-three images and the project enjoyed 186 user contributions, 137 comments, and 3,722 views. The project design respected the horticulture staff member's desire to produce very little content while opening up dialogue with people around the world about plants.

In contrast, Tench helped the MLS animal keepers set up a blog to share the behind-the-scenes stories of caring for their often mischievous charges.[2] While at first the animal keepers were skeptical of the project, they were eventually rewarded with a dedicated and eager audience and a new sense of institutional importance. The animal keepers update the blog several times a week with stories, images, and video about their work with the museum's animals. They also started a "MunchCam," uploading short videos to YouTube showing how different animals eat.[3]

In addition to online efforts, Tench hosted a weekly happy hour at a local pub, bringing together small groups of staff members each Friday for brainstorming, networking, and relationship-building. In 2009, she ran a personal project called *Experimonth* in which she chose a monthly goal

---

2   Follow the MLS animal keepers' blog at http://www.participatorymuseum.org/ref11-2/

3   View the MunchCam in action at http://www.participatorymuseum.org/ref11-3/

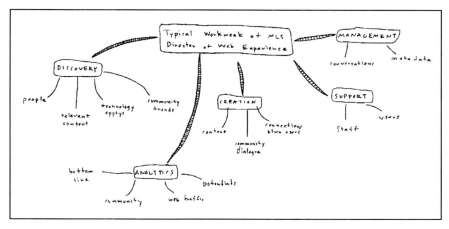

Beck Tench's visual representation of her work. Despite the title "Director of Web Experience," she defines her work activities as covering broad topics like discovery, creation, support, management, and analytics.

(i.e., eat only raw foods, do push-ups every day, share a meal with someone every day) and encouraged others—co-workers and friends—to experiment and share the experience using a multi-author blog.

These activities all contributed to a growing sense of the Museum of Life and Science as a safe space for experimentation, even if individuals only opted in to a few discrete opportunities. As Tench put it, "A lot of my work has been just encouraging staff and making them feel that their jobs and reputation will not be threatened through various forms of digital engagement." By helping staff members find comfortable starting points, she helped make the institution more participatory overall.

Changing the Culture

How can staff teams transition from conservative experiments to more significant forays into participation? If you want to pursue a project that may be a true "stretch" for your institution, you need to find deliberate ways to build comfort, encourage staff participation, and provide continual opportunities for feedback and progressive evaluation.

Consider the basic challenge of becoming more responsive to visitors' interests. I've worked with several institutions where staff members have said, "We want to engage in conversation with visitors, but we have no idea where to start." At these museums, employees who do not work on the front line have little interaction with visitors, and they are often uncertain about who visitors are, why they come, and what interests them. Many staff members may even have a preconceived adversarial relationship with visitors, demeaning their lack of attention and fearing their destruction of the venue and artifacts.

The simplest way to address this is to encourage the staff to spend time working on the front line with visitors. By engaging directly with visitors in low-risk situations, talking to them about exhibits and asking them about their experiences, staff members can start to see visitors as potential collaborators and trusted participants.

Some institutions ask back-of-house staff members to serve as outdoor greeters or help check people in at events. The New York Museum of Modern Art (MoMA) requires all staff members to spend a few hours per month working at the information desk. In MoMA's case, staff members have remarked that just spending a bit of time answering visitors' questions helps them keep visitors' needs in mind when working on other projects. It may not be full-blown participatory engagement, but it's a start.

Other institutions take this further, encouraging staff members to stay connected to visitors' needs by leading programs or conducting visitor research. New York's Tenement Museum, which provides public one-hour tours of historically accurate downtown tenements and the immigrant experience, requires every staff member, no matter how "back of house," to lead at least one tour per month. This helps everyone stay connected to the institution's core mission and its visitors.

CASE STUDY

PROMOTING INSTITUTION-WIDE TRANSPARENCY AT THE INDIANAPOLIS MUSEUM OF ART

When Maxwell Anderson, the Director of the Indianapolis Museum of Art (IMA), wanted to make his institution more transparent, he knew he had to find a way to involve staff members across the institution in the change. In a 2007 article in *Curator*, Anderson wrote:

> Art museum directors can no longer afford to operate in a vacuum. Transparent leadership requires the disclosure of information that has traditionally been seen as sensitive, such as details on what museums acquire and from whom, how museums attract support and spend it, who they have succeeded in serving, and how they measure success.[4]

To provide more disclosure, the IMA launched an internal project to collect and share data about all aspects of museum operation—how many visitors come from different zip codes, how many pieces of art are on display, how much energy the building consumes each day, and so on. In the fall of 2007, the data was made public on the IMA's website in an area called the Dashboard.[5] On the Dashboard, visitors can access real-time statistics with information from across the institution. Visitors can access data commonly considered private, such as the real-time size of the endowment, number of staff members, operating expenses, and retail sales.

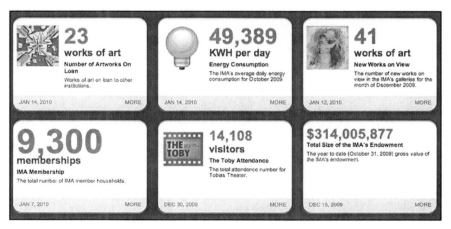

The IMA Dashboard provides current and historical data
across a wide range of functions of the institution.

---

4   See Anderson, "Prescription for Art Museums in the Decade Ahead" in *Curator* 50, no. 1 (2007). Available at: http://www.participatorymuseum.org/ref11-4/
5   Explore the Dashboard at http://www.participatorymuseum.org/ref11-5/

The Dashboard is a tangible project with several small sub-elements that touch every part of the institution. Everyone, from groundskeepers to registrars, reports their data through a Web-based system to update the Dashboard. Chief Information Officer Robert Stein described the Dashboard this way:

> One of our goals was for the Dashboard to reflect the institutional priorities of the museum, and to serve both as an information source for the public, but also as a tracking tool for staff at the museum. If we say energy conservation is important to us, we need ways to track that information over the long term and to monitor whether or not we are being effective. The way the Dashboard works, staff members from around the museum are assigned dashboard statistics which relate to their area of responsibility. These are metrics which are a part of their job responsibilities already. The Dashboard provides a reminder mechanism to keep those statistics fresh, and in context of previous performance. Our goal was to encourage top-of-mind knowledge about statistics we say are important while minimizing the actual data-entry work required to keep up-to-date statistics.

The Dashboard isn't just for visitors. It's also a tool that helps build a culture of transparency and participation throughout the IMA. Every time a staff member consciously logs, uploads, and shares data, he participates in the broader institutional effort. Every time a volunteer or museum member logs on to learn more from the Dashboard, she gains a better understanding of the institution that she supports. While not all staff members may like "airing their dirty laundry" on the Web, doing so in such a discrete, tangible, and distributed way helps the whole institution become more comfortable with how the museum is changing. The Dashboard isn't just a project for the IMA's Web team. It's for everyone.

Staff Strategies for Managing Participation

Managing community projects requires a fundamentally different skill set than managing traditional institutional projects. For this reason, many institutions that pursue major participatory projects—whether internally or with outside partners—hire dedicated "community managers" to facilitate them. Community managers may hold positions in community relations, human resources, or strategic planning. Because many participatory projects start on the Web, it's also common for online managers (like Beck Tench at MLS) to serve in this role.

What makes a good community manager? Community managers need to be skilled at motivating participation and building relationships with diverse participants. Unlike project managers, who are responsible for keeping track of the budget and schedule, community managers are responsible for keeping track of and supporting people. For this reason, community managers' abilities and unique personalities often have a significant effect on the makeup, attitudes, and experiences of participant populations.

The ideal community manager is someone who connects staff members, volunteers, and visitors to each other in diffuse communities of interest, not a person who engages directly with all participants across all projects. When community managers are the sole masters of visitor engagement, two problems arise. First, their efforts may not be fully integrated into the overall work of the institution, which can lead to conflicts between institutional and community needs. Secondly, the communities they manage often become unhealthily centered on the managers' personalities and abilities, causing problems when those community managers choose to leave the institution. Healthy communities are not fiefdoms; they're networks.

Communities can struggle when a single person manages them. When I was at The Tech Museum developing and leading *The Tech Virtual* community (see page 245), I tried to involve a wide range of staff members in the online exhibit development community so we could spread out the interactions and relationships built between amateurs and experts. Unfortunately, The Tech Museum's director decided that spending time with participants was a "waste of time" for staff members whose roles were not explicitly focused on that community. The engineers and fabricators who had enthusiastically engaged early on were forbidden to continue participating. Left on my own, I put on my friendliest, most dynamic face and cultivated a couple of volunteers to help manage the growing community of amateur exhibit designers.

I became participants' sole source of information about the frequently changing project. We started to form unhealthy relationships in which I served as the cheerleader, coach, and point person to all community members.

While my energy and enthusiasm as a community leader held the group together, when I left the museum, the community dwindled. Subsequent museum employees have kept the project going, but the community had connected with me as their focal point. There has not been a new person able to comparably rally participants to high levels of involvement.

I don't tell this story with pride. It was partly my fault that *The Tech Virtual* community did not thrive beyond my tenure. The system we set up to perform that management and cultivate the community was ill-considered. The project looked good—it kept attracting new members—but it was not sustainable. It's a warning sign when community members make comments like, "it was only boundless encouragement from Nina that prevented me from giving up more than once."[6] This participant was one community manager away from leaving the project. It may be easiest to quickly rally a community around one dynamic or charismatic person, but that doesn't make for a healthy, sustaining project.

Decentralizing Community Management

Why does this happen in the first place? There are two good reasons that organizations tend to focus community activities around a single individual: it consolidates resources spent on a particular strategy, and it simplifies interactions for community members.

Institutions are accustomed to associating individual staff members with specific projects and associated resources. But community managers, like front-line staff, are responsible for interacting with a vast and varied group of people who engage with the institution. They are like development officers who cultivate small, targeted sets of individuals via personal relationships. But they are also the face and voice of the institution to everyone who participates in a project: a front-line army of one. This is a problem. If only one person worked in the galleries of a museum, and he was incredibly charismatic and quirky, his personality would put a unique and specific

---

6   Read Richard Milewski's longer reflections on my June 2008 blog post, "Community Exhibit Development: Lessons Learned from The Tech Virtual" at http://www.participatorymuseum.org/ref11-6/

stamp on the onsite experience—one that might attract some visitors and repel others. The same is true for online and participatory communities.

If an institutional community is focused around one person, staff must plan for succession and think about what will happen if that community manager leaves. Even the most well-intentioned community managers may not be able to transfer their unique personality and style to new staff. Imagine the most popular person in a friend group moving away and trying to anoint a new, unknown person to take her place in the social network—it's nearly impossible.

The more voices there are in the mix, the more the community management team can effectively welcome community members of all kinds. The *Science Buzz* blog, which is managed by a team of exhibit developers, science writers, and front-line staff members at the Science Museum of Minnesota, is a good example of diversified community management that models the inclusion of a range of voices and opinions. The Buzz staff representatives even argue with each other in blog comments, modeling a kind of healthy scientific debate that would be impossible for a single community manager to conduct herself.

Strong community managers are educators as well as implementers. They help other staff members understand opportunities for connecting with communities of interest, and they provide support and training so that many individuals across the institution can work with their communities in ways that are sensitive to staff abilities and resources. Consider Beck Tench at the Museum of Life and Science, who helped staff members across the museum start their own participatory projects, including everything from science cafés to animal keeper blogs to exhibits that incorporate visitor feedback. While Tench tracks and supports all of these projects, she's not the lead on any of them.

The ideal community manager is more like a matchmaker than a ringmaster. He points visitors to the networks of greatest interest to them and helps staff members connect with communities that they want to serve. He is energetic and passionate about serving the needs of the institution's communities. It's fine to have a community manager who is the "go to" person—the face of all of the projects—as long as that person is ultimately pointing visitors to other venues for engagement. After all, it's not desirable for everyone who visits your institution to have a relationship with just one person. Visitors should be able to connect with the stories, experiences, and people that are most resonant to them. A good community manager can make that happen.

Taking a Strategic Approach to Encouraging Staff Participation

Diffusing the institutional voice among multiple staff members can generate confusion for visitors, who may be searching for a single individual to whom they can direct queries. This is a valid concern, especially when community projects are spread across many initiatives or online platforms. For clarity, it is useful to have a single individual as the point person for community engagement. But that person should function as a coordinator and manager of community interactions, not the sole provider of those interactions.

This is as true for both internal and visitor-facing projects. For example, when Josh Greenberg joined the staff of the New York Public Library (NYPL) as Director of Digital Strategy and Scholarship, one of his goals was to "unleash the expertise" of staff librarians and scholars. He encouraged staff members across the institution to engage in community outreach via blogs and other digital projects. The outcome was a slate of new NYPL content channels including blogs, podcasts, and video series about cooking, crafts, poetry, and older patrons' interests, each written by a different staff member or staff team.[7] By focusing on coordinating and supporting staff rather than producing visitor-facing content, Greenberg was able to effectively manage and inspire an internal community of new digital content producers.

Greenberg is a high-level staff member at NYPL. While community managers don't have to be at the director or VP level, it is useful for them to be able to think strategically about the overall goals and mission of the organization. High-level community managers are more able to interface with directors across the institution to coordinate reasonable levels of community involvement for various staff members. One of the common

---

7   Peruse the New York Public Library's blogs, audio and video offerings at http://www.participatorymuseum.org/ref11-7/

challenges of a diversified community management plan occurs when low-level staff members become overly absorbed in community outreach and lose perspective on how those projects fit into their overall job requirements. When community projects are coordinated at a high level, it makes it easier for administrative staff to collectively negotiate and balance different staff members' involvement.

In the case of the New York Public Library, Greenberg is pursuing a three-phase strategy for encouraging staff involvement in participatory projects:

1. *Open experimentation.* In this phase, the NYPL leadership granted Greenberg permission to work with energized staff members across the library to start blogging and producing digital content. By "unleashing the expertise" of those who were truly invested and engaged, Greenberg's team was able to start exploring the potential for digital content sharing at NYPL.

2. *Development of institutional policies.* Buoyed by the success of initial experiments, Greenberg began working with other NYPL managers to devise strategies for more widespread staff involvement in digital and community initiatives. Toward that end, he crafted a Policy on Public Internet Communications that put forward an encouraging approach to staff engagement on the Web. By ratifying this policy, the NYPL board indicated that staff could safely initiate digital engagement projects with institutional blessing. Greenberg also worked with the Office of Staff Development to develop new professional development programs to help staff members across the NYPL branches understand how they might use technology to connect with communities of interest around their services and collections. To help the marketing team feel comfortable with diffusing the "voice" of NYPL and to provide consistent and clear expectations for digital engagement, staff members are required to attend one of these training sessions before they can produce digital content on the NYPL website.

3. *Institutionalization of efforts.* This phase is still in the future as of 2010. Greenberg is hopeful that evaluation of digital community

engagement techniques, coupled with increased participation throughout the staff, will help NYPL managers see these efforts as core services of the library. Only then can the NYPL integrate expectations for community engagement and digital outreach into hiring practices, job requirements, and policies on staff advancement.

The NYPL is able to take an ambitious and comprehensive approach to digital community engagement due to Greenberg's leadership. If participation is a strategic goal for your institution, it is useful to have champions at the top who understand what is required from both the management and community engagement perspectives.

Managing Participatory Projects Over Time

The most challenging part of executing participatory projects isn't pitching or developing them; it's managing them. Participatory projects are like gardens; they require continual tending and cultivation. They may not demand as much capital spending and pre-launch planning as traditional museum projects, but they require ongoing management once they are open to participants. This means shifting a larger percentage of project budgets towards operation, maintenance, and facilitation staff.

Consider the management of the *Weston Family Innovation Centre (WFIC)* at the Ontario Science Centre. Sustaining the *WFIC* requires several different kinds of ongoing content production, maintenance, and support. In one area, visitors can use found materials, scissors, and hot glue guns to design their own shoes, which they can then display informally on a set of plinths throughout the gallery. Supporting this activity requires:

- A continual influx of materials, which are acquired monthly both through donations from local factories and bulk orders
- Exhibit maintenance staff to prepare materials for use each day, which involves tasks such as cutting sponges and fabric, replacing glue sticks, and filling bins

- A WFIC coordinator to sort through each day's shoes, saving the best examples for showcases and passing the others to maintenance staff for recycling
- Electronics staff to check the glue guns and tools daily to ensure they are safe for visitors' use
- Host staff to monitor the space, keep bins stocked, and help visitors create, display, and take their shoes home
- Cleaning staff to perform a deep clean of the area each week

The shoe-making activity is highly resource and labor intensive. It is also a high-value, popular activity that has been shown via evaluation to promote the specific innovation skills that the *WFIC* seeks to support. For this reason, the staff continues to support it, while also seeking ways to make it more efficient.

Other parts of the *WFIC* have evolved over time to balance their visitor impact with the cost required to manage them. For example, the *Hot Zone* features video and host-facilitated shows about contemporary science stories. When the *WFIC* opened, the staff offered five new stories every day. This was incredibly labor intensive, and the staff realized that few, if any, visitors

WFIC staff changed their approach to producing content for shows on up-to-the-minute science news to make the shows more manageable without negatively impacting the visitor experience.

were coming back daily for new content. The team changed their approach and began offering one evolving major story per week, supported by two or three fresh, short daily updates. That way, staff members could present up-to-the-minute content with a reasonable amount of labor.

WFIC manager Sabrina Greupner described running the WFIC as being like running a newspaper. "It involves juggling a list of priorities that changes on a daily basis," she commented, "and we take a 'systems' approach to the effort." Unlike the other areas of the Ontario Science Centre, the WFIC has dedicated coordinators as well as a dedicated manager. Each morning, the coordinator goes through his area, making a list of prioritized issues to pursue throughout the day. Managers and coordinators focus on the systems and infrastructure needs, which allows hosts to focus on creatively facilitating visitor experiences.

Not every participatory project is as complex as the Weston Family Innovation Centre, but they all require approaches that are different from standard program and exhibit maintenance strategies. Even a simple comment board requires ongoing moderation and organization of visitor content. Developing consistent systems for maintaining, documenting, and supporting participatory platforms can prevent this work from becoming overwhelming. This was the problem that doomed the Haarlem Oost library book drops. The staff didn't have a good system in place to deal with the shelf overflow and crowding that the tagging activity introduced.

Developing a good system for dealing with participation requires setting boundaries as well as creatively supporting participation. This is particularly true for online community engagement, which can easily extend beyond the workday. While it may make sense for online community staff members to continue to connect with visitors on nights and weekends, managers should help staff develop reasonable boundaries for times when they will not be "on call." When that information is available to visitors, it helps everyone understand when communication is and isn't expected.

CASE STUDY

MANAGING PARTICIPATION AT THE SAN JOSE MUSEUM OF ART

For small museums, setting reasonable boundaries for participatory platforms is essential to their success. For example, in 2008, staff members at the San Jose Museum of Art wanted to create an element for their upcoming *Road Trip* exhibition that would both promote the exhibition and add an interactive component to the physical gallery. They decided to solicit postcards from real people's road trips to be displayed in the exhibition. They created a quirky video promoting the postcard project, put it on YouTube, and waited for the postcards to roll in.

What happened? For the first eight weeks, not a lot. There were about 1,000 views of the YouTube video and 20 postcards submitted by August 15th, at which point something strange happened. Manager of Interactive Technology Chris Alexander left work that Friday afternoon having noticed the YouTube view count on the video suddenly rising. By the time he got home, 10,000 new people had seen the video. After some puzzling, he realized that the video had been featured on the homepage of YouTube. YouTube had anointed the *Road Trip* video with top billing, which shot the views way up (over 80,000 to date) and sent comments and video responses pouring in. The comment stream, which was previously unmoderated, suddenly became overloaded with opportunists who wanted their voice to be heard on the YouTube homepage. Alexander spent an exhausting but rewarding weekend moderating comments and managing the video's newfound fame.

The attention gained from being featured on YouTube's homepage prompted an energized burst of postcards from around the world. Overall, the museum received about 250 postcards. They were featured in the exhibition in a little sitting area along with the video and will be kept in the museum's interpretative archive at the end of the project.

This was a relatively quick project that generated a lot of positive publicity and participation for the museum. But the staff was only able to take it so far. The museum team could not afford to scan or transcribe the postcards, so they were only viewable in the museum, not online. The staff also did not have the time to personally connect with the people who had sent in

The postcards received during *Road Trip* mostly featured hokey roadside attractions. This was in keeping with the YouTube video, in which SJMA staff visited the World's Largest Artichoke in Castroville, CA.

postcards.[8] This was a one-shot approach—put out the video, collect the postcards. The people who sent in postcards weren't able to see their content as part of the collection (unless they visited the exhibition in person), and they weren't recognized for their contribution in a place online where they could both spread the word and enjoy a little fame. This project could not take on a life of its own beyond this exhibition.

From a management perspective, the *Road Trip* postcard project team made clear decisions about how far they would take their engagement with the postcards. They received, organized, and displayed them, but didn't digitize them. Even with this self-designated, budget-related constraint, they still ran into management surprises. Alexander gave up a weekend to manage the onslaught of online participation and spam that arrived with the YouTube homepage feature.

---

8   Note that both of these activities could have likely been performed with the help of volunteers.

The combination of controllable design choices with pop-up surprises is common to many participatory projects. When projects are built to change, staff members must be ready and willing to embrace their evolution.

Sustaining Participation

Many of the projects described in this book are one-time events, programs, or exhibits. How can cultural institutions move from experimenting with visitor participation to integrating it into core functions and services over the long term? To make this happen, staff must be able to demonstrate that participatory techniques help institutions deliver on missions and are appealing and valuable for staff and community members alike.

This can happen from the top down, with new strategic directions focused on the "museum as forum" or the institution as community center. As of 2010, there are several museums and institutional networks reorienting themselves toward community engagement, with staff members at the highest levels publicly advocating for visitor participation and new ways of working. Institutional leadership is essential when it comes to changing institutional culture and fostering supportive environments in which staff can experiment with participation and learn new engagement skills.

But change is also possible from the bottom up. Ultimately, participation succeeds and is sustained not by CEOs and board directors but by the staff and volunteers on the ground. Every institutional stakeholder has a role to play in supporting and leading participatory engagement. Every time a front-line staff member makes a personal connection with a visitor, she builds a relationship. Every time a curator shares his expertise with an amateur, he helps that participant develop new skills and knowledge. Every time a designer develops a showcase for visitors' contributions, she honors their involvement and creative work. Every time a manager finds a more effective way to maintain a participatory experience, he enables staff members and visitors to keep working together.

Consider the story of Jessica Pigza, a staff member at the New York Public Library (NYPL) who evolved from a rare book librarian into a participatory project leader. Energized by Director of Digital Strategy Josh Greenberg's open invitation to staff to "unleash their passions," Pigza started a library blog that focused on handicraft-related items in the NYPL's collection.[9] The blog slowly attracted a dedicated audience who, like Pigza, were interested in lace making, quilting, and bookbinding.

When Pigza started blogging, she was also teaching a class for general audiences on how to use library collection resources (or, in library-speak, "bibliographic instruction"). These classes were offered in conjunction with the public programming department, and they tended to attract about ten attendees. Pigza realized there was an opportunity to take an audience-centric approach to this outreach and hopefully increase participation by developing a bibliographic instruction class specifically targeted to crafters.

Pigza started offering *Handmade*, a class for crafters to learn "how library materials can inform and inspire you in your own DIY endeavors." At the same time, she teamed up with an outside design blogger, Grace Bonney of Design Sponge, to co-create a series of mini-documentaries called "Design by the Book." The series featured five local artists who came to the library, learned something from the collection, and then went home to make creative works based on their experiences. The videos received tens of thousands of views on YouTube and many enthusiastic comments.[10] The classes and the films inspired a range of new partnerships and effusive responses from crafters.

At that point, Pigza realized, "there was a huge audience of regular, curious people in New York who would love to use the library if they knew they could get access to visual collections and get support from friendly people." Pigza formed another partnership, this time with Maura Madden, the author of a book called *Crafternoon*, to offer a series of events called *Handmade Crafternoons* in which crafters could come learn about the library and make art together.

The *Crafternoons* were collaborations between Pigza, Madden, and guest artists. Each month, a guest artist would come in to talk about his work, teach a technique, or discuss something from the library's collection that

9   Visit Pigza's NYPL blog at http://www.participatorymuseum.org/ref11-9/
10   Watch the "Design by the Book" series at http://www.participatorymuseum.org/ref11-10/

inspired him. After about thirty minutes of presenting, audience members were invited to socialize, make crafts, and check out collection materials related to the topic at hand.

The free events drew anywhere from 40 to 120 people, many of whom contributed their own materials (as well as financial donations) to share with others during the craft sessions. *Crafternoons* injected bibliographic instruction with a spirit of collaboration and creativity. Participants approached Pigza with comments like: "I didn't know I could come into this building," or "can you help me with research on this personal project related to 1940s women's knitted hats?" Pigza made new connections with artists, young professionals, and older crafters who started to see the library as a place that supported their community and interests.

At an event in September of 2009, *Crafternoon* participants made embroidery punch cards, using books from the NYPL collection (including this vintage children's book) for design inspiration.

All of these projects were implemented over a matter of months. No one was paid for their time or contributions, including guest artists and collaborators. While the NYPL is moving towards formalizing compensation for participatory projects, they're not there yet. Ideally staff members and partners would receive compensation for community work, but for now it's worth it to Pigza and her cohorts to have the opportunity to engage with the craft community through the library. Pigza noted:

> My boss knows that I find this to be very satisfying, but he also recognizes that it's a good thing for the institution in general. He also is one of the people who recognizes the connection between handicraft and history and rare books. I mostly do this work on weekends and nights and days off. It's not always easy but I have an amazing opportunity to work here and pursue my passion. Not all institutions would support me in this. It's good for me professionally, and it's satisfying. I don't think I'd want to give it up.

The mission of the New York Public Library is "to inspire lifelong learning, advance knowledge, and strengthen our communities."[11] Pigza's participatory work with crafters gave her—and the institution—the opportunity to achieve these goals in ways that were previously unimaginable.

When institutional leaders trust their employees' (and visitors') abilities to contribute creatively, extraordinary things can happen. No one told Jessica Pigza that craft outreach was outside the purview of her job or that she was overstepping into public programming's domain. No one told her she couldn't do her own marketing or form outside partnerships. Instead, her managers encouraged and supported her passions in a mission-specific direction.

Participation becomes sustainable when institutions develop systems to support enthusiastic staff members like Jessica Pigza. It's a matter of flexibility, focus, and trust. For managers, it's a question of helping staff members see what is possible, and then developing mechanisms to guide their efforts in the most effective direction. For employees and volunteers, it's a matter of finding new ways for participatory mechanisms to enhance the value and impact of their work.

There are already people in every institution—managers, staff, volunteers, board members—who want to make this happen. I encourage you to be the one to introduce participatory engagement in your institution. You can do it across a department, with a few colleagues, or on your own if need be. Find a participatory goal that connects to your mission, and develop a

---

11 The New York Public Library's mission is one of the clearest I've seen, matching values to programs. Read the full document at http://www.participatorymuseum.org/ref11-11/

way to achieve it. Start small. Ask a visitor a question or invite a volunteer to help you solve a creative problem. Listen, collaborate, test your assumptions, and try again. Soon enough, participation will be a part of the way you do your work, and by extension, the way your institution functions.

———————

You've reached the end of the strategic section of this book. Now onto the final section, which provides a glimpse of what the future of participatory techniques might hold—a future I hope we can create together.

IMAGINING THE PARTICIPATORY MUSEUM

THROUGHOUT THIS BOOK, I have argued that participatory techniques are design strategies that have specific value and can be applied in cultural institutions to powerful effect. These techniques represent an addition to the design toolkit, not a replacement for traditional strategies. Participation is an "and," not an "or."

I believe in these arguments. I also believe in the potential for participatory techniques to give rise to a new kind of institution, just as interactive design techniques led to the ascendance of the science centers and children's museums in the late twentieth century. While today museums of all types incorporate interactive techniques to some extent, most children's museums and science centers can be described as wholly interactive. Some contemporary leading science centers and children's museums, like the Boston Children's Museum, are radically transformed versions of traditional institutions. The Exploratorium and many others were born in the 1960s and 1970s to offer new kinds of visitor experiences. These institutions use interactive engagement as the fundamental vehicle to promote visitor learning, recreation, and exploration.

I dream of a comparable future institution that is wholly participatory, one that uses participatory engagement as the vehicle for visitor experiences. Imagine a place where visitors and staff members share their personal interests and skills with each other. A place where each person's actions are networked with those of others into cumulative and shifting content for display, sharing, and remix. A place where people discuss the objects on display with friends and strangers, sharing diverse stories and interpretations. A place where people are invited on an ongoing basis to contribute, to collaborate, to co-create, and to co-opt the experiences and content in a designed, intentional environment. A place where communities and staff members measure impact together. A place that gets better the more people use it.

The final result may not resemble today's museums. It may look more like a coffee shop or a community arts center. It may function with models found today in a co-working space or a sewing lounge. It might feature content based on democratic rather than top-down processes. It might prioritize changing displays over traditional conservation and accession practices, multi-vocal content over authoritative catalogs. It might be owned cooperatively or funded by members. It might allocate more dollars to dialogue facilitation than exhibit construction.

Could your institution become such a place? While imagined participatory institutions may appear fundamentally different from traditional museums, so does the modern Boston Children's Museum look different from the display of children's objects that preceded it. That institution shifted from being "about" children and families to being "for" them. What would it look like if it evolved to being "with" them?

This is a question that many institutions are already pondering, and with good reason. The cultural and technological shifts that accompanied the rise of the social Web have changed people's expectations of what makes experiences worthwhile or appealing. People assume the right to co-opt and redistribute institutional content, not just to look at it. They seek opportunities for creative expression, both self-directed and in response to the media they consume. They want to be respected and responded to because of their unique interests. They crave the chance to be recognized by and connected to sympathetic communities around the world. These shifts will change the way that cultural institutions of all types, from museums to libraries to for-profit "experience vendors," do business.

All of these expectations can bring cultural institutions closer to their fundamental goals. Object-centered institutions are uniquely equipped to support creative and respectful community dialogue. Interpersonal interactions around content can strengthen relationships among diverse audiences. Participatory activities can provide valuable civic and learning experiences. Most importantly, the idealistic mission statements of many cultural institutions—to engage visitors with heritage, connect them to new ideas, encourage critical thinking, support creativity, and inspire them to take positive action—can be attained through participatory practice.

There are millions of creative, community-minded people who are ready to visit, contribute to, and participate with cultural institutions that support their interests. While many people explore their passions in online communities, there is enormous potential for them to come together in physical spaces organized around stories and objects that matter to them. These physical spaces may be historical societies or science cafés, art centers or libraries. They may be museums of all sizes and types.

When people have safe, welcoming places in their local communities to meet new people, engage with complex ideas, and be creative, they can make significant civic and cultural impact. The cumulative effort of thousands of participatory institutions could change the world. Rather than being "nice to have," these institutions can become must-haves for people seeking places for community and participation.

How will you integrate participation into your professional work? How do you see it benefiting your institution, your visitors, and your broader audience of community members and stakeholders?

These questions are not rhetorical. I hope that you will join the online conversation about this book at **www.participatorymuseum.org**. There you can find the entire text of this book, along with links to all references and space to share your participatory case studies, comments, and questions.

This book is just a start, a rock tossed in the water. I hope that it will help you in your design thinking and that you will share your ideas and innovations with all of us so we can move forward together into this new, participatory world.

ACKNOWLEDGMENTS

Thank you for investing your time, money, and attention in this book. I hope it is useful to you as a practical guide to developing, implementing, and evaluating participatory audience experiences. If it is, it is in no small part due to the fabulous group of people who inspired, shaped, and edited it.

I have been most greatly influenced in writing this book by three professional heroes: Elaine Heumann Gurian, Kathleen McLean, and John Falk. If this book excites you, I highly recommend that you "go to the source" and read their books as well. I am honored to consider Elaine, Kathy, and John as mentors and friends, and I would not have written this book without their inspiring example.

This book was not only inspired by colleagues; it was also directly improved by their active involvement in its development. If you think peer review in the museum field is dead or languishing, I encourage you to open your work processes to the eyes and opinions of your colleagues. I wrote this book publicly on a wiki site and invited colleagues and enthusiastic readers of the Museum 2.0 blog to add their comments, insights, and examples along the way. Their contributions, particularly during the editing stage, were invaluable. They pointed out what was valuable and not, shared new examples, and gave me the courage to make major changes to the content, organization, and tone of the book.

Several people contributed many hours of their attention towards improving this book. Some of these editors are colleagues whom I solicited directly, but most are museum professionals and interested folks with whom I had no prior relationship. In no particular order, I'd like to thank the content reviewers: Conxa Rodà, Sarah Barton, Mark Kille, Barbara Oliver, Bruce Wyman, Cath Styles, Susan Spero, Chris Castle, Claire Antrobus, David Kelly-Hedrick, Ed Rodley, Georgina Goodlander, Linda Norris, Kevin Von Appen, Darcie Fohrman, Maria Mortati, Haz Said, Jody Crago, Jonah Holland, Kerrick Lucker, Kristin Lang, Daniel Spock, Eric Siegel, Lauri Berkenkamp, Rebekah Sobel, Andrea Bandelli, Louise Govier, Lynn Bethke, John Falk, Peter Linett, Ruth Cuadra, Maureen Doyle, Marc Van Bree, Patricia Sabine, Heidi Glatfelter, Susan Edwards, Jane Severs, Phillippa Pitts, Jana Hill, Mariana Salgado, Melissa Gula, Robert Connolly (and his museum practices students), Becky Menlove, Mia Ridge, and Michael Skelly.

Copy-editing was also a collaborative volunteer effort. Thank you to: Dave Mayfield, James Neal, Buster Ratliff, Lizz Wilkinson, Tikka Wilson, Jody Crago, Erin Andrews, Lisa Worley, Monica Freeman, Matthew Andress, Barbara Berry, Kaia Landon, Rhonda Newton, Jonathan Kuhr, Lynn Bethke, Susan Edwards, and L. Corwin Christie for making all the little punctuation and grammatical fixes that make this book read smoothly.

Thanks to Robin Sloan and Scott Simon for their editorial efforts to improve the book overall. Thanks also to Sibley Simon and Sarina Simon, who generously responded to many out-of-the-blue requests for feedback. Great thanks to Jennifer Rae Atkins, who designed the beautiful front and back covers, and to Karen Braiser, who formatted many of the Web-based images for inclusion.

This book was heavily informed by conversations and interviews with professionals across many institutions. Thank you to Evelyn Orantes, Shelley Bernstein, Wendy Erd, Tsivia Cohen, Kris Morrissey, Jeff Grabill, Kirsten Ellenbogen, Kelli Nowinsky, David Chesebrough, Stephanie Ratcliffe, Jane

McGonigal, William Cary, Jamee Telford, Barbara Henry, Kathleen McLean, Kevin Von Appen, Sabrina Greupner, Vishnu Ramcharan, Robert Stein, Chris Alexander, Bridget Conley-Zilkic, David Klevan, Nancy Zinn, Jackie Copeland, Josh Greenberg, Jessica Pigza, Lori Fogarty, Beck Tench, Jeff Stern, and countless others who have generously provided information, images, and inspiration for this book.

I take full responsibility for all errors and omissions in this book, and I encourage you to share new case studies, comments, and questions on the website at **www.participatorymuseum.org** That site also includes direct links to all the references in the book, which I will try to keep updated over the years to come. Please share your feedback. It improves everyone's experience with the content and it opens up the opportunity for multi-directional conversation.

Finally, thank you for considering these ideas and, hopefully, integrating them into your work. I can't wait to hear where you take it.

IMAGE CREDITS

Cover artwork and interior illustrations by Jennifer Rae Atkins
page 15: ADKAP youth summit: Photo courtesy The Wild Center
page 24: *Side Trip* posters: Photos courtesy Denver Art Museum
page 44: Bookshop Santa Cruz staff picks: Photo by Dave Mayfield
page 48: *Heroes* cards and tag: Images courtesy Walters Art Museum
page 49: "Talk to Me" label: Photo © Carolin Seeliger
page 53: Apartheid Museum entrance: Photo by Charles Apple
page 69: *Skyscraper Challenge*: Photos courtesy Chicago Children's Museum
page 77: Tina, We Salute You loyalty wall: Photo by Jessie Cutts
page 80: *1stfans* event with Swoon: Photo by Melissa Soltis
page 89: *Near*: Photo © Scott Snibbe
page 96: *Spinning Blackboard*: Photo © Exploratorium
page 99: *Internet Arm Wrestling*: Photo by Ryan Somme
page 103: *Human Library*: Photo courtesy Human Library
page 131: *Race: Are We So Different?*: Photo by Terry Gydesen
page 134: Visitors in Phillips Collection: Photo by Linda Norris
page 143: *Side Trip* rolodexes: Photo courtesy Denver Art Museum
page 148: *World Without Oil* comic by Jennifer Delk
page 160: *Question*: Photo by Darcie Fohrman
page 163: The *Odditoreum*: Photography by Paula Bray. Reproduced courtesy of the Powerhouse Museum, Sydney.
page 170: *MP3 Experiments*: Photo by Stephanie Kaye
page 185: Winter Birding: Photo by Deborah Phillips, courtesy NAS
page 199: COSI *Labs in Life*: Photo courtesy of COSI
page 205: Denver Community Museum: Photo by Jaime Kopke
page 209: *MN150* at the State Fair: Photo courtesy Minnesota Historical Society
page 217: *On the Road*: Photos courtesy Lowell National Historical Park
page 220: *From Memory to Action* pledge wall: Photo by U.S. Holocaust Memorial Museum/Max Reid
page 229: *In Your Face* make stations: Photos © Art Gallery of Ontario 2007
page 234: *Investigating Where We Live*: Photos courtesy National Building Museum
page 241: Vietnam Museum of Ethnology editing session: Photo by Pham Minh Phuc
page 265: Wing Luke Asian Museum: Photograph by Dean Wong, courtesy of the Wing Luke Asian Museum
page 270: *SFZero Doorhenge*: Photo by anna one aka Alanna Simone
page 276: *Days of the Dead* ofrenda: Photo courtesy Oakland Museum of California
page 284: IMA "Free" banner: Image courtesy Indianapolis Museum of Art
page 285: Jumping in the FotoMuseum: Photo by FotoMuseum Provincie Antwerpen/Sofie Coreynen en Tanja Vrancken.
page 297: Detroit's Chinatown timeline: Photo courtesy Detroit Historical Society
page 299: *Rethinking Picasso* illustration by Jose Luis (Oze) Tajada Gracia
page 326: *MN150* vetting session: Photo courtesy Minnesota Historical Society
page 329: "A Day in the Life" illustration by Beck Tench
page 339: *Question of the Day*: Photo © Ontario Science Centre 2010
page 342: *Road Trip* postcards: Image courtesy San Jose Museum of Art
page 345: *Crafternoons*: Photo by Shira Kronzon

SELECTED BIBLIOGRAPHY

This bibliography provides a selection of long-format works critical to the development of this book. For a complete list of up-to-date references, please consult **www.participatorymuseum.org**

Abergel, Ronni, Antje Rothemund, Gavan Titley, and Peter Wootsch. *The Living Library Organiser's Guide*. Budapest: Council of Europe, 2005.

Allen, Sue and Josh Gutwill (2004). "Designing with multiple interactives: Five common pitfalls." *Curator* 47(2): 199-212.

Center for Advancement of Informal Science Education. *Public Participation in Scientific Research: Defining the Field and Assessing Its Potential for Informal Science Education*. Washington D.C.: Center for Advancement of Informal Science Education, 2009.

Chinn, Cassie. *The Wing Luke Asian Museum Community-Based Exhibition Model*. Seattle: Wing Luke Asian Museum, 2006.

Falk, John. *Identity and the Museum Visitor Experience*. Walnut Creek: Left Coast Press, 2009.

Falk, John and Lynn Dierking. *The Museum Experience*. Washington D.C.: Whalesback Books, 1992.

Falk, John and Beverly Sheppard. *Thriving in the Knowledge Age: New Business Models for Museums and Other Cultural Institutions*. Walnut Creek: AltaMira Press, 2006.

Hein, George. *Learning in the Museum*. London: Routledge, 1998.

Heritage Lottery Fund. *A Catalyst for Change: The Social Impact of the Open Museum*. London: RCMG, 2002.

Heumann Gurian, Elaine. *Civilizing the Museum*. London: Routledge, 2006.

Humphrey, Thomas and Josh Gutwill. *Fostering Active Prolonged Engagement: the Art of Creating APE Exhibits*. San Francisco: Exploratorium, 2005.

IDEO. *Human-Centered Design Toolkit*. San Francisco: IDEO, 2008.

Illich, Ivan. *Deschooling Society*. New York: Harper and Row, 1971.

InterAct. *Evaluating participatory, deliberative, and co-operative ways of working*. Brighton: InterAct, 2001.

Jenkins, Henry. *Convergence Culture: Where Old and New Media Collide.* New York: New York University Press, 2006.

Jennings, Gretchen, ed. "Visitor-Generated Content and Design." *Exhibitionist* 28(2).

Koke, Judy and Marjorie Schwarzer, ed. "Civic Discourse: Let's Talk." *Museums & Social Issues* 2(2).

Li, Charlene and Josh Bernhoff. *Groundswell: Winning in a World Transformed by Social Technologies.* Boston: Harvard Business School Publishing, 2008.

McLean, Kathleen. *Planning for People in Museum Exhibitions.* Washington D.C.: Association of Science and Technology Centers, 1993.

McLean, Kathleen and Wendy Pollock, ed. *Visitor Voices in Museum Exhibitions.* Washington D.C. Association of Science and Technology Centers, 2007.

National Endowment for the Arts. *2008 Survey of Public Participation in the Arts.* Washington D.C.: National Endowment for the Arts, 2009.

Norman, Donald. *The Design of Everyday Things.* New York: Doubleday, 1990.

Shirky, Clay. *Here Comes Everybody: The Power of Organizing without Organizations.* New York: Penguin Press, 2008.

Stanton, Philip, ed. *Repensar el Picasso.* Barcelona: Agpograf, 2009.

Zorich, Diane, Gunter Waibel, and Ricky Erway. *Beyond the Silos of the LAMs: Collaboration Among Libraries, Archives, and Museums.* Dublin, Ohio: Online Computer Library Center, 2008.

CASE STUDY INDEX

A Complicated Collaboration at The Tech Museum 245

Aligning Co-Creators' Goals in Wikipedia Loves Art 271

A Networked Show at the Anne Frank Museum 92

Assessing the Value of Hosting the 888 Toronto Meet-up 289

Climate Conferences at The Wild Center.. 14

Co-Creation as a Way of Life at the Wing Luke Asian Museum 264

Co-Creation Inspires Reinvention at the Oakland Museum of California 276

Community-Based Video at the Vietnam Museum of Ethnology 239

Conducting Research with Visitors at the United States Holocaust Memorial Museum 254

Engaging Front-Line Staff as Researchers at the Museum of Science and Industry Tampa 307

Engaging Teenagers as Collaborators at the National Building Museum 233

From Me-to-We with Nike Plus 29

Getting Personal with PostSecret... 141

Hosting Teenagers at the Experience Music Project and Science Fiction Museum 293

How Internet Arm Wrestling Mediates Social Engagement.................................. 98

How the Victoria & Albert Museum Asks for Contributions 212

Imaginative Object Descriptions at the Powerhouse Museum.............................. 161

Learning with Strangers in The Human Library.. 100

Making Visitors' Comments an Art Experience at the Rijksmuseum..................... 226

Managing Participation at the San Jose Museum of Art....................................... 340

Niche Memberships at the Brooklyn Museum and the Center of Science and Industry 79

Object-Rich Theater at the Indianapolis Children's Museum 155

Pandora—An Expert Recommendation Engine 63

Personalized Relationships with Harrah's Casinos.. 81

Promoting Institution-Wide Transparency at the Indianapolis Museum of Art 330

Real-Time Visitor Collaboration at the University of Washington.......................... 257

Sharing Artifacts at the Glasgow Open Museum 175

Structured Dialogue in the Signtific Game 111

Studying the Conversations on Science Buzz.. 310

Taking Instructions at the San Francisco Museum of Modern Art.......................... 165

Testing the Wisdom of Crowds at the Brooklyn Museum 115

The 39 Clues and Cross-Platform Engagement 72

Using Participation to Reinvigorate the Center of Science and Industry 197

Using Take-Homes for Deep Engagement at the Chicago Children's Museum....... 69

What if We Lived in a World Without Oil?.. 146

INDEX

1stfans 79, 80. *See also* Brooklyn Museum
21st century skills 193, 195. *See also* learning theory, participatory
The 39 Clues 72–73
826 tutoring program 244, 248
888 289–292. *See also* Ontario Science Centre

A
Adaptive Path 236
Advice: Give It, Get It, Flip It, F**k 103, 257–260. *See also* University of
        Washington
Alexander, Chris 341. *See also* San Jose Museum of Art
A Matter of Faith 52. *See also* Stapferhaus Lenzberg
The American Image 222. *See also* University of New Mexico museum
Anderson, Maxwell 330. *See also* Indianapolis Museum of Art
Angel Island State Park 184
Anne Frank Museum 92–94
antiboredom 269–270. *See also* SFZero
Apartheid Museum 52
Arab American Museum 183
Art Gallery of Ontario 228, 229, 230
artifacts
   as social objects 127–182
   sharing 173, 175–176
The Art of Participation 165. *See also* San Francisco Museum of Modern Art
audio tours 37
Avesta blast furnace 38, 66. *See also* historic sites

B
Bernstein, Shelley 80, 118, 119, 192. *See also* Brooklyn Museum
Beyond the Silos of the LAMs: Collaboration Among Libraries, Archives, and
        Museums 323
Bibliotheek Haarlem Oost 6, 321
blogging 310–314, 328
   front-line staff 57–58
Bonney, Rick 185–186
bookmarking 67
Boston Children's Museum 46, 286, 349, 350
Bottled Up! 204. *See also* Denver Community Museum
Brooklyn Museum 66, 79, 80, 115, 118, 124, 174, 192, 261, 271, 272

C

Cambodian American Heritage Museum & Killing Fields Memorial 184
Cantor Art Center 160
Cardiff, Janet 169. *See also* Words Drawn on Water
casinos. *See* Harrah's casinos
Center for Advancement of Informal Science Education (CAISE) 185–186
Center Of Science and Industry. *See* COSI
Chesebrough, David 197, 198, 199, 201. *See also* COSI
Chew, Ron 265. *See also* Wing Luke Asian Museum
Chicago Children's Museum 69, 71, 124
Chicago Cultural Alliance 184
Chicago Japanese American Historical Society 184
Children of the Lodz Ghetto. *See* US Holocaust Memorial Museum
citizen science 185, 186, 287
Clarke, Wendy 149. *See also* Love Tapes
Click! A Crowd-Curated Exhibition 111, 115–120, 130, 187, 192, 261. *See also* Brooklyn Museum
climate change 14, 15, 283
comment stations 13, 57, 90, 108, 111, 151, 162, 177, 187, 209, 215, 216, 258–259, 305, 316, 340
  design 13, 150
  placement 222
  video 110–111, 226–227, 229
community advisory boards 237, 266, 267, 277
  youth 194–195
community galleries 295–299
community management 122–123, 332–340
  staff roles 243–245
  strategic 337–338
Comparisons: An Exercise in Looking 159. *See also* Hirshhorn Museum and Sculpture Garden
Conner Prairie 154–155
constraints 22
contests 248
Cornell Lab of Ornithology 185
COSI 47, 79, 80, 197, 198–201
  premium membership 81
Cousins, Jay 49
Crafternoon 344–345. *See also* New York Public Library
crowdsourcing 208, 245

D

Daisy 143. *See also* Exploratorium
Darkened Waters 210. *See also* Pratt Museum

Dashboard 331, 332. *See also* Indianapolis Museum of Art
Days of the Dead 237, 276–279. *See also* Oakland Museum of California
Deller, Jeremy 104. *See also* It Is What It Is: Conversations About Iraq
Denver Art Museum 23–25, 124, 143, 150, 287, 292
Denver Community Museum 204, 205, 206, 207
Deschooling Society 120. *See also* Illich, Ivan
design challenge 238
Detroit Historical Society 296, 297
dialogue 111–113, 117
　facilitation 157–158
　programming 100–105
　research 311–314
Dialogue in the Dark 153, 154
Dinosaur Trail 223, 224. *See also* Museum of Life and Science
Discovery Tree Walk 152. *See also* Nature Park, Hebrew University
docent tour. *See* guided tours
donors 43, 54, 78, 179, 200, 201
Do's, Don't's, How-To's, Why Not's: A Zine For Teens About Museums And Art 194.
　　See also Walters Art Museum

E
e-cards 67, 178
EgoTrap 99. *See also* Experimentarium
Eina School of Design and Art 298. *See also* Rethinking Picasso (Repensar el
　Picasso)
Eklund, Ken 146–147. *See also* World Without Oil
Engeström, Jyri 128, 133. *See also* social objects
Erd, Wendy 239, 242. *See also* Vietnam Museum of Ethnology
exhibits
　multi-user 89, 95, 98, 164
　personalized 42, 65, 65–67
Experience Music Project and Science Fiction Museum 293–295
Experimentarium 99
Experimonth 328. *See also* Museum of Life and Science
Exploratorium 44, 57, 95, 143, 195, 208, 349

F
Facebook 8, 40, 125, 224
Facing Mars 86, 87, 88, 90, 91, 92, 226. *See also* Ontario Science Centre
Falk, John ii, 18, 43, 55
Field Museum 184
Field to Factory 52. *See also* Smithsonian National Museum of American History
Fill the Gap 150, 151, 196. *See also* Smithsonian American Art Museum

Fishing for Solutions 57. *See also* Monterey Bay Aquarium
Flickr 9, 124, 128, 133, 134, 135, 136, 137, 151, 163, 172, 174, 271, 272, 328
Flickr Plant Project 328. *See also* Museum of Life and Science
Fohrman, Darcie 161. *See also* Question (exhibition)
Follow the North Star 27, 154, 155. *See also* Conner Prairie
Forrester Research 8
For the Love of God 226–227. *See also* Hirst, Damien; *See also* Rijksmuseum
FotoMuseum 285
Free2Choose 92–94, 122. *See also* Anne Frank Museum
Freer Gallery 169
Friere, Paulo 120
From Memory to Action 70, 219, 221. *See also* US Holocaust Memorial Museum
front-line staff 28, 39, 55, 56, 57, 58, 74, 75, 107, 177, 257, 307, 308, 334, 335, 343
futurecasting 111–113. *See also* Signtific

G

game 30, 98, 124, 132, 170–171, 269
  cross-platform 72–74, 99, 146–151
  game nights 288
  mechanics 60
  online 95, 111–113
Ghosts of a Chance 124. *See also* Smithsonian American Art Museum
Glasgow Open Museum 175, 176, 187, 264
Goodlander, Georgina 196, 2. *See also* Smithsonian American Art Museum
Google 85
Grabill, Jeff 311. *See also* Take Two
Greenberg, Josh 336, 343. *See also* New York Public Library
Greenwalt, Toby 288. *See also* Skokie Public Library
Greupner, Sabrina 340. *See also* Ontario Science Centre
Groundswell: Winning in a World Transformed by Social Technologies 8
guided tours 152–153
Gurian, Elaine Heumann ii, 5

H

Hächler, Beat 53
Hammer Museum 104
Harrah's casinos 81–83
Henry Ford Museum 284
Heroes: Mortals and Myths in Ancient Greece 42, 43, 45, 47, 48. *See also* Walters Art Museum
Hirshhorn Museum and Sculpture Garden 159, 169
historic houses 28

historic sites 38, 66
Holocaust Museum. *See* US Holocaust Memorial Museum
Human Library 100–105, 122

I

identity-building 68, 312, 313
IDEO ii, 236
Ideum 222
If Tired Hands Could Talk: Stories of Asian Pacific American Garment Workers 264.
  See also Wing Luke Asian Museum
I Like Museums 36–37
Illich, Ivan 120
Immigration Sites of Conscience 183–184
Improv Everywhere 169. *See also* MP3 Experiments
innovation skills 193. *See also* learning theory, participatory
Institute of Museum and Library Services 310
International Spy Museum 155
Internet Arm Wrestling 98–100
Investigating Where We Live 233–235, 237. *See also* National Building Museum
In Your Face 228, 229. *See also* Art Gallery of Ontario
It Is What It Is: Conversations About Iraq 104

J

Japanese American National Museum 184
Jenkins, Henry 3, 172
Jumping in Art Museums 285. *See also* blogging
Just Letters 95–98

K

Klevan, David 254. *See also* US Holocaust Memorial Museum
Kopke, Jaime 204. *See also* Denver Community Museum

L

Lawty, Sue 206, 207. *See also* World Beach Project
Learning Strands in Informal Environments 312
learning theory
  instructional scaffolding 12, 22, 94, 104, 269, 270, 297, 327
  networked learning 120
  pull content 37–38
libraries 4, 41, 52, 101, 102, 103, 282, 283, 288, 321, 351
Library of Congress 135–137
LibraryThing 40–43, 61–63, 85–87, 128
LinkedIn 40
LITMUS 318. *See also* research

London Science Museum 209, 210
loud hours 282
Love Tapes 149. *See also* Clarke, Wendy
Lowell National Historical Park 216

M

Magnes Museum 211
Make a King's Crown 315. *See also* Powerhouse Museum
Make History 122. *See also* National September 11th Memorial and Museum
Maryland Historical Society 44, 159
McGonigal, Jane 18, 112
membership 43, 55, 75, 77, 78, 79, 80, 81, 200, 201
  niche 79–81
Memory Lab 211. *See also* Magnes Museum
Menchies 76
Metropolitan Museum 124
Michigan State University 311. *See also* Take Two
Mining the Museum 44, 159. *See also* Maryland Historical Society; *See also* Wilson, Fred
Minnesota Historical Society 7, 132, 192, 208, 325
Minnesota History Center. *See* Minnesota Historical Society
Minnesota's Greatest Generation 193. *See also* Minnesota Historical Society
mission statement 16, 192
MN150 192, 208, 209, 228, 229, 325, 326. *See also* Minnesota Historical Society
mobile phones 66, 99
models for participation
  co-creation 263–280
  collaboration 231–262
  contributory 203–230
  differences 186–191
  hosted 281–300
Monterey Bay Aquarium 57
MOSI 307
MP3 Experiments 169–171
MunchCam 328. *See also* Museum of Life and Science
Museum of Broken Relationships 225
Museum of Jurassic Technology 161
Museum of Life and Science 56, 223, 304, 328, 329, 335
Museum of Science and Industry in Tampa. *See* MOSI
Museum of Transport and Technology 132
Museu Picasso 298, 299
Music Genome Project. *See* Pandora

N

Nanoscape 195, 207, 208. *See also* Exploratorium
National Academies of Science 312
National Building Museum 233
National Constitution Center 157
National Endowment for the Arts i
National Library of Scotland 109
National September 11th Memorial and Museum 122
Nature Park, Hebrew University 152
Near 88, 89, 90. *See also* New York Hall of Science
Netflix 60, 61, 63, 85
New Economics Foundation 306
new media literacies 193, 211. *See also* learning theory, participatory
New York Divided 144. *See also* New York Historical Society
New York Hall of Science 43, 50, 88, 99
New York Historical Society 144–146
New York Public Library 336, 337, 338, 343, 345
Nielsen, Jakob 9
Nike Plus 29, 31, 83
Norman, Donald 236

O

Oakland Museum of California 237, 276
Odditoreum 146, 162, 230. *See also* Powerhouse Museum
One Minute Sculptures 165–166. *See also* San Francisco Museum of Modern Art
Online Computer Library Center 323
Ontario Science Centre 39, 86, 107, 194, 215, 222, 226, 256, 289, 290, 292, 338, 340
On The Road 216. *See also* Lowell National Historical Park
Open House: If Walls Could Talk 132, 133. *See also* Minnesota Historical Society
Operation Spy 155. *See also* International Spy Museum
Orantes, Evelyn 278. *See also* Oakland Museum of California
O'Reilly, Tim 85
Our Green Trail 46. *See also* Boston Children's Museum

P

Pandora 63–64
participation
  inequality 9
  reasons for iii–iv
  types 8, 12
  value of 5, 16, 193–201, 236–237
  with staff 47, 327–332

with youth 233–235, 275, 293–295
photography
  for personalization 68, 70
  on Flickr vs. in-museum 133–137
  policies 176
Pigza, Jessica 343–345. *See also* New York Public Library
Placeography 193. *See also* Minnesota Historical Society
Playing with Science 209, 210. *See also* London Science Museum
Polish Museum of America 184
postcards 71, 141, 142, 143, 177, 178, 224, 341, 342
PostSecret 141–143, 224
Powerhouse Museum 124, 146, 161, 315
The Power of Children 155–157
The Power of Children. *See* Indianapolis Children's Museum
Pratt Museum 210
Princessehof 107
profiles
  for staff 50
  in the real world 41–43
  online 40
  prescriptive 51
  wearable 47–50
Public Participation in Scientific Research 185–186
punch cards 75, 76

Q

Question (exhibition) 160–161. *See also* Cantor Art Center
Question of the Day 222. *See also* Ontario Science Centre
questions
  personal 141–146
  placement 149–181
  speculative 146–147
  writing good ones 140–141

R

race 44, 137, 155, 158, 159
Race: Are We So Different? 131. *See also* Science Museum of Minnesota
RadioLab 218–219
Ramcharan, Vishnu 39. *See also* Ontario Science Centre
Rapid Idea Generation 256. *See also* Ontario Science Centre
recommendation engine 60–62
REFLECTS 307–308. *See also* MOSI
REI 75

Reimus, Alison. *See* Jumping in Art Museums
Remix 287. *See also* Seattle Art Museum
remixing ii, iii, 8, 23, 24, 25, 142, 172, 174, 188, 350
research
  adaptive 314–316
  goals 304–305
  indicators 305–306
  with front-line staff 307–308
  with participants 317–319
Rethinking Picasso (Repensar el Picasso) 298–299. *See also* Museu Picasso
RFID 42, 65
Rijksmuseum 44, 226
Road Trip 341–342. *See also* San Jose Museum of Art

S
San Francisco Museum of Modern Art 165, 166, 285
San Jose Museum of Art 340
scaffolding 12, 22, 25, 94, 103, 104, 171, 269, 270, 297, 327. *See also* learning
      theory
Scholastic Books 72. *See also* The 39 Clues
Science Buzz 57, 310, 311, 312, 313, 314, 335. *See also* blogging; *See
      also* Science Museum of Minnesota
Science Museum of Minnesota 57, 131, 158, 311, 312, 335
Seattle Art Museum 287
Second Life 245, 246, 247, 249, 251, 252
SFZero 269, 270
Shards & Happiness 107. *See also* Princessehof
Shirky, Clay 17
Side Trip 23–25, 124, 143, 150. *See also* Denver Art Museum
Signtific 111–113, 122, 146, 150–151, 224–225
Skokie Public Library 288, 289
Skyscraper Challenge 69–70, 124. *See also* Chicago Children's Museum
Slavery in New York 144–146
Smithsonian American Art Museum 124, 150, 196
Smithsonian National Museum of American History 52
social networks 8, 39, 40, 88, 125, 128, 135, 172, 176, 291, 306
social objects
  active 130
  gifting 177–178
  personal 130
  provocative 131–132
  relational 132
  sharing 172–173

social Web ii, 3, 4, 9, 12, 29, 172, 174, 275, 323, 350
Sony Wonder Technology Lab 42–43
Sound Off! 293–295. *See also* Experience Music Project and Science Fiction
    Museum
spaced repetition 71
Spinning Blackboard 95–97
staff picks 44, 45, 60–62
Stapferhaus Lenzberg 52
Stein, Robert 332. *See also* Indianapolis Museum of Art
St. Louis Science Center 274, 275, 317
Subsidized Times (Thoi Bao Cap) 239. *See also* Vietnam Museum of Ethnology
Swedish American Museum Center 184
Swedish Interactive Institute 38. *See also* Avesta blast furnace

T

tagging 7, 135
Take Two 310–314. *See also* Science Buzz
The Tate Modern 37
Tench, Beck 304, 328, 329, 333, 335. *See also* Museum of Life and Science
theater 75, 155–157
The Design of Everyday Things 236
theme parks 35
The Tech Museum 245, 247, 249, 252, 261, 333
The Tech Virtual Test Zone 245–253. *See also* The Tech Museum
Tina, We Salute You 76
Titanic 45
Top 40 106, 261. *See also* Worcester City Gallery and Museum
transparency 330–331
  in research 319–320
Tropenmuseum 68

U

University of New Mexico 222
University of Washington 103, 108, 257
Unsuggester 61, 62, 63. *See also* LibraryThing
Untitled 287, 292. *See also* Denver Art Museum
US Holocaust Memorial Museum 45, 219, 254

V

Victoria & Albert Museum 124, 174, 206, 212, 213
Vietnam Museum of Ethnology 239–242
visitor-generated content 109
  art 166, 204–207, 276
  artifacts 209–210

curating 109–110, 115, 125, 221–225
exhibits 245–253, 266–268, 276, 295–299
inappropriate content 222–224
labels 162
model content 215–221
ownership 123, 213
privacy 123, 213
research 253–255
video 289–292
Visual Thinking Strategies 153–154
Von Appen, Kevin 291. *See also* Ontario Science Centre
voting 7, 86, 92–94, 106

W
Walters Art Museum 42, 45, 47, 194, 195
Warren, Frank 141–143, 224. *See also* PostSecret
Web 2.0 85, 125, 315
Weston Family Innovation Centre 107, 194, 215, 256, 257, 338, 340. *See also* Ontario Science Centre
Wi-Fi, providing to visitors 283, 284
Wikipedia 174, 256, 271, 272, 273, 274, 314
Wikipedia Loves Art 271–274
  Dutch 273
The Wild Center 14, 15, 283
Wilson, Fred 44, 159, 161. *See also* Mining the Museum
Wing Luke Asian Museum 6, 264, 265, 266, 267, 268, 269, 278, 295, 303
The Winking Lizard Tavern 77
Worcester City Gallery and Museum 105, 105–106, 106, 126
Words Drawn on Water 169–171. *See also* Cardiff, Janet
World Beach Project 206, 207, 212, 213. *See also* Victoria & Albert Museum
World Without Oil 146–148

Y
youth 15, 194, 233–235, 274, 289–292
Youth Exploring Science 274. *See also* St. Louis Science Center
YouTube 8, 9, 10, 122, 123, 146, 172, 289, 290, 291, 292, 328, 341, 342, 344

ABOUT THE AUTHOR

Nina Simon is an independent experience designer with expertise in participatory design, gaming, and social technology. She is the principal of Museum 2.0, a design firm that works with museums, libraries, and cultural institutions worldwide to create dynamic, audience-driven exhibitions and educational programs.

In addition to design work, Nina lectures and gives workshops on visitor participation. She is an adjunct professor of social technology in the University of Washington Museology program. Nina authors the Museum 2.0 blog, which also appears as a column in *Museum* magazine.

Previously, Nina served as Curator at The Tech Museum of Innovation in San Jose, CA, and was the Experience Development Specialist at the International Spy Museum in Washington, D.C.

Nina lives in Santa Cruz, California.

CPSIA information can be obtained at www.ICGtesting.com
Printed in the USA
BVOW012142051211

277640BV00005B/123/P

9 780615 346502